'This book is a must-read for every per
earth would God choose me?" It is a me
fails to move and encourage me. Paul's
can be transformed when God gets hold of us. This book inspires me and makes me want to keep going.'

Nikki Marfleet, Governing Governor, HMP Woodhill

'This is the story of a redeemed man. A man whose life God changed through circumstances and events, relationships and conversations. A man whose life story brings hope to all who read it. Hope not simply in what someone can do when they are put to work by God. Hope not simply in the power of relationships of friendship and family. But hope in the God who makes all things new.'

Justin Welby, Archbishop of Canterbury

'A powerful story of brokenness and transformation by grace. Uplifting, humorous and full of hope.'

Justin Walford, Legal Director, News Group Newspapers Ltd

'The story of Paul Cowley is heart-stirring. Having been taken into HM Prisons on several occasions by Paul, I can testify to his complete commitment and work among the marginalised. I highly commend this book and wish its author all continued success in his important work.'

Prince Michael of Kent GCVO, KStJ, CD

'This is an inspirational story of hope and belief. For our veterans who struggle to find purpose in their lives, Paul's journey serves as a guiding light towards fulfilment.'

Lieutenant General JI Bashall CB, CBE, President, Royal British Legion

'In desperate times Paul Cowley's memoir is a much-needed reminder that love wins and hope prevails. This is a story of redemption for our time.'

Pete Greig, 24-7 Prayer International and Emmaus Rd

'Life is about the journey! If you are willing to let go and let God, that journey becomes a story that writes itself. This is exactly what you experience in this marvellous book – the journey Paul Cowley has experienced from thief to prisoner to soldier to priest.'

James Ackerman, President and CEO, Prison Fellowship USA

'A modern-day story of the astonishing kindness of God . . . Paul's account of his transformation from despair to hope is a moving and truly inspiring source of encouragement to all of us . . . highly recommended.'

Bishop Sandy Millar

'Paul Cowley's book is a very brave "warts and all" read. *Thief Prisoner Soldier Priest* is a call to arms and Paul's strategic advice, based on such a depth of practical experience, should be taken on board.'

General David John Rambotham, Baron Ramsbotham, GCB, CBE

'I once read that the two most important days in anyone's life is the day they are born and the day they realise the reason why, discovering a sense of identity and purpose. After many struggles throughout his early life Paul discovered both an identity and purpose in Christ; and everything changed.'

Major General Timothy Cross, CBE

'Paul Cowley's story is wonderful evidence of the life-changing power of Jesus Christ. For many years his life was one of violence, crime and family instability. That changed when he encountered Jesus Christ on an Alpha course and was filled with the Holy Spirit. I have known Paul for more than twenty-five years and have witnessed his remarkable ministry firsthand. His story is one of faith, hope and love. It is one which will inspire you.'

Reverend Nicky Gumbel

'Through his own experience of personal transformation, Paul Cowley ably communicates how a life can be changed, but calls too for a reform of the prison system based on repentance, rehabilitation and mentoring to ensure that all are given a second chance. I highly recommend this book to anyone who is frustrated with their own life and longs to live differently.'

Baroness Philippa Stroud

'An exquisite account of turbulence and trouble making that eventually turn to orderly obedience and optimistic opportunity; his life is a record of triumph and disaster. He is a living St Francis of Assisi – where there is pain, Paul brings hope.'

Lord Hastings, Baron Hastings of Scarisbrick

THIEF PRISONER SOLDIER PRIEST

Paul Cowley

with Amanda Cowley

First published in Great Britain in 2020 by Hodder & Stoughton
An Hachette UK company

4

A CIP catalogue record for this title is available from the British Library

Trade Paperback ISBN 978 1 529 30376 6
eBook ISBN 978 1 529 30377 3

Typeset in Celeste by Palimpsest Book Production Limited, Falkirk, Stirlingshire

Printed and bound in Great Britain by Clays Ltd, Elcograf S.p.A.

Hodder & Stoughton policy is to use papers that are natural, renewable and recyclable products and made from wood grown in sustainable forests. The logging and manufacturing processes are expected to conform to the environmental regulations of the country of origin.

Hodder & Stoughton Ltd
Carmelite House
50 Victoria Embankment
London EC4Y 0DZ

www.hodderfaith.com

This book is dedicated to my wife, Amanda,
my shield-bearer and my best friend.
And to my children, Clinton and Phoebe.
I love you to the moon and back.

*

And to all those who find themselves in
a hopeless situation – be encouraged.

Contents

Foreword

Paul Cowley was born to serve.

He started early by serving a prison sentence in 'Grisly Risley', a notorious Lancashire jail for young offenders, which turned him off crime. Toughened by his dysfunctional and brutalised upbringing, he yearned for action. So his next move was to serve in Her Majesty's Armed Forces. He saw the world and, desperate for promotion, he served in Northern Ireland, the Falklands, Gibraltar, Cyprus and Germany. His military exploits and escapades make colourful reading.

During the selection process Paul turned down an opportunity to join the SAS. He stayed close enough to the Special Forces to be invited to become manager of the SAS Squash Club in London. It did not exist. What transpired was an opportunity to serve Mark Birley, the Mayfair Club owner extraordinaire, who founded Annabel's, Mark's Club, Harry's Bar and the Bath & Racquets Club.

As manager of the Bath & Racquets Club, Paul moved in high society, serving many a health-conscious celebrity. Yet, curiously dissatisfied by his successful lifestyle, he was persuaded by a military colleague to start searching for God. He attended various churches until landing at Holy Trinity Brompton in Knightsbridge. As his messy personal life consisted more of sinning than serving, former Sergeant Cowley did not look like a good potential HTB recruit. But God moves in mysterious ways.

I entered Paul's life in a small way some twenty years ago. I accompanied him to HMP Dartmoor and other prisons when he was leading and developing Alpha courses. He was further down the road on his spiritual journey than I was, but as ex-cons who were doing a bit of public speaking, we bonded over our shared passion for prison ministry and became close friends.

The chapters in this book that strike the deepest chords for me are those which describe Paul's inner journey to a new Christ-centred life of service as an ordained priest, prison chaplain, pioneer of Alpha Prisons, and founder of Alpha Forces and Caring for Ex-Offenders. He is also the Bishops' Advisor to Prisons, and the Ambassador for Social Transformation at HTB and Alpha International.

The cast of characters in this part of the Paul Cowley story are even more extraordinary than those he met on the wilder shores of his youth. Some of them I know well, such as Bishop Sandy Millar, Nicky Gumbel, Jack Cowley, Bishop Graham Tomlin, Emmy Wilson, and the true heroine of the book, Paul's wife and co-author, Amanda. All have played pivotal roles in the unfolding tapestry of Paul's transformative – and still growing – life of service. They would all agree that both the story and the service is remarkable.

But what is this book really about at its deepest level?

Paul Cowley is only its narrator. The story is about a man's redemption. Unconditional love changed the direction of Paul's life from self-service to God's service.

The self-service chapters of part one make for a fast moving and compelling read. But why was Paul left unsatisfied by its worldly excitements and successes? The answer, as made clear in part two, is because he had an unexpected call to a higher level of service and vocation.

Revd Jonathan Aitken
November 2019

Acknowledgements

I frequently ask myself the question: how does a man, born into a dysfunctional family, with very little formal education, and subsequently a criminal record, become a priest in the Church of England? On some days, I am truly perplexed but have come to realise it is the love of God and the help of some wonderful family, friends and work colleagues.

A huge thank you to my wife, Amanda, for her unceasing dedication to write my story, which hasn't always been an easy journey for either of us. I salute you! To my son, Clinton, for having the grace to forgive me. To my daughter, Phoebe, for teaching me how to be a father. A special thank you to Anna, who has shown me love over the years and who took care of my father when I couldn't. To Amanda's mum, Tricia, for her editing skills and to her and her husband, Andrew, for their love and support over the last few decades. Thanks also to my wife's brother, James, and the Willison family who have become my own. With particular thanks to Eric Martin who set me on a course of searching for God and for his continued companionship, and to Nick and Deborah Henderson who, in friendship, challenged my behaviour on several occasions. Friends who have loved and supported Amanda and me over the years include Kristina Page, Lisa Ashton, Amanda Tucker, Bishop Ric and Louie Thorpe, the Reverend Andy and Sue Keighley, Martin and Catherine Bennett, Nick and Jane Oundjan, Nick and Annie Chance, Tan and David Buxton, Olga and Nicholas Goulandris, Justin and Anna Walford, Dan and Susan Hague, the Reverend Simon and Sue Kirby.

Huge thanks to the Reverend Jonathan Aitken who has been a mentor and dear friend, sitting with Amanda and me over the past two years, advising us on the content and style of the book. Fortunately, Jonathan and I are able to rejoice together at how God has changed us for the better.

Also, a big thanks to my publisher, Hodder & Stoughton. To Andy Lyon, Jessica Lacey and the whole team, who had a strong conviction to publish this story. To Mark Elsdon-Dew who believed in the story and helped us connect with Hodder, and to Amanda Elsdon-Dew for some early editing.

The Most Reverend Justin Welby, who has encouraged me personally – but also by his example – with his passion for the lost, lonely and marginalised.

I am forever grateful to Bishop Sandy Millar, who has been like a father to me, chastising me and encouraging me in equal measure, and to Annette for copious amounts of tea and friendly reassurance. To Bishop Graham Tomlin for his unceasing enthusiasm for prison ministry and for appointing me as Bishops' Advisor to Prisons. Thanks to the Reverend Nicky Gumbel and his wife, Pippa, who have supported and encouraged me in my vision for numerous social transformation projects at Holy Trinity Brompton (HTB).

Thanks also go to the Reverend Emmy Wilson, who is like a sister to me, and without whom I may have never embarked on prison work. I am indebted to her for being so prayerful and obedient in her belief that God had a call on my life.

To work colleagues including my line manager and friend, Tricia Neill. The Reverend Nicky Lee, my prayer partner, and his wife Sila, both having counselled Amanda and me on many occasions, especially in raising our daughter. Will van der Hart, a sensitive man with the heart of a lion, and a wonderful ministry to those with mental health issues. Andrea Graham, my exemplary EA. Also thanks to members of the Ministry Team at HTB who have spurred me on. And to Steve Page, Reverend Bill and Clare Birdwood and Reverend Matt Boyes.

The Reverend Tom Jons, a truly kind and gentle man, whom I first met when he was one of four assistant chaplain generals to the prison system; his love and belief in me were extraordinary. The Reverend Ann Colman, my tutor at theological college, without whose encouragement and listening ear I would never have completed my first year of training.

Thanks to my friends and work colleagues over the pond. Jack Cowley (Alpha Prisons USA), a friend and a mentor in the prison work. John Mackay and Mike Timmis for their friendship and for being instrumental in the prison ministry in the USA since it was formed. Dorthe and Truett Tate for their hospitality and sense of fun. James Ackerman, the President and CEO of Prison Fellowship, who was eager to include Alpha Prisons. Jim Liske, Chair of the board of Crossroads Prison Ministries, for his friendship and pastoral support. Thanks also to Melinda Dwight and Jono Green in Australia, who adopted the William Wilberforce Foundation and really embraced working with the marginalised.

A big thank you to others who have encouraged me in my work, including Prince Michael of Kent, Simon Rufus Isaacs the 4th Marquess of Reading, Lord Michael Hastings, Sir Paul Boateng, Dame Philippa Stroud, Lord David Ramsbotham, Major General Tim Cross CBE, Lady Williams of Elvel, Peter Welby, Lady Jane Williams and the Rt Hon Rory Stewart MP.

Thanks also go to the amazing men and women who work in the chaplaincy departments of our prisons and our military bases around the UK. Working in some of the hardest environments, they bring light into dark places, often lonely in their quest to help change people's lives. I'm constantly humbled by their dedication and passion.

Having witnessed the power of the Holy Spirit truly transform their lives, I wish to thank a few inspiring reformed characters: Michael, Brian, Finny, Shaun, Eddie, John, Dave, Shane, Gram, Ross and Darren.

Prologue

We can make our plans,
but the Lord *determines our steps.*
Proverbs 16:9 NLT

Mine is the story of a man who eventually succumbed to God knocking on his door.

When I first met with God it was a bit of a shock, possibly for both of us! Because I didn't think God bothered with people like me. I was stubborn and opinionated and certainly self-sufficient.

The purpose of this story is to give people hope.

It is not the tale of a gangster or a violent man. I didn't do a life sentence or commit a horrendous crime and I wasn't a military hero. In that respect it is not a dramatic story, but for that very reason there may be many readers who can identify with my experiences, especially from my early years.

The word 'sin' may seem old-fashioned, but one definition is 'to miss the mark' and that's what I did. Much of my early life is embarrassing and makes me feel ashamed. Some of the stories may be difficult to read, but it is the truth as I remember it. I have therefore changed some people's names in order to give them anonymity.

A good friend of mine, who works for a charity dealing with dysfunctional kids from inner-city estates, told me how on a train heading out to the country one teenage girl in the group was staring out the window. Asked if she was okay, she turned to him and responded, 'I didn't know my eyes could see this far.' Without hope and vision, our faces, our attitudes and our self-esteem start to turn downwards, when really they should be looking upwards towards new horizons. So, when your mum reinforces a negative stereotype of your dad, screaming at him that a Cowley man will never achieve anything and the only thing they are good at is drinking, fighting, womanising and being in debt, as a child, you believe you are no better. And when your father belittles your mother, and spends his time chasing women and drinking, then you assume that's what men do.

Words are powerful, given and received at any age, and what I've come to understand is, if teachers, parents, peers, friends or family speak negatively into our lives, then those words can stick. Seeds of self-doubt start to take root and grow, making us believe we are nothing more than useless, slowly knocking out any hope we might have had.

I have learnt that this type of upbringing has a profound effect on your brain as 'a single word has the power to influence the expression of genes that regulate physical and emotional stress'.[1] In the first half of my life, my parents and their friends furnished me with a mindset that justified the direction my life was taking. If you are not careful it can become a self-fulfilling prophecy. I wasn't careful!

The words and Scripture spoken and revealed to me in the second part of my life, after my conversion, made the hairs on my arms stand up and brought a tear to my eye. They were powerful, dynamic, poetic, inspiring, romantic and challenging, but mostly they were encouraging.

This is the story of my fall and my redemption – my journey of discovery – and an insight into how I got the help I needed when I missed the mark.

In the words of John O'Donohue:

> You can suffer from a desperate hunger to be loved.
> You can search long years in lonely places, far outside yourself.
> Yet the whole time, this love is but a few inches away from you.

It is at the edge of your soul, but you have been
blind to its presence.
We must remain attentive in order to be able to
receive it.[2]

I therefore encourage you, whatever your start in life, or whatever troubles you are facing today, to remain attentive. Take a real hard look at yourself and ask the question: is my plan the only way or could God be offering me something better? If, like me, you have fallen down in the first half of your life, you have a chance to get up in the second half. You can, with the help of God, and a loving, supportive group of people, be literally reshaped and transformed by the 'renewing of your mind' (Romans 12:2). It is such an exciting journey – trust me, I am still on it.

Part One

The first half of my life

. . . 'For I know the plans I have for you,' declares the L*ORD*,
*'plans to prosper you and not to harm you, plans to give
you hope and a future.'*
Jeremiah 29:11

1: Life started with a bang!

I don't doubt that my dad loved me, although I am unable to feel or remember much love from him. He was a larger than life character, with a Liverpudlian accent and charismatic charm disguising his darker and more forceful side.

Arthur Cowley had a difficult upbringing and it is therefore not surprising that he struggled with communication. His father had been a bare-knuckle street fighter in Toxteth, Liverpool, and by all accounts was very successful, supporting his ever-growing family. His mother, Florence, a large woman, over six foot with jet black hair, had a huge drink problem and was apparently quite promiscuous. His parents' relationship was volatile and, in 1931, when my dad was five years old, the neighbours complained to the authorities that the three Cowley children were left too long on their own. His parents were taken to court by child welfare services and when the judge asked them who would take care of their son, in turn they replied, 'I don't want him.' The judge said he would have to go to a care home for boys. His mother whispered into his ear, 'It will be the best thing for you.'

My dad went straight from that courtroom to a 'home' in the Dingle area along the Liverpool coastline, and only when he was in his seventies did he tell me about it. 'Me mother was right! It was the best thing to happen to me. I was well fed and clothed, taught skills such as woodwork and calligraphy as well as doing some basic cooking and cleaning.' I asked him if he had missed his mum and dad. 'There wasn't much to miss. At the home, I was taught to sew up hems of trousers and darn socks and thread beads.' When I teased him, he replied, 'I loved threading beads for the women who took care of me. It made me popular.'

Leaving the home at fourteen he was sent to Shenton's Farm

in Cheadle for three years. 'The work was hard. Up at four in the morning, out milking cows and collecting eggs, then back in at seven-thirty for breakfast – porridge and a cup of tea – and then out again for ploughing or reaping. The farmer often beat me.' When I asked why, he said, 'I never knew. Just took a stick to me, with any excuse, but it made a man of me. I grew to be a big strong teenager. They should send more kids there instead of letting them roam the streets.'

Many years later, he went back and knocked on the farmer's door. Apparently, the farmer took one look at him and said, 'Crumbs, you turned out to be big.'

'Do you want to beat me now?' said Arthur.

He could have borne a grudge, but he chose not to. He shook hands with the farmer and always referred to the time he spent on the farm as good.

In my early days my dad played a huge role in my life, and ironically, he continues to be a big part of my life today even though he died many years ago.

*

My entry into the world started with a bang. Late on Bonfire Night, 5 November 1955, when returning from the pub, some kids threw a firecracker that landed at my mum's feet, scaring her enough that her waters broke. Arthur drove like a madman to Crumsall Hospital and I was born in the early hours of the seventh, delivered by the nuns from the St Paul's order, from which my name was secured.

My mum, Brenda Saxon, was an attractive woman with piercing blue eyes, high cheekbones and a winning smile. She was thirty years old when she met Arthur on a ferry crossing the Mersey, on the way to the Isle of Man. He was two years younger, six foot two, muscular and tanned with huge hands, a good-looking man, who on entering a room immediately became the focus of attention. Arthur and Brenda were both excited when they realised they would be working together for the whole summer at Howstrake Holiday Camp – a sort of early Butlins on the cliff face of the island near Douglas. There followed a whirlwind romance and I was conceived. On returning to Liverpool Arthur wasn't expecting Brenda to say, 'I'm married to a man who beats me. He will kill me when he finds out about us.'

Arthur took matters into his own hands. Turning up at Brenda's home, he beat the living daylights out of her husband. Leaving her two children, she moved in with Arthur.

Their first home was on Great Jackson Street, Manchester. Rows and rows of terraced houses with entrances at the back like you might see on *Coronation Street*. Basic houses with no frills. Two up, two down – with an outside toilet in a yard often filled with a washing line and large white bed sheets flapping in the wind.

Arthur also had a family, of which I know little, except that he had a son about five years older than me. I met him briefly when I was around ten. Dad brought him to the house, but due to him being rude and bullish towards me, my mum said, 'He needs to go!' Dad took him by the arm and they left.

My parents both had a series of jobs, but most of the money they made went on drink and my dad's passion for cars. When I was five years old, he bought a Ford Popular and when I was eight, a Morris Minor Traveller. At ten, a Ford Zodiac. It was one of his proudest moments when he drove his new MG Magnette Mark IV out of a car showroom in Wilmslow. Unsurprisingly his pride in cars rubbed off on me.

I believe my dad's care for me was evident, but in some ways it was inept, and this came up time and time again. One of my earliest memories, aged five, was going to Manchester Royal Infirmary to see a specialist about a squint in my right eye. My parents were told that I needed an operation in order to correct it. In the car park, Dad said to Mum, 'No son of mine is having an eye operation!' I was taken back to the doctor, who gave me a patch for my left eye to make my right eye work harder. I still have a lazy eye to this day.

Another time, when I was eight years old, he took me to Gorton Park and sat me on a high wall. It was a game of trust and dare. Crouching on the wall I took a small jump and he caught me and swung me round. Confidently, I stood on the wall and dived into his arms again. As he moved further and further away, the jumps became longer and riskier – until the time I leapt into the air, he stepped to the side and I fell to the ground. I was shocked, hurt and embarrassed, thinking it was my fault. On the way home we didn't speak, but I was used to that. Mum cleaned the grazes on my hands and knees with Dettol and sent me upstairs. She proceeded to yell at him. The house was small and so I could hear them clearly. 'What the hell were you thinking, Arthur?' she said.

Dad shouted back, 'I was teaching him a lesson! Not to trust anyone, because they will always move away from him or disappoint him.'

Mum, screaming at the top of her voice, replied 'Teach him a lesson? All you are doing is teaching him to hate you!'

But Dad was right about the impression his lesson had left me with. Unfortunately, it was a lesson that stayed with me for too many years.

I also remember a time when I was eleven. I returned home from school one afternoon to find a party in the front room, with my dad serving drinks from the bar in the corner. I asked a stranger what the party was for, and she told me, 'Their wedding, of course!' I had no idea they weren't married. It was a subject they never raised with me and I didn't feel I could talk to them about it.

*

Unlike my parents, I didn't experience World War Two, but a flak jacket and tin helmet might have given me some protection from my parents' crossfire. They smoked a lot, drank a lot and swore a lot. Their dramas had a cyclical pattern and, as a child, I absorbed it without question. It began on Friday nights around 6.00 p.m.

as I walked with my parents to the local working men's club. Once inside, Dad picked a table and we became entrenched for the next three or more hours. Monty, our huge German shepherd, sat quietly by my side, while Dad and Mum played the slot machines, pints of Guinness and glasses of rum and blackcurrant stacking up on small round tables, ashtrays overflowing, until closing time.

Saturday was a repeat of Friday and then on Sunday Mum spent an age preparing lunch, to be eaten on trays in the front room often watching a World War Two movie. After lunch it was as if a bell had been struck to announce the beginning of round one: ding, ding. Dad, wanting to get to the pub, always started an argument – an excuse to leave, slam the door and find solace among friendships that never went deeper than commiserations and crude jokes. When he rolled in late and very drunk Mum wouldn't speak to him for the next thirty-six hours. By Tuesday morning he was remorseful enough to cuddle her and apologise by making tea and toast. For the next two days, they would even be a little romantic. On Friday at 6.00 p.m. we went back to the club to start the weekly routine. Their arguments frightened me because they were so cruel to each other. It wasn't just the abuse but the volume at which they shouted, screaming and belittling one another. There was always the chance my mother would push my dad too far – always the fear he would overreact.

As a young boy my favourite place in the world was the Isle of Man. We went there regularly to stay at Howstrake, where my parents had met. I felt connected to the island and the people; the locals always commented favourably on my Viking complexion, blond hair and blue eyes. It was many years later that I discovered our surname 'Cowley' originally derived not from the cow pastures of England, but from MacAuley, the shortened form of Mac Amhlaoibh, Anlaf's or Olaf's son. In the ninth century, the Norse sea king Olave the White, having reached Ireland with a large fleet, then migrated to the Isle of Man and the adapted Cowley name was everywhere.

I often spent the summer weeks with Dad's mum, Florence Cowley. Nana Florrie loved me and gave me special attention, maybe because she had abandoned my dad when he was young and wanted to compensate by spoiling me. I loved her simply because she made me laugh when I sat next to her in the buttery at Howstrake where she worked. She had an air of importance about her as she was in charge of around thirty women, which meant they all respected her and spoilt me.

In 1960, when I was five, Dad got a new job as a security officer for Belle Vue, the largest amusement centre in England, and so we moved into a run-down flat opposite the main gates on Hyde Road. Belle Vue was set in 165 acres of land, with a large zoo, amusement park, exhibition hall complex, speedway and greyhound racing stadiums. With more than two million visitors a year it soon became one of the North's most popular attractions. A year later, Dad was promoted to chief security officer and could afford a two-bedroomed house in Rosemary Street in Gorton. I liked living in Rosemary Street because it had a sense of community, with a corner shop, a butcher's and a grocery shop. There was a short time in my life when I played in the streets with a ball and I made a few friends. Gorton Park was nearby and there were often gatherings throughout the year including Christmas and Easter parades and Palm Sunday events, and I remember being fascinated by the spectacle of them. At Belle Vue I was so proud of Dad, dressed in his dark blue uniform, an Alsatian guard dog at his side. I liked nothing better than to accompany him on his patrol around the site as he received a great deal of attention, especially from women. At other times he left me watching the circus or the wrestling or holding the hand of one of his many female admirers while he carried out his duties.

One morning, coming downstairs, I saw two men standing in the front room arguing with my mum. They removed the television and some other things from the house. My dad came home that night and was furious, stomping around and shouting at Mum for letting the bailiffs take 'his' stuff. This was a regular occurrence, and we often had to wait a few weeks for Dad to get paid before getting our belongings back.

My dad, however, was my hero because he was big and strong and never appeared to be scared of anything. He acquired guard dogs, mainly Alsatians, by retrieving them from building sites. Once I saw him take hold of a raging Alsatian that had been left on the end of a rope in a scrap yard. As it bit into his hand, he held it tightly round the neck until it became subdued. He then brought it home and rehabilitated it. After that incident, he became a bit of a legend in the neighbourhood, and for me it became a powerful memory that I have relayed time and time again when working with men coming out of prison. Unfortunately, a series of events occurred over the next few years which would change the opinion I had of my dad.

After the incident on the wall, Mum discovered that Dad was carrying on with several women he had met at Belle Vue. His drinking was increasing, along with the lies. Driving back after a drinking session at the Conservative Club one afternoon in his Ford Popular, he took a short cut home. I was sitting in the back while Mum was in the front passenger seat shouting abuse at him. Dad's hands were firmly fixed to the wheel. 'Quiet!' he shouted.

Suddenly, he reached over, opened the passenger door and pushed her out.

I screamed, 'Mum!' but he didn't care. He closed the door and carried on driving.

I remember looking out of the back window and seeing her lying on the pavement, being helped up by a young woman who had witnessed the event.

At home my mother became withdrawn. I knew she was shocked because I felt it deep down, too; she was never really the same after that. Mum was not an easy woman to live with, she wound Dad up, but she didn't deserve his cruelty and indifference.

Sometimes I would find her in a darkened room listening to Patsy Cline's 'Three Cigarettes and an Ashtray' on the record player, waiting for my father to appear, expecting some excuse. I've learned that indifference can kill a relationship even more than hate; it weakens someone's spirit deep within and changes them.

When I was ten years old, we moved to my parents' first business, a sweet and tobacconist shop on the corner of Donnison Street. Attached to the shop at the back was a large yard where my dad built a carport with a fence around it and a corrugated roof to protect his brand-new MG Magnette Mark IV.

Having left Belle Vue, he was working late shifts as a security guard for British Road Services (BRS), an enormous warehouse based in Manchester: a distribution centre for mail-order products. The Cowley household seemed to acquire an enormous amount of new stuff, electrical goods, clothing and more. Mum, meanwhile, was running the shop, but it wasn't going well due to her rudeness and impatience with customers, mostly neighbours, who ran up debts.

Opposite our house was a dry-cleaning shop run by a tough Irish family with three huge adult brothers whom my dad hated due to an ongoing feud that was started by my mum in the shop. One Saturday afternoon, when Dad returned home from the pub, he parked the car on the road outside the house. Unbeknown to us, he had thrown a house brick through the large glass window of the dry cleaners'.

A few hours later he left the house to go back to the pub, but within minutes stormed back in, shouting, 'Brenda! Have you seen the state of my car?' Mum and I ran out to take a look. Paint stripper had been poured over the bonnet, and paint was peeling off down to the metal. I remember my father's face; he looked menacing. 'They won't get away with it. I'll show 'em', he said.

What unnerved me most was how he sat down and did nothing, because his normal reaction would have been to act immediately. Over the years I had experienced him bursting into fits of rage – in pubs and working men's clubs, or on the street, thumping someone for staring at Mum, or for giving him a disapproving look. He was being unusually passive, and it wasn't what I expected. I now know that he was weighing up the situation and, like a curled snake, was waiting for the opportunity to strike.

The brothers had their own idea.

That evening, when I was in the bath, I heard one of the men shouting, 'Come out, Cowley! You coward!'

The front door slammed. There was to be no talking, no negotiating. Still dripping from the bath, a towel held around my waist, I arrived on the doorstep to see a man lying on the pavement holding his head; blood splattered on the ground. Dad's hand was around the neck of another man. He lifted him off the pavement, pressed him against the wall of the house and punched him in the face repeatedly. The third brother ran up the street. It was never a good idea to call my dad a coward.

Mum, grabbing my arm, removed me from the carnage but the shock of seeing Dad's brutality at such close range made me throw up on the stairs. At that moment I knew the brothers were bad but realised my father was far worse.

I'm not sure how, but in 1966 I passed my eleven-plus and was to go to Manchester Grammar School. I was excited when I visited the school and saw its vast playing fields, but my parents moved yet again to a small bungalow in Windmill Lane in Denton, and I was sent to Egerton Park Secondary Modern. There was no discussion on the matter, but I remember being quite devastated. I can only think that the journey to the grammar school was awkward for them while Egerton Park was a mile away from our house. My parents never valued education, so they didn't understand how going to a grammar school could have helped me in life. My mother, meanwhile, became one of the first traffic wardens in the area and very quickly gained a reputation for giving out the most tickets.

Egerton Park was enormous, with a bad reputation. At twelve years old I was a small-framed kid with blue eyes and wavy blond hair; Dad nicknamed me 'Blue' after Billy Blue Cannon in *The High Chaparral*. I think he fancied himself as Big John Cannon, the Arizonian rancher played by Leif Erikson, a striking and manly actor, typical of the John Wayne era. Mum loved to make a feature of my hair, brushing it over and over, but once I got to school I would run to the sink, wet a comb and flatten it down before the dreaded school day began. As it dried, it bounced upwards, becoming the focal point for the school bullies who thumped and kicked me in the playground at break time.

What made things worse was that my surname incurred nicknames including 'cowpat' and 'cowshit' which echoed around the playground every day. I went from one explosion at home – Mum hitting me around the head whenever I disagreed with her – to another at school where some kid wanted to show off by bullying me at the gate or in the playground. Unfortunately, I also had a speech impediment, often mixing up my Ls, and my Rs. Liverpool became 'Riverpool' and river became 'wiver'. The drama teacher gave me some elocution lessons, but even today I can mix up some letters. Added to this I was blighted by frequent cold sores, my lips often covered in red crusty blisters, and I was totally uncoordinated. This meant I was the last to get picked for a team on sports day, the two team captains arguing over who had to take Cowley. Lastly, I had my lazy right eye, which when I got stressed or tired moved over to the far corner and must have made me look strange.

I dreaded the name-calling, the punching and bullying. I wanted to melt into the wooden seat in my classroom to avoid the bell which would mean facing the bullies in the corridor. The bell also indicated the end of the school day, when they would get me as I walked home. I simply hated school and cannot recall having even one friend. I often woke in the night in a sweat from reoccurring nightmares, fuelled by the events of the day or from watching war films with my dad late into the night.

Most days I returned home from school in tears and my father, annoyed at my weakness, would say, 'If you can't hit 'em, kick 'em. If you can't kick 'em, get a big stick!' By the age of fourteen I decided to take his advice and put an end to the bullying, so I agreed to accept the offer of a fight on the sports field near our home. I imagined I would be triumphant (like the heroes in the spaghetti westerns I watched with my dad) and that the worst bully would leave me alone for good. But unfortunately, he beat the living daylights out of me, and I was left in the mud watched by a large crowd of my peers that had gathered. Not my finest hour.

I started to resent my father because he wouldn't teach me to fight and I felt vulnerable for years. But perhaps he wanted a different life for me. Just maybe he didn't want me to turn out like him.

Meanwhile, my studies at school were suffering and I started truanting to avoid any more confrontations with bullies and teachers. Everything started to go downhill, and Egerton Park could not prepare me for what was to happen next.

2: Never come to anything

By the time I was sixteen life at home had deteriorated. Mum was preparing the Sunday roast when an almighty row broke out yet again and my father raised his hand to strike her. Dashing to defend her, I felt the full force of his hand across my face and I was knocked over. It was the first time my dad had ever hit me. Mum had slapped me across the head many times but not my dad. He told me to 'get out and don't come back', so I threw some clothes in a bag and walked out of the house. Fifty metres later I stopped and realised what I'd done. I had no plan, no money and no hope. All I knew was that I had to escape the war zone. It had to be better out of the house than in it. After my dad backhanded me, he came crashing down off the pedestal I had placed him on. I not only lost respect for him but the powerful giant of a man that I had adored as a very young boy never quite shined for me again.

*

You might wonder how my mother got over the car incident when I was eight years old. I think in many ways it put my parents' relationship under huge pressure, but time heals, or so they say. Or maybe it was Dad's haemorrhoids. They were so bad that he had to have an urgent operation. The doctor advised him to take a long rest, so he went on his own for two weeks to Tarragona on the Spanish coast. To Mum's annoyance, she had to remain working in the shop.

Returning with a deep suntan, he presented Mum with a huge box. When she opened it, she laughed out loud. 'What the hell is it?'

'What do you mean? It's bloody obvious what it is! It's a bull's head!' he said. It was menacing and as black as coal, made of papier mâché and mounted on a wooden plinth. He didn't care what she thought. He loved it.

I was presented with my gift of two shiny bullfighting swords wrapped in newspaper. 'Wow, Dad, they're brilliant! Can I use them?'

'No, son, too dangerous! Give them 'ere.'

Taking the two swords he attached them to either side of the bull's head on the wooden plinth and mounted it over the fireplace. As we watched television that evening the bull glared down at the three of us, its horns spanning the chimneystack. Such a fixture provoked laughter from friends that popped in to have a drink, but Mum defended Dad. 'I think the bull is strong and courageous like Arthur', she said, caressing its nose as she passed by. But when the arguments restarted, I imagined the swords being drawn from the wall and a battle taking place in the living room.

When Dad painted 'La Casita' on to a plaque and put it at the side of the front door, Mum said, 'Arthur, what does that mean?'

He said, 'It means small house, woman! Don't you know anything? *Mi casa es su casa!* My house is your house!'

Mum decided we all needed to go to Spain and immediately booked our summer holiday.

I loved time with my dad, the two of us preparing the MG Magnette for the long drive, pouring oil into a smaller can for the trip and stashing bottles of water for the windscreen, as well as hiding a plentiful supply of rags and tools in every spare nook and cranny. Meanwhile, Mum bought biscuits and bottles of orange squash, magazines and a new pair of fashionable sunglasses that shrouded her small features. The night before our departure she made spam sandwiches, placing them into a Tupperware box in the fridge ready for the journey at the crack of dawn.

At 5.00 a.m. we left the house, driving off on the epic trip from the dark, damp streets of Manchester to Dover, taking a Townsend

Thoresen car ferry across the channel to Calais. As we drove down through the centre of France heading for Tarragona near Barcelona, I lay on the back seat for hours, with no restriction – or safety – from a seat belt. When it turned dark, I was lulled to sleep by watching light from the street lamps pass over the car. From the moment we left Manchester the burden of cohabiting evaporated. Holidays were my parents' happiest times together, as passion was relit and their marriage was safe, for a time.

Once they had checked into the Hotel Marina, a three-star establishment on the coast, Dad immediately unpacked the car. He changed into his trunks and walked over the road to the beach, hiring two sun beds for himself and Mum, and then plonking himself down with an ice-cold San Miguel. His deep sigh of relief was a sound that Mum and I genuinely loved because we knew he was happy at that moment. The beach was so hot we had to walk on the mats provided – my dad insisting we play the game of seeing who could stand on the sand the longest. Of course he always won.

One evening we were all sitting outside at the hotel bar when a stray dog, which Dad had grown fond of, came timorously looking for food. A Spaniard drinking his beer kicked the dog and it yelped. Within a split second Dad backhanded the man off his bar stool and walked calmly back to the table muttering, 'Bloody peasant! That's no way to treat a dog.' A small Spanish man was no match for my dad, and no one ever dared to challenge him. Mum sat quietly smoking, and drinking her rum and coke, used to his dramas. Dad would have rescued all the stray dogs in the vicinity if he had had somewhere to take them.

Bullfighting appealed to Dad's masculinity and he insisted on going back each year. However, he battled with respecting an age-old tradition versus the pointless act of cruelty to a living beast. When the bull was finally defeated with the matador driving his sword into its heart, he had to turn away. The heat and the smell of death made me feel nauseous, but Mum refused to take me out and we all sat there until the spectacle was over. Dad found some solace in the rumour that the meat from the bull was given to the poor.

It was the beginning of the Spanish-themed bungalow in Windmill Lane. Dad bought wallpaper with a recurring print of a matador holding a red cloak posing over a bull in mid-charge. Mum didn't want it but gave up arguing as she realised how determined he was. He decorated the front room with me by his side mixing the powdered wallpaper glue in a saucepan with the handle of a wooden spoon. When it was finished, he called Mum in. She was speechless, but Dad and I were chuffed with the result. Constructing a bar in the corner of the living room, he suspended optics of every type of spirit, and beer mats from the local pub were strewn upon the surfaces. We lived our lives in a parallel universe with our own language, a form of Spanglish, being spoken in the twilight hours; Dad turning on the charm: 'Ola, Brenda. You bueno?' Mum replying, 'I'm bueno, Arthur. Gracias!' Dad holding up a bottle of Bacardi and pouring in some Coke. 'Una Cubra Libre por favor?'

'Si!' said Mum. 'Get me a shot too while you're up there, Arthur!' All of us watching TV in a cloud of smoke as they puffed away together. Dad eventually rising from the smog. 'Right, Brenda, let's go to the pub.'

I always went with them, except on rare occasions, such as when the moon landing was televised in 1969. I sat on my own in the kitchen, watching it on a tiny black and white portable TV. The spectacle of it gave me a sense of belonging. Fifty years later, I had the same feeling when I watched a BBC documentary commemorating the event. It occurred to me that during this moment in history, when half a billion people were in awe of this remarkable achievement, my parents were in the pub.

Most of my childhood memories begin and end in smoke-filled pubs listening to adult stories and jokes, hundreds of them, made at the expense of some race, be it Irish, Scottish or African. Dad cried with laughter, his joviality was infectious. Soon everyone had tears rolling down their faces and bellies that ached for days.

I didn't understand the jokes, but I got the fun of them, although now I understand they were all highly offensive. In the 60s and 70s there was little awareness about the language of prejudice. Jokes were, in some way, a break from the anger and the daily grind of life. Unfortunately, the daily grind permeated my world like the nicotine stained walls and ceiling tiles of our home.

In 1970, I was fifteen years old and still at Egerton Park Secondary Modern. It had never occurred to my parents to remove me from the continual bullying by placing me in another school. Fundamentally, I think they were just too self-absorbed with their own dramas to take mine seriously. However, the teachers were noticing my bad attitude and my regular truancy. 'Paul is a waste of time!' said the maths teacher. 'He will never come to anything', echoed another.

I don't ever remember my parents attending a parents' evening, so I was able to keep my shortcomings to myself for a while, but not for very long.

At that time two things happened to me that shaped my life.

First, I was expelled from school, mostly because of truancy. I left with no qualifications, except a 25-yard swimming certificate. Since my parents were not academic, they didn't seem too upset about my being expelled. They were just happy that a good friend of theirs, a policeman, had taken me through my life-saving proficiency awards. But I was relieved I didn't have to go into school every day.

Second, I got caught up in the middle of my parents' arguing over Dad's womanising. I shouted for them to stop but they wouldn't. I could bear it no longer. I went to the nearest wall and started banging my head against it. 'Stop it. Please stop it', I shouted. It had the desired effect. Mum grabbed me and held me in her arms. Even now, I can remember that moment, the intimacy, the softness and the smell of her; there was peace for a while, but it wasn't to last for long.

My father soon secured a job as a caretaker for a block of flats and so we moved, yet again, to a small terraced house in Didsbury, and the bull's head and swords came with us. Mum insisted that I start contributing to the household finances, which meant I took the first job available: an apprenticeship in Pollard's family butcher's. An apprenticeship appealed to me as I wanted to learn a trade. I was hired immediately by the two brothers and they put me to work. I started at the bottom, sweeping the floor, making the tea and mincing all the scraps of meat, lungs and offal, to be sold as dog meat. Playing numerous pranks, the brothers crept up behind me and dropped large steel trays, which made me jump, and they were frequently locking me in the walk-in freezer. The meagre wage of £5 for the first week's work did not entice me to stay and I never went back.

In a space of twelve months I had many jobs including working in a freezer centre in Stockport and being an assistant in a camping equipment store, a salesman for Corona soft drinks company, and a plumber's mate.

It seemed I was following in my dad's footsteps as he continued to go from job to job. After working as a security officer at BRS he then went self-employed, starting his own company: a security firm using security officers (friends from the pub) and Alsatians he had rescued and trained. Having found some of his letter-headed paper years later, I discovered it was called Argos Guard Dogs, named after Odysseus' faithful dog in Homer's epic Greek poem, *The Odyssey*. My father's capacity to love dogs was extraordinary and I think it possibly happened because he found the relationship more straightforward than dealing with people who challenged him. Studying in the evenings, he then went on to fulfil a lifelong dream of becoming a private detective. He took on many divorce cases, following people and taking photos of them in compromising situations. I think he fancied himself as Dick Tracey.

I subsequently became a driver's mate working for Express Dairies, a large milk company based in Stockport. After a few weeks in the job I realised that some of the drivers had ways of making extra cash. Once I was trusted to say nothing, I became involved in their scam. It was simple but effective. The driver (of the three-tonne truck) kept the shop owner talking while I went into the back of the shop. Counting the number of full crates of milk, I shouted out a reduced number to the shop keeper. He then asked for more than he actually needed. Throughout the day, with around twenty shops on the delivery round, we could sometimes resell fifty crates to other shops. Every transaction was in cash and at the end of the day we split the profit. The scam lasted a while until one of the shop owners reported us for fiddling. The driver was sacked, and I was asked to leave. I wasn't bothered because there were always jobs available.

*

After my father backhanded me, I left the house with my bag and spent the first night walking around the streets of Manchester and the second night sleeping in a doorway and then a bus shelter in Manchester's Piccadilly station. In the early hours of the morning a tall, thin skinhead, wearing red Doc Marten's, Levi jeans and braces, kicked me awake. Handing me a cup of tea, he showed me his collection of photos of women he had slept with – his conquests. Passport-sized pictures stuck together with tape in a concertina display as long as my arm, it made me laugh. For some reason Photo Booth Boy liked me, and possibly saw me as a new recruit for his lucrative business. He could see that I had nowhere to go and invited me to move into 'his place', a squat in a large semi-derelict Victorian house near Stockport.

Living in the house were all types: drug addicts, middle-aged men, young men and women, and a gang of skinheads who were to be my new friends. Each room was dark and squalid with mattresses on the floor, broken windows, tatty curtains blocking out the light, milk bottles made into bongs (a sort of glass pipe) and plenty of cannabis (dope) and alcohol. I tried dope once, but it made me feel as if I had lost my legs, and that was the end of my drug taking. I preferred the taste and effects of alcohol.

The skinheads taught me lots of things and Photo Booth Boy became my role model. For kicks and easy money, he taught me how to rob houses and then small factories. Breaking into a printing factory in Heaton Mersey, we robbed the cigarette vending machines. Pooling all the stuff we had nicked, the money from the sales was divided between us, though I never seemed to end up with much. This went on for months, but I was often the one that a policeman grabbed as my leg hung out from a window trying to escape. Frequent trips to the police station ensued, followed by more visits to the probation office, and I was fined repeatedly.

The Mods and Rockers were on the scene and I fancied myself as a Mod. Somehow, I managed to get a scooter on hire purchase. It was a sky blue Lambretta 150, with added chrome side panels, a back-rest and a head-rest. I particularly liked stealing the expensively chromed side panels from scooters and selling them to Mods who couldn't afford to have them chromed. Decorated with two 5-foot aerials on the back with small triangular Union Jacks flapping in the wind, I was particularly proud of the three spotlights and the twenty-five wing mirrors I had nicked from numerous cars, attached to three rods on either side at the front; it was a stunner!

One night the police caught me trying to take a leaping jaguar from the bonnet of a Jag – not that easy to get off I found out. The intention was to mount it on the front wheel arch of my scooter. I was arrested and put in a cell overnight and released in the morning. Struggling to pay the fines I was eventually sent to the magistrates' court in Stockport. I was building a rather impressive record of petty crimes.

Eventually I progressed to stealing cars. Although I hadn't passed my test, my dad had taught me to drive. Joyriding meant nicking cars from the local area on a Saturday night and driving them up and down the motorway. Compared to all the sophisticated security devices on cars nowadays, it was easy then to get into a car, hotwire it and be off in seconds. There were no steering locks, alarms or tracking devices in the 1970s.

One Friday night, along with Photo Booth Boy, I stole a navy blue Austin 1100 from a side road in Stockport, drove it out of the area, and started heading along the East Lancs Road towards Liverpool. I wanted to visit my uncle Sydney who owned a pub on the Springfield Road near the city centre. The car began to run out of petrol and the police, who had been tailing us for some time, drove up behind us as we pulled on to the hard shoulder. A police officer came to the window and said, 'Is this your car, son?'

'No, officer', I said.

The officer paused. 'Have you stolen this vehicle, son?'

I thought for a moment. 'No, officer,' followed by a pause . . . 'Yes, officer.'

'You're nicked, son!' said the officer, manhandling both of us into the back of the police car.

I was just seventeen years old when I was driven back to a Manchester police station, where I spent the weekend in a holding cell with my accomplice. We were interviewed together at first then separately; they were trying to pin burglaries on to us that we hadn't done, or maybe we had, and I couldn't remember. I now see what I was like. I may not have had my father's strength, but I had my mother's tongue and I was a highly annoying teenager with an attitude.

But what I remember most about that time was being scared. I had lost my sidekick and was on my own in a very grown-up world. I was taken into a room and interviewed. Two male officers sat behind a desk, whispered something to each other, smiled, and then ordered me to remove my trousers. Considering I didn't have the luxury of underwear, I stood with my thin legs protruding from my t-shirt, clutching my bits, for an hour while officers came and went. I guess it was fun for them, but it was embarrassing for me. When a woman officer entered the room with a tray of tea for the two policemen, I blushed. I just couldn't understand why I had had to remove my trousers; I guess it was a tactic to humiliate me, and it worked.

I slept two nights in that holding cell because it was a Friday night and the courts wouldn't be open until Monday morning. I had asked to see my dad, but they never informed him I was there. On Monday morning I was in Manchester magistrates' court. I was scruffy and dirty, as I hadn't been able to wash for three days. I was scared, and I can still remember the panic I felt as I climbed into a van and was handcuffed to a bar.

Standing in the witness box, I was asked to swear on the Bible, 'to tell the truth, the whole truth, and nothing but the truth, so help me God'. The magistrate must have seen so many boys like me. He read out a list of previous offences: petty theft, driving without a licence and insurance, missing probation, non-payment of fines, breaking into warehouses, stealing clothes and raiding vending machines. The list went on and on. I was a useless thief, always getting caught, bound over to keep the peace or fined. Eventually the magistrate looked at me and said, 'You are just not listening to the authorities, Cowley. I'm sending you to Risley Remand Centre for six months, where I hope you will learn a lesson.'

It was that quick. I was taken back downstairs, put in a police van with only the clothes I stood up in and driven away. I was on my own and petrified, and I had no idea where or what Risley was, but I was soon to find out exactly what the magistrate meant by learning a lesson.

3: Never coming back

I had been awake all night and was already dressed and pacing my cell at 5.00 a.m. I could hear the officers on the wings talking but I was terrified they would forget today was my release day. My cell mate, a big black lad from Birmingham, said, 'Relax, Cowley; they won't forget you.'

'I'm never coming back here!' I said.

'Yeah, we all say that! I've been back five times already.'

'No way! I'm never coming back!' I said.

To my surprise my father met me in the reception area, dressed as usual in a blue shirt, beige trousers, a navy-blue blazer, an Irish Guards tie and a trilby. He looked uncomfortable and anxious. We didn't speak much. I just repeated to him what I had said to my cell mate.

'That's what I told myself when I was let out', he replied.

It was the first and last time my father mentioned he had been in prison.

*

Risley Remand Centre was built in 1963. It was a prison for young offenders and held about a thousand boys and girls. I don't remember ever seeing the girls, so we must have been segregated. Risley had a bad reputation in the seventies (Grisly Risley) and from the moment I entered its gates I sensed something oppressive fall on me. It was like a heavy shroud; a malevolence – a darkness, despite the brightness from neon lights in the reception area. I had sensed the same malevolence on my dad when he beat up those men in the street and when he pushed my mum from the moving car. It shrouded my mum when she hit me for answering back, and it was on both of them as they ripped into each other night after night. I felt it at the school gate when I was bullied and when I walked the streets of Manchester not knowing where to sleep. It was on the faces of the men who teased me as they smoked reefers in the squat and injected who-knows-what into their white, emaciated arms and legs. The difference for me at Risley was that I couldn't escape it. It got into my hair, up my nostrils, under my skin, and I was determined to get away from its pungency and weight as quickly as possible.

When the prison officer told me to strip down to my underpants I was not prepared to be humiliated again, so I answered back with sarcasm. He gave me a swift backhander across the head, so I shut up and handed over my clothes and a few belongings: a wallet, a cheap watch, a comb and some change. All my worldly goods were put in a box with 'Cowley' scrawled across it in black ink and placed on a shelf behind the desk.

Everything appeared large to me – the prison, the guards, the rooms, the inmates. I was given a set of clothes: denim bib and brace dungarees and a striped blue shirt. There was an induction about the dos and don'ts, and I was marched off down the noticeably clean wings, with their overwhelming smell of disinfectant. Young men of various shapes and sizes viewed my arrival with interest. When the cell door was shut, I came face to face with a large black guy, sitting on the bottom bunk, a year older than me, with a strong Brummie accent. The cell was about 8 feet by 6 feet, with two bunk beds on the right, each with a sheet, a blanket and a pillow. There was a bucket in one corner and a sink.

I blabbed something about how they must have made a mistake as I had only nicked a car, and hadn't hurt anyone, so why had they given me six months? I think I truly believed in my innocence. 'Take the top bunk, keep your head down and you will only do half.'

He was kind; he knew I was scared stiff. Later that day an officer collected me, and I was taken for orientation. I visited the education wing, the health care unit, the gym and the canteen. The food that evening was bland. My cell mate sat with me. He didn't say much but I knew he could take care of himself, so I decided to stick with him.

The noise started when the lights went off, and the din was endless; doors slamming, officers shouting, teenagers shouting, keys turning.

Over the next few weeks many jobs were given to me, mostly in the form of cleaning. The job that no one wanted was cleaning the porcelain toilets and the white tiles in the showers. But I enjoyed it as it gave some order to my day.

If you ask my wife, Amanda, how I relax at home, she will laugh out loud and talk about how I like to hoover or take a damp cloth and a bottle of cleaning fluid around the house removing any scuff marks on the walls. I always assumed it was because of my army training but now I wonder if it all started way back in Risley.

Jonathan Aitken, the former Conservative MP jailed for perjury in the 1990s, was the 'wing cleaner' when he was in prison. 'I was issued with a huge book called *The Toilet Cleaner's Manual*,' he told me. 'It went into elaborate detail: "Take the Harpic in one hand, take a brush in the other, put on rubber gloves, four clockwise movements, four anti-clockwise movements . . ." so it was very easy to comply with, but at the end of the day, because clean toilets in that environment were essential, it was a worthwhile job, and I got used to it and I didn't mind it at all. In fact, I felt I'd done something which had a real point to it in the community in which I was living.' Jonathan was at one point Minister of Defence in the John Major government and chief secretary in his cabinet, even tipped to be a future prime minister of the country. Talk about being humbled! When he speaks in prisons, he jokes about once being a 'privy counsellor' and how he became 'counsellor to the privies'.

I also got very used to cleaning the corridors with a big manual floor cleaner called a bumper and, once I got into a rhythm, swinging it from side to side, I found it quite therapeutic. The floor on the wings was so clean I could have eaten off it – not that you would want to because the food was awful. Taking a stainless-steel tray, uninterested inmates dolloped out portions of some sort of stew and mashed potato, followed by, if we were lucky, treacle pudding or spotted dick. I sat with my cell mate for three meals a day and we ate in silence. The food didn't bother me that much as I was used to my mum's cooking which included a strange variety of sheep's head stew, tripe, and pigs' trotters. While I can appreciate a good steak or fish pie, to this day I've never really been that interested in food, seeing it only as fuel.

Each day for an hour we walked around a fenced courtyard area. It was great being out of doors. I wore a standard prison-issue, smelly-but-warm donkey jacket, and unlike most of the boys I didn't smoke so I didn't bother with all the bartering. I took a few educational courses while I was there but was never really that interested, taking myself off to the library where it was warm and safe with plenty of magazines and detective novels. I enjoyed reading about crooks getting caught!

At Risley I kept myself to myself. I was constantly scared of being beaten up. I think I survived by never looking people in the eye, avoiding certain wings, and never complaining about the TV channel in the community room. Time passed quickly, and after three months I was given a resettlement interview with a woman from the probation service. She spoke to me about employment and staying out of trouble. I began to feel quite anxious. *What next?* I thought.

*

My father must have been informed of my release date by a resettlement officer as he was there to meet me in the reception area. The officers were a little surprised he was my dad as his tie gave away his army background. He had grown a moustache, which I thought made him look older, but more distinguished.

In the car I told him what had happened at the police station, about standing semi-naked and being humiliated, especially in front of the female police officer. He didn't seem particularly interested but nodded.

Looking back, I remember my dad was desperate to get away from Risley. I found out many years later, from his sister, that he had served some time in a military prison. It's not clear what he was in for, but most likely he was doing some scam somewhere.

He was keen to let me know that he had left my mum and was in the process of divorcing her and that he had moved into a small flat in Heaton Moore. 'I only stayed for you', he said. His comment angered me because I felt he was blaming me for all their years of fighting. We stopped off at a pub and he told me about his new independent life and how he was 'rid of her'. He suggested I go back home and live with her for a while so that she wouldn't be lonely. I wasn't sure if he was trying to offload me, or if he had a tiny bit of compassion for her.

When I went to the house Mum was happy to see me, but within minutes was telling me how terrible Dad was. She was vitriolic. Leaving her job as a traffic warden, she had become a salesperson for Victoria Wines – right next to where my dad worked. Dad then decided to leave and go to work as a security officer in the John Myers catalogue storage warehouse. There he met Anna, his partner for the rest of his life.

A couple of months after having left Risley, my father told me to get dressed in my smartest clothes as he had arranged an appointment with the chief of police in Manchester. I panicked and said that I hadn't done anything wrong since coming out of prison. *Why were we going to the police station?* He reassured me that I wasn't in trouble. When we arrived at the police commissioner's office I waited outside while my father spoke with him. I was then asked to recount what had happened to me the night I was arrested. The commissioner opened the door and two male police officers and one female officer walked in. They were told to stand to attention while I identified them.

Two weeks later I received a letter from the chief commissioner apologising for the way I had been treated by three of his officers and letting me know that they had all received a reprimand. I remember thinking, *Wow, my father did that for me*. His response was, 'That will teach the bastards to mess with a Cowley.'

Wanting my independence, I moved into a small bedsit in Didsbury and got a bar job working evenings at the Didsbury Inn, a very popular watering hole in the middle of the town. Having learnt some tricks at HMP Risley I made some decent money, especially as I was promoted and put in charge of the restaurant bar; it meant I could fiddle as much as I wanted to and yet balance the books at the same time. The cash in my room was mounting up under my bed, so I decided to invest in some driving lessons. Since I'd been driving with my dad from the age of fourteen, I only needed a few and I passed first time.

Having money felt good but I wanted more and so I took a driving job for a chrome electro plating company in Stockport during the day. My job was to drive a truck laden with huge industrial chrome-plated valves to Hindle Valves in Leeds. I had company in my father's dog, an Alsatian called Rebel, but the driving was tedious, so after a few months I packed it in and went for a job as a driver for a flower shop in Chorlton.

The job was fun as there were several attractive girls working there, so plenty of flirtation and laughter. Having asked one of the girls out I soon got more than I bargained for. At the end of the evening I offered to drop her off at her home. When we arrived, I gave her a kiss, but immediately she began to shake. At first, I thought it was the 'Cowley charm', but then it got worse and she went into a fit. She had forgotten to mention she had epilepsy and for the next twenty minutes I had to stay with her to make sure she was alright. I was completely shocked as it was the first time I had ever encountered the condition. The relationship didn't go any further as I soon left to earn more money.

I was a little awkward around women as I hadn't had much experience of them. The only understanding I had of sex was an incident which happened in my parents' bedroom. There was a wooden wardrobe with ornate handles which was always locked. One day when I was thirteen years old, I noticed the key had been left in the lock. On opening the wardrobe, shoes and clutter filled the space on the floor, as well as a brown cardboard box in the corner. I lifted the box out onto the bed and started to look through the contents: men's magazines. Looking through such graphic pornography scared me, and I panicked and started putting the magazines back, but those images were ingrained on the hard drive of my mind. Girls scared me a little, but the more time I spent with them the more I liked the attention I was getting.

I drove a transit van for a furniture company during the day and continued as the restaurant barman at the Didsbury Inn at night. My dad, propping up the bar opposite me most nights, nagged me about how my mother had ruined his life and that I should avoid her because she was bad news. When seeing my mum, she said the same about my dad. I decided that in order to protect them and myself it was easier to lie, telling each in turn that I hadn't seen the other. Unfortunately, this became a pattern over the years and lying became second nature to me.

Seth Salter, in his article 'Why Do We Lie?', states, 'Lying can bail us out of awkward situations. Spare the feeling of others, preserve or strengthen alliances, enhance social standing, keep us out of trouble, even save lives.' Salter goes on to say, 'Most of us humans, though, bear out the veracity of Mark Twain's statement', which is that 'a man is never more truthful than when he acknowledges himself as a liar.'[3]

I was a long way off from being truthful.

At times my stupidity even exceeded my own expectations. Much of it revolved around drink.

Steve, a friend of mine, and I were drinking at our local pub in Heaton Mersey when I noticed two young women sitting together in the corner. I asked them if they would like to join us for a drink. Surprisingly, they agreed and then the chat up lines started. One of the girls owned the new yellow Ford Capri I had admired in the car park. It was one of my favourite cars as it was fast and stylish. I, however, was driving a very old Renault R10 at the time, certainly not the fastest or even the nicest looking car on the market, but it was all I could afford. Steve was waffling on about how we might be starting our own dog business. I hadn't heard that one before, so I just smiled as he looked at me for affirmation.

Sensing our new friends weren't interested in our business plan, or in us come to that, Steve said, 'Paul used to race cars and he's an amazing driver, and he could easily beat your Capri!'

Desperate to keep the girls interested I nodded.

One of them replied, 'If you can get to Mersey Square before us, then we can all go out together.'

Spotting my Renault, the girls laughed out loud, especially when they saw Rebel, my Alsatian, and Steve's Afghan hound on the back seat. The Capri hit the main Stockport Road and raced off, but I was hot on their tail. Taking me by surprise they took a sharp right with ease, unlike the Renault. Hitting the bend fast, I lost control of the car and it tipped up onto the two offside wheels and slid across the road. As if in slow motion the car flipped onto its roof and we ended up in the middle of the road. The windscreen and back window popped out and my door flew off. I stumbled out of the car and was instantly sick. A witness told me later that the only funny thing about the crash was seeing an Alsatian and an Afghan hound come flying out of the rear window and run off up the street. Fortunately, the dogs were unharmed and came back to Steve's house a couple of hours later.

Someone grabbed my arm and helped me up. He walked me across the street to his home, asking me questions about what had happened and if I was hurt. He took me inside his house and gave me some water and then suggested I lie down. I must have fallen asleep immediately. On waking me, he said the police were downstairs and they wanted to interview me about the accident. He had told them that I had been throwing up and that

I may have concussion. He then said, 'Your mate is downstairs on the settee talking to them now, but I can't stall them any longer or stop them seeing you. I think you are okay now.'

I was in a daze during the interview but didn't mention chasing the Capri. Whether or not they believed me I'll never know. But I didn't hear from them after that. My car was picked up and scrapped the next day. Fortunately for me it was the era before breathalysers otherwise I would certainly have been prosecuted. Steve and I had suffered no major injuries, just a few cuts and bruises and, of course, a massive dent in our pride. We didn't see the Capri girls ever again. It was a great story to tell the guys in the pub, who gave me the nickname Steve McQueen, and it earned us a few beers.

During the next few months I was pretty fed up with life. I ventured out with a friend who suggested we go to a nearby disco held in the basement of a church in Heaton Moore. He said there were always nice girls there and drink, and he was right on both counts. After a few drinks I met a girl called Katie. I walked her home and kissed her goodnight. I asked if I could see her again, she agreed and that was the start of our romance. She was a lovely girl, eighteen months younger than me, well educated and sweet-natured. I met her mum and became fond of her because she was kind to me, especially in the difficult years that followed.

In September 1975, I was twenty years old and still driving a van somewhere in Manchester's Deansgate area when I saw a poster that caught my attention. It showed two soldiers dressed in camouflage uniform, skiing down a snow-capped mountain, backed by an azure blue sky. Bright red capital letters underneath read: 'DO YOU WANT A LIFE OF ADVENTURE? JOIN THE ARMY.'

That was exactly what I wanted: a life of adventure!

I went immediately to the army recruiting centre in Fountain Street. The recruiting sergeant was friendly, but his first question was, 'Do you have a criminal record?' He had 'you can't fool me' written all over his face. I knew I had to tell the truth. I told him about my time in prison and that it hadn't been for long, but he shook his head and told me I couldn't join up. I was gutted. I tried persuading him, but he just walked off, stopping for a moment and saying, 'If you keep trying, then you never know what might happen. Now f*** off!' That little offer of hope was all I needed. I was determined to get in. It felt to me as if it was my only option for escaping my boring life.

Revisiting the recruiting office every week for the next few months I became a familiar face, but each time I received the same answer: 'Not today, but keep trying.' Then on one visit the sergeant suggested I see the duty officer and tell him my story. The young officer appeared and shook my hand; he spoke with a posh accent. After a chat he said, 'Why don't you come through and meet the major. Be polite and address him as Sir. Do you understand?' I nodded.

The major was in a smart uniform, an older man with a kind face. He asked me to take a seat and then said, 'Do you have any qualifications?'

'I have my bronze, silver and gold life-saving proficiency awards.'

Giving a wry smile, he told me that he had been informed of my persistence over the last few months and that it had impressed him. He said that he had the power to enlist me if he thought I was good enough. I could then be sent for a three-day initial selection and induction course. 'Would you like that, son?' he said.

I nodded and felt my heart beating in my chest, wondering if I should trust him or whether he would let me down just as my father said people would. I was sent into another room while they talked. The major called me back in. 'I've decided to take a chance on you.' He took a small Bible out of a drawer and placed a sticker inside. It said, 'This Bible is given to Paul William Cowley 27 January 1976' and I was told to put my hand on top and read from a printed card from which I swore allegiance to the crown. He told me to expect a letter detailing what I should do next.

I walked out of that office on air. It is a day I shall never forget.

A big organisation, the army, represented by a senior officer, was prepared to take a chance on me. This Salford kid had been accepted and I felt deeply excited. I went home and told my mum, who was happy for me, but also a bit gloomy about the whole thing. I didn't care what she thought. At last I had a sense of excitement and nobody could take that from me.

A month later I was on a three-day selection course at St George's Barracks, Sutton Coldfield, in the Midlands. Over the next few days I took a series of assessments including maths, English and psychometric testing. I also had to get through a medical and a sight test. Due to my lazy eye, I looked through a gap in my fingers when reading the chart. I flew through every test, excelling in my new environment.

I filled in my form to choose my regiment and headed for the final interview. The officer went through my test results and it seemed I had done well. Unfortunately, my scores weren't good enough for my first choice, the Royal Army Veterinary Corps. Neither was I tall enough for my second choice, the Irish Guards. The officer said, 'But you could get into the Royal Artillery as a gunner.' I had no idea what the artillery was, but he made it sound good. My papers were stamped, and shaking my hand he said, 'Well done, you're in.'

Returning home, I went back to the bedsit and within the week received a letter with a rail warrant and directions to Woolwich station in London. I had been spending time with Katie, who was by now my girlfriend. She was pleased for me but anxious about what it meant for the two of us. My mum became soft with me; maybe she had an idea that being in the army could be dangerous. It never crossed my mind. She offered to do my laundry. I was packed and ready to go.

The short sharp shock of Risley worked for me but for many it is the beginning of the revolving door of repeat offending. I wasn't a saint after Risley, that's for sure. Avoiding prison a couple more times, thieving and behaving badly was still on my agenda. At this stage of my life, I had no real awareness, and no accountability. The army was going to make a man of me, but it wasn't going to be easy. It was like carving my character out of stone. It was going to take a few knocks and scrapes to get me into shape.

4: No pain, no gain

Adventure came within a few months, but not in the way I expected.

My first tour of Northern Ireland, like my birth, started with a bang. I was twenty-one years old when I went from my regiment as part of an advance party for my first deployment. I flew out to Ireland on 3 October 1976; the rest of the regiment followed a week later. The pressure was immense, on a daily basis, and within the first few weeks one of the lads committed suicide in the communal showers with a standard issue 9 mm pistol. My new friend, Geordie, and I were tasked to clean up the mess. We then packed all his kit and personal belongings into an MFO box (packing crate) to be sent on to his family. Cleaning the toilets and showers at Risley was one thing, but wiping splattered blood, tissue and bone off white tiles was something I shall never forget.

*

Before Northern Ireland I went through sixteen weeks' basic training, which started as soon as I got off the train at Woolwich station in March 1976. A full bombardier, quite an awesome-looking figure standing in his No.2 peaked cap with his pace stick tucked under his arm, met the sixty or so recruits on the platform. After taking a roll call, he walked us up to the barracks.

Passing through those gates of the training facility at Woolwich I told myself that my new life was to start here, and that no one was ever going to lay a hand on me or bully me ever again.

There were five blocks of accommodation, each named after a great battle involving the artillery, and I, along with twenty-six others, was allocated to Colenso block. We all had to report to the barber immediately and my head of thick blond hair was cut to a short crop.

Next came the clothing store where we collected lightweight trousers, a No.2 tailored uniform, socks, underpants, a heavy wool jumper and No.2 dress shirts, a tie, a beret, blue and red running PT vests and shorts, plimsolls, combat boots, ammo drill boots, combat jacket and trousers, webbing and a gas mask with its carrying case. After placing it all in a sausage-shaped kit bag, I carried it back to the block. It was then on to the bedding store for a mattress, sheets, blankets and a pillow.

Each day began with fitness: running, boxing, and drill. It didn't take long for me to become exceptionally fit; having been mocked at school for having skinny legs, I soon discovered they were fast. It was the best of times for me, as I felt I was growing in confidence every day, always something new to learn – a new skill, a new challenge.

One month into the sixteen weeks' basic training I went to my training sergeant and told him I wanted to change my enlistment order from three to nine years as I was enjoying the process so much. He was delighted. The thought of returning to that bedsit in Didsbury held no appeal for me and I was determined to succeed. The time flew by and I was surprised and honoured to be awarded the title of Best Recruit (Satisfied Soldier) which meant an extra two weeks' leave at the end of the training.

In the final week, after the pass out parade, a list was put up in our dormitory and my name was next to 49th Field Regiment RA. I had no idea where they were based. All I knew was that it was a field gun regiment using 105 Howitzer guns mounted on a vehicle called an Abbot. It was, in fact, part of a large garrison called Haig Barracks in Hohne, West Germany. During the Cold War it had been a major British garrison, home to the 7th Armoured Brigade and most of its subordinate units.

However, I had one problem, so I went to the training sergeant and said, 'Sarge, can I take my girlfriend with me?' He replied, 'No girlfriends, only wives!' Having heard that the army gave a house (married quarters) and more pay to a married soldier I decided there was only one thing to do.

There was little time for romance and I'm not even sure if I ever asked Katie to marry me. I went with her to her nearest church (Heaton Norris) and found the vicar, telling him I would like him to marry us on my next break as I was being posted to Germany. Looking at me with surprise, he said, 'Don't you want to attend church before you get married? Or talk about this commitment?'

'No. Why would I do that?' I replied.

Knowing that my regiment had been put on a warning order for an operational tour of Northern Ireland that began in October, I suggested a date for the wedding and then we left. Katie didn't say a word – I think she was in shock. I can only assume that she went to the church and heard the banns being read.

It was mid-July 1976 when I flew out to Germany to join my regiment with a few of the recruits including my new friend, Geordie. Billeted together in a four-man room, we did everything together as a team ('brick'). The Northern Ireland training involved fitness sessions and daily weapon handling on the firing ranges, intelligence courses explaining how to recognise known terrorists, and urban map reading. It was necessary to brush up on our military skills and our radio communications because if we got it wrong we could pay with our lives.

The most worrying part of the training was having to load our weapons with live ammunition in the loading bay, which was basically a sand-filled bunker. On returning to the base we had to unload our weapons in the same bunker, trying desperately to avoid an NG (Negligent Discharge), which was a court martial offence. So, the phrase 'magazine off, cock, hook and look' became embedded in our brains.

The army was the new start I needed, a place where I could recreate myself. However, I simply replaced one way of behaving with another. A stronger tougher Cowley was to emerge.

*

It is estimated that 100 soldiers committed suicide during the Troubles and I witnessed just one of them. I cannot imagine the horror experienced by their parents or loved ones on hearing the news. At the age of twenty-one I was in some ways tougher than I am today because I was emotionally immature and oblivious to danger, but it definitely made an impact on me.

Operation Banner was the name given to the army's operational tour in Northern Ireland between August 1969 and July 2007, and it was the longest continuous deployment of British troops in that land. At the peak of the operations in the 1970s about 21,000 troops were deployed and 1,441 serving personnel died. Most people assume it was a religious war but primarily it was political and fuelled by historical events.

In 1972 the army took over the Grand Central Hotel in Belfast (GCH) for use as a military base in the height of the Troubles. Troops based there were protected by anti-rocket wire screens constructed in front of the building. It was one of the most bombed hotels in the world, attacked more than 150 times by the Provisional IRA and other groups.

Training in Germany for Northern Ireland had been challenging but also fun. When we were actually in a war zone it was a very different matter. Despite my squint, I was considered a good shot and had qualified as a marksman, eventually becoming a sniper. I wore the envied badge of crossed rifles with the small 'S' above them on my arm and my personnel weapon in NI was a 303 Lee-Enfield rifle: a single shot bolt-action rifle, very accurate (with an effective firing range of 730m) and very dangerous in the wrong hands. I was the sniper in our 'brick' of four, and we patrolled the streets of central Belfast on foot, searching houses and looking for IRA suspects.

A week later my section was on Quick Reaction Force duty; first on the scene if anything went off in the city. It was boring, as much of the time we sat in full combat gear with weapons ready, watching TV and eating egg banjos (sandwiches). Then one day, we got the call that there was a suspect bomb in the front window of Burton, the men's clothing outfitters on Grand Avenue. *Great,* we thought, *some excitement at last,* and we all dived into the Land Rover. I was the driver that day and as we approached the shop the adrenalin was high. Suddenly, there was an almighty blast coming from Burton's doorway. Once our ears stopped ringing and the dust cleared, we were stunned by what we saw – body parts lying everywhere. It looked like a disaster movie. When we got nearer, one of the team jumped out and ran forward and picked up a leg. We thought he had lost his mind, especially as he was laughing his head off. Gradually we realised the joke. He was holding the leg of a mannequin from the shop window display. Plastic pink body parts were strewn everywhere.

Fortunately, the shop was closed on that day, and no one was injured. Luckily for us the bomb had been triggered far too early. Once we had made the area and the shop secure for the police we left with a few pairs of socks and underwear. Old habits die hard and most of the soldiers had come from a similar background to mine. There are no excuses for crime, but I have come to realise that many young men do not have much of a conscience.

The next week the IRA blew up a sports shop on Gresham Street, which was very near to our accommodation. One of the lads, looking out of our window, said, 'That's a bit too close for comfort.'

Rioting in the streets was a frequent occurrence and the army was often called in to disperse the crowds. I decided to volunteer for the snatch squad: three soldiers dressed in lightweight trousers and red T-shirts who would run out from between the uniformed soldiers and grab troublemakers. In training it was exciting but when it came to doing it for real it was nerve racking. We had no weapons and so were very vulnerable as we relied on the soldiers to let us back in behind their protective shields. This was not always easy as the soldiers themselves were scared and didn't want to re-open their tight defensive line. They also had to defend themselves from petrol bombs containing sugar, which were often thrown at them to cause the most damage to the shields and clothing. In all the times my snatch squad went into the crowd we only managed to grab one person, as they always turned on us. I was relieved when I was called to do a different job.

Patrolling the streets in our brick, we gathered information about certain individuals, checked car number plates, and passed on information to the intelligence officer at HQ. Other tasks mostly consisted of guard duties, often in a hut (known as a sanger). One night when we were back at base in the Grand Central Hotel I was on guard duty in one of the six sangers positioned around the hotel with my colleague, nicknamed 'The Bear' due to his size and his eating habits. The sergeant major occasionally checked on us, to make sure we weren't sleeping. If you got caught sleeping, you were in big trouble!

It was around 3.00 a.m. when we both thought we heard a noise. There was a thick mist and visibility was bad, so we decided it must be in our heads. Suddenly there were shots fired straight at us! It frightened the life out of both of us and we jumped up. It was at that moment that the training kicked in. The Bear got on the radio shouting, 'Contact wait out.' This informed the operation room (OPS) that we had been fired at. More shots came our way and I returned three rounds of fire from my personal weapon, a 7.62 SLR. Within seconds we had the duty officer, the sergeant major and numerous officers with tracker dogs, in our area.

The next morning, we heard that the sniffer dogs had found a trail and followed it until it went cold a couple of miles away. The Bear and I were complimented on our handling of the situation and everything returned to normal. After a couple of days my group were back on patrol around the hotel and we thought we would try and see where my shots had landed. One of the lads shouted for me to come and look at the damage. 'Good grouping, Paul!' he said.

'That gets you a few beers when we get back to base', said one gunner.

The only thing that troubled me was that my three well-placed shots had destroyed part of the entrance to a small church. I wasn't a man of faith, but I felt bad about hitting a church. Somewhere deep down I must have had a bit of reverence for the institution.

Five months passed, and we were coming to the end of the first tour. Being a young soldier and not knowing all the army protocols, I had not even thought to ask permission from the commanding officer (CO) to leave the tour a week early for my wedding. The troop commander told me I was an idiot and that I needed to see the CO immediately and might even have to call the wedding off. Eventually, after a heated discussion, the CO gave permission for both me and Geordie (my best man) to go back to England. Armed with my grey suit with its wide-lapelled jacket and trendy flared trousers, bought from a tailor's shop in Belfast, I flew back on a VC10 into RAF Brize Norton airbase.

When I arrived back in England, Katie was pleased to see me but insisted that I should not have my stag night just before the wedding on the Saturday. She obviously knew me better than I knew myself.

On the Wednesday night, Geordie, my father and I started drinking early in the Didsbury Inn. Heading for the city centre, we went to numerous pubs. By 2.00 a.m. we started towards home, stopping at a fish and chip shop. I could barely stand up as I was so drunk. Noticing someone trying to push in front of us, and without thinking, I took a swing at him to teach him a lesson. Missing my target, I crashed through the plate glass window of the shop, and ended up on the floor, badly injuring my hand, arm and back. My dad called for an ambulance and I was rushed to hospital with three slashed tendons in my right hand and a large piece of glass stuck in the middle of my back close to my spine.

I woke up the next morning in Manchester General Hospital with my right hand raised above my head, in plaster up to my elbow. The doctor told me how Geordie had stopped me from bleeding to death by making a tourniquet from his shirt. Once at the hospital, my father was asked to sign a consent form for the operation, as there was a risk to life due to the amount of alcohol I had in my system. The surgeons spent hours sewing the tendons of my right hand together with titanium wires and Geordie slept under my bed all night while my father walked home.

Katie arrived and was not impressed. I checked out and we headed to her home in a taxi. The cocktail of alcohol, anaesthetic and drugs they had given me in the hospital didn't mix well and I had to stop the taxi to be sick several times before we got back.

Two days later I was getting dressed for my wedding when I realised I couldn't get my arm into the sleeve of my jacket because of the plaster cast. Geordie jumped into action and split the seam and safety-pinned it together. 'Job done!' he said, feeling very proud of himself.

Although Katie and I had been dating for over a year when we got married in February 1977, there were problems right from the beginning. I knew in my heart that we were fundamentally unsuited. I was reckless and self-centred and young; she was hopeful, like many women, that she could change her man. However, the honeymoon set the scene.

When we arrived at the Mellieha Bay in Malta we were informed that there was a reception for all newly married couples that evening. Thrilled, we went to experience our all-inclusive buffet, champagne and dancing. Katie and I were having great fun, the drink was flowing, things were going well, and we even became friendly with another young couple from the north who shared our table for the evening, dancing together into the early hours. When the music changed to slow songs we changed partners, but in a holiday haze of music and drink I started to kiss my new dancing partner, who didn't resist my advances. Katie strode across the dance floor, pulled us apart and slapped me hard across the face, walking off in disgust. Like a scene from a western, when the stranger walks into the saloon and everybody stops and stares at him, I was being stared at by a group of disgusted newlyweds. After a lot of apologising on my part, Katie and I made up and then spent the rest of the week desperately trying to avoid our new friends. I blame my age and the drink, of course. Young men are often wayward and with no accountability. I was something of a loose cannon!

After the honeymoon I went back to Germany and my four-man room. Katie had to wait for me to get quarters before she could join me. I was excited to get qualified to work within a team of five men on the 'workhorse' of the artillery, the Abbot 105 field gun that looked like a tank. It was an amazing piece of weaponry, weighing in at 16 tonnes with a muzzle velocity of 1,550 ft/sec and could project a shell over 15 km. After a while the level of noise created by the gun firing was unbearable. Even with ear defenders it felt as if my head was exploding. Deciding I needed a quieter job, I became a command post assistant, which involved working in a track vehicle much further away from the noise of the guns.

During the winter I managed to go to Oberjoch in Bavaria and get my British Association of Ski Instructors certificate. I was finally living the 'life of adventure' as depicted on that poster in Deansgate.

When I went into the army my life improved dramatically. Educationally, I had to do numerous tests as well as learn practical discipline towards fitness and personal hygiene. Washing, ironing, bulling boots and keeping my living area spotless was all good for my character. Each day there was a new challenge and I realised I was capable of pushing myself further, both mentally and physically. Going to the gym and doing weights gradually changed my body from scrawny to a muscular physique. The change in my body and mind gave me an adrenalin rush, a sense of achievement in everything I did. Although the work was hard and challenging and almost killed me at times, it was the first time in my life I felt I was getting somewhere. I was also able to relate to a group of men and they respected me.

Katie eventually joined me in late March 1977. Due to a lack of married quarters we were given emergency accommodation in what I can only describe as a Portakabin. There were about a hundred of them in a field, at the back of the garrison camp. Life was exciting at first, with a wife, a new home and a great job. What else could I have wanted? The trouble was, I was restless. I therefore put myself on any course that I thought would help with promotion. This meant I was away from Katie once again as some of the courses were in the UK. She would fly back home and stay with her mum and then both of us would return to the emergency accommodation, which was proving stressful due to its size and lack of warmth.

It was around this time that I had the crazy idea of asking my mum to visit. I felt sorry for her as Dad now had a girlfriend. Picking my mum up from Hanover airport, all was well for a couple of days. Then things started to deteriorate. I'd come home to find her arguing with Katie, criticising her cooking skills or telling her how she was supposed to look after me. At times both of them ended up in tears and I couldn't handle the conflict. The Portakabin was small and for three strong-minded adults each hour that passed, the tension increased, and something was bound to happen. One evening, Mum was telling Katie how to cook a curry, when the pressure cooker exploded. Curry sauce went everywhere. I sided with Katie, shouting at Mum that she had to stop nagging, as Katie was doing her best and it was more than I deserved. But Mum ranted and ranted and just wouldn't stop, so I packed her case and took her to a village, checking her into a hotel.

The next day, I told her it wasn't working out and that I needed to take her to the airport. Katie wanted to leave too and spend a few weeks with her mum. I guess she was worn out living with me and being in a constant state of isolation. When Katie came back it was even harder for her to settle down as we just seemed to argue about everything. I tried spending time with her but it was proving difficult. I took her to the battery bar at night, but she wasn't impressed because often the soldiers were rowdy and crude. Sometimes we would go into Celle, the nearest town to the camp, for a meal or a drink.

Celle is an old town, with a lot of history and culture, and it is nice to walk around. Unfortunately, as a young man I wasn't very stimulating to be with. My life revolved around work, drink, cars, men's humour and gossip, and of course, me. It was difficult for us to find a real connection as we were both quite inexperienced and hadn't really developed any interests, shared or otherwise. Katie had the added disadvantage of not having many friends on the camp. She took to going back to England to spend time with her mum and I kept myself busy with training, fitness and getting into trouble with women and drink.

When Katie was away, I went across the road to the local bar called the Astra. It was the soldiers' favourite bar on a Saturday night as it had a great atmosphere and also doubled as a brothel. One night we played a drinking game. After several rounds, I lost and so ordered a round for the lads and looked at my change. Believing that the barman had ripped me off, I started to have a go at him and like lightning he landed such a punch to my temple that he completely knocked me out. I didn't see that coming! As I opened my eyes, all I could see were deep red curtains and soft furnishings. My vision cleared, and I saw two gorgeous women looking down at me, smiling. Then I saw Geordie, who started to explain what had happened.

The barman hated British soldiers because one had run off with his wife. Since he had also been a boxer in another life, he saw red when I started arguing with him about my change. Geordie had carried me, with the help of a couple of the 'ladies of the night', into the back room where they had looked after me; I had been unconscious for over half an hour. The next morning when I looked in the mirror, I had a one-inch cut above my right eye. I should have had stitches but I didn't want to go to hospital so the women put a sticky plaster on it. The area around my eye turned a dark yellow with the bruising and today I still have the scar and the memory of it. When Katie returned from one of her trips, she asked me what had happened, and I made something up about getting hurt during a training exercise.

Fortunately, we moved into far superior married quarters and in December 1977, Katie fell pregnant, which was an exciting time for both of us as we thought having a child would fix all our problems.

Meanwhile, I had heard that Sergeant Major Payne, nicknamed 'No Pain, No Gain', was putting together a group of twenty-seven men, known as the Close Observation Platoon (COP), and that I might be suitable. Always looking for adventure I volunteered and was accepted on the six-week selection course. Payne organised the training around areas of the camp, setting up road blocks, snap car checks and various covert operations. Using lots of military equipment, including numerous weapons, was great fun as well as challenging, and the variety suited me.

At the end of the training I walked into the office and Payne said: 'Cowley, if you want to be in COP there is one more thing you have to do. Go over there to the sergeant.'

The sergeant handed me a plastic bag and said, 'You need to crap in this bag.' I was a bit confused, but being a man under authority I replied, 'Where, Sarge?' He replied, 'Right here, right now.'

Of course, I did as I was told and offered him the bag. The sergeant shook his head. 'You can dispose of it,' he said. 'But well done, you have passed the final test.'

I found out later that three soldiers had failed the course because they couldn't poo in a bag in front of other men. It may seem ridiculous to non-military people reading this, but I was to learn of its importance on my second tour, which began in the May of 1978.

Based in Flax Street Mill on the corner of the Ardoyne and the New Lodge area, we were all warned to be cautious as there had been several soldiers killed in this region by IRA snipers.

Although I was with 49 Field Regiment, I was now part of COP, eating together and living together in separate accommodation. We were given special treatment, clothing and equipment, and it felt good to be a part of something different. One covert operation lasted three days and three nights in the attic of an empty house. As we left, we had to remove everything, including our poo bags and bottles of urine.

On another occasion, after a long briefing session, and after a couple of days of reconnaissance, four of us were tasked at nightfall to take up positions in the hedgerow of an unoccupied house in the Ballysillan area of Belfast. Our role was to report back any suspicious movement around the area of the main post office, which was opposite the garden in which we were hiding. There had been a tip off to the Royal Ulster Constabulary (RUC) that the IRA were going to rob the post office. If the IRA did come along they would be in for a surprise, that was for sure. However, on the third night of living in the hedge we were told to retreat from the garden, because the Special Air Service (SAS) were now being tasked to take over. When the IRA tried to rob the post office that night, they met with the SAS, who shot all but one of them dead.

Having spent six months previously in NI, to be there for another six was tedious, and Geordie and I were constantly trying to find some excitement.

One night, a woman on the gate who was part of the Civilian Search Unit recommended we meet her for a drink in a bar in the White Rock area of Belfast near the Springfield Road. Against military orders, Geordie and I took off in a cab. Having signed out a 9 mm pistol I was feeling quite confident. When we stepped into the pub we both sensed it was the wrong place to be. Men turned and stared at us. It was very difficult to hide the fact that we were soldiers. Two women came over and said, 'What are you doing here? You need to leave now.'

'But we are meeting someone', said Geordie.

'No, you are not. You need to leave', replied one of the women.

The darkness, the malevolence I had experienced in Risley and in my home, was back with full force. I knew we had to leave. I grabbed Geordie and we went outside and picked up a taxi straight away. Neither of us knew that there had been several notorious incidents on the Springfield Road only a few years earlier. The Ballymurphy Massacre and the Springhill Massacre had resulted in civilian deaths being carried out by members of the British Army, and the locals were not in favour of soldiers being in their pubs.

Remarkably, thirty years later, when I visited HMP Belmarsh in south London to help on an Alpha course, I met Sergeant Major Payne. He had become the senior prison officer in charge of security at the gate and was known as Mr Payne. Recognising him, the colour drained from my face. He addressed me without looking up. 'Name?' he said, and I replied, 'No Pain, No Gain.' He then looked straight at me and said, 'Ah, Cowley!' Nothing more was said, and he let me through security.

Northern Ireland was not a good experience for me. But I did learn about teamwork and how you couldn't do anything on your own. Being in the army meant I had to trust people with my life. It contradicted my understanding of never trusting anyone – the message my dad had given me as I leapt from the wall when I was eight years old.

The birth of my child would be another chance for me to develop, but I wasn't convinced I had the skills or the maturity to be a father.

5: Promises like pie crust

Katie went into labour just before the end of the tour, so once again I was released a few days early. I made it just in time to see my son born in Stepping Hill Hospital in Stockport, on the day before Katie's twenty-first birthday. The birth wasn't easy as there were complications. But I was proud of my young wife as she showed such grit and determination. Naming him Clinton, after Clint Eastwood, I think it was in some way a tribute to my father, as Eastwood was one of our mutual heroes.

I loved my son as soon as he was born. Everyone said he had the Cowley look. I started to get used to having another person in our lives and I was happy for a while. Several soldiers known to me, including a close friend, had lost newborns in cot deaths. Out of concern, I had his cot next to me at night, and placing my hand on his chest, I would constantly check his breathing. Sometimes he turned over in the night and by the morning he was awake on my hand.

I thought of all the things my own father had never done with me and I made promises to myself that I wouldn't be like him. I wanted to be with my son, play with him and teach him to trust me. I had plans to play football with him, teach him to swim and ride a bike, and watch him grow into a fine young man. My mother used to say to my father, 'Your promises are like pie crust; they are made to crumble.' I didn't know what she meant at the time, but I soon found out that my promises too were made to crumble and that I wasn't any better than my father. In fact, he had stayed with my mother until I left home, which was more than I was able to do for my son.

*

Katie tried to love me. She was a good woman, but I was messed up and at the time was not very loving. I gradually felt restricted by the responsibilities of having a child and wife to support. My marriage was in threads and I had little interest in trying to make it work. I was now on my way to making full bombardier and that was all that mattered to me. I was hungry for my next promotion, but promotion was slow in the regiment.

The first opportunity I had, I took a posting to Chester as a staff car driver for Brigadier Stagg, who was in charge of the UK Territorial Army.

Moving to large married quarters on Saighton Camp, Katie was happy that she was nearer to her mum and sister. I was out most days driving Brigadier Stagg to various Territorial Army units. It was always a big event for the unit when the Brigadier arrived, as the visit would last most of the day. It started with an inspection of the guard and a walk around the camp. Then it was lunch in the Officers' Mess, followed by a small show put on to demonstrate the unit's skills; tea was served in the Sergeants' Mess, and then a visit to the junior ranks club to meet the younger soldiers. Finally, it was polished off with dinner in the Officers' Mess hosted by the Commanding Officer. As a result, I was hanging around for hours entertaining myself. Most visits included an overnight stay with the Brigadier in a local hotel. Once the boss had gone to bed, I would hit the bar and start drinking. There was usually someone to chat to, a barmaid, housekeeper or waitress, and often that led to a one-night stand and rather embarrassed smiles at breakfast, which the Brigadier politely ignored.

*

Time spent with my son was special to me – the days we had together were important – but I was away a lot, and when he was three years old I knew I was failing him as a father.

After arguing with Katie for weeks, I made up my mind to leave. Then I returned home late from work one night and found my uniform hanging in the hallway. Katie, who had never really taken any interest in my work before, had pressed my shirt and trousers, placing my red stable belt and side cap neatly on the stairs next to a pair of very shiny black work shoes. I knew she was trying to be kind and keep the marriage together, but it was too late. I was addicted to chaos and betrayal. I was irresponsible and reckless. I was split in two; the world of the army and combat was out of sync with my home life. You might have thought I would have craved the security of a wife, a nice home and a child, but I didn't. I just felt trapped. I wanted my freedom.

After five years of marriage I packed up a few belongings and checked myself into what I can only describe as a large wooden shed on the army base. I tried making it homely, having taken the tropical fish tank from my married quarters, as Katie disliked it. We divorced quickly, and Katie and Clinton moved in with a friend across the road. Clinton was a good kid and when I look back, I can see now how I let him down. I regret the time I lost with him, but it was my fault – my lack of care – and I will never have those days again.

Since my long-standing goal was to make sergeant, I soon became bored with being a staff car driver. I was prepared to take any postings necessary to secure those three tapes on my arm and get into the Sergeants' Mess.

When I wasn't working, I stayed in much of the time and began to regret my divorce. One night when I was getting the staff car out of the military compound, I spotted Katie coming out of her friend's married quarters with a man. She was laughing and the guy put his arm around her as he helped her into his car. I wondered if I had been a bit hasty in my decision to leave. I would have belted him, but I think I was depressed, as I was becoming passive and introverted. I have never liked spending a lot of time on my own. Maybe because it reminds me of the loneliness I felt growing up.

Eventually, Katie left her friend's in Chester and went to live with her mother in Stockport. Fortunately, Katie met a good man who took care of her and loved her as she deserved to be loved. He also helped raise my son until he was sixteen years old, for which I am very grateful.

One night, a friend of mine came to see me and we had a couple of beers in my room. He told me I had to get some fun otherwise I would go mad. He persuaded me to go with him for a drink at the Royal British Legion Club in Chester. I was playing darts with a few locals when a girl walked in who looked as if she had just come off a fashion shoot. She was certainly not dressed for the British Legion darts night. Her name was Julie and we made immediate eye contact. I offered to buy her a drink, oblivious, at first, to the fact that her boyfriend was standing next to her. After sizing him up I worked out he was no match for me, and he must have felt the same because he kept quiet. In a pub full of longstanding darts players, Julie was an impressive player. I asked her out on a date, and she said yes.

We met a few days later and really hit it off. She was fun, with a great sense of humour, carefree and very tactile – something I had missed. We continued to date for a few months and then in July 1982 we were married in a registry office in Chester only five months after my divorce from Katie. The wedding was fun, with lots of people – mainly Julie's friends, as I didn't have many. I thought to myself that this time it would be different. I was determined to make it work. I was twenty-seven years old and believed I could change.

Julie was attractive, and she knew it. And I was highly jealous of any man looking at her. One night, when we were in a bar in Chester, I came back from the toilet and found two guys chatting her up. I was furious. One of them had his hand on my wife's shoulder and she looked uncomfortable. The other man threatened me and made a sarcastic comment about Julie. Remembering my dad's words – 'Make sure your first punch counts, because you won't get another' – I went in for a hit, but all of a sudden, I felt a punch to my face. I hit back with the full force of my pent-up jealousy, grabbed Julie and left the pub. Glancing back, I saw my opponent being held up by his friend and clutching a cloth to his bleeding nose. No one would have been proud of me that day, except maybe my father. We never went back to that bar again, and after a while it started to get difficult to find a bar where there hadn't been an incident or where we didn't run into the same people.

Once again, I was on the move and given quarters on Shooters Hill, which suited us both. I was now the personal assistant to Major General Tomlinson, Director General of the Royal Artillery (DGRA). I was to run his large Victorian house in the grounds of Woolwich Barracks. The job was good but hard work. The staff could be difficult, and I didn't enjoy standing around in my uniform at dinner parties, feeling like a waiter, but I threw myself into the job and was determined to be a success. I decided I needed some extra training and so took some courses. I achieved distinctions in City & Guild's certificates, including food and beverage, silver service, management, wine selection, and I particularly enjoyed the flower arranging!

Some of the general's guests were very pompous and rude at times, but I learned to be polite and manage their questions or complaints. On the positive side I had lots of time to myself once orders were given for the day's duties. I kept busy by going to the gym, running and spending time with Julie.

Fortunately, the general liked me, as I was conscientious and good at the job. After six months, when I was feeling really settled, he came home one night and as I prepared him his usual gin and tonic, he called me into his study. 'I have something for you, Bombardier Cowley!' He handed me a piece of paper. It was an official memo, which stated, 'Major General Tomlinson gives authority for Bombardier Cowley to be promoted with immediate effect to the rank of substantive sergeant.' I looked at him and he smiled. 'You've earned it, son.'

I'd made it to sergeant at last. I was elated and so was Julie. That night she sewed three tapes on to my uniform, as I didn't want to wait for the military tailors. It was one of the happiest days of my life.

With the promotion came more money and a slightly bigger married quarters. For a while I was happy. The kid from Salford was so proud to hear people addressing him as 'Sarge'. But my happiness was short lived – lasting four months – because I always seemed to resort to my default position of being unsettled and restless. I was finally in the Sergeants' Mess, which was my dream, but now I was there, I was looking for the next thing to occupy me – something unknown to me – something to give me that excitement I'd craved most of my life.

The work continued to go well with the general, but little did I know he had a plan for me. Another major general and his team were visiting, and it was my job to put on a dinner event. There were to be about thirty people, all high-ranking officers and their wives, plus a couple of Ministry of Defence people, and a couple of MPs. The pressure was on, so I made the staff have two dress rehearsals, plus I insisted that the chef give the general and his wife two tasting sessions prior to the evening. They were suitably impressed, as they had never had a house sergeant go to so much trouble before.

The following morning General Tomlinson called me into his office. He told me that the supper party had been a very special event, but it had also been a test to see if the visiting major general liked me. I had passed with flying colours and the visiting general asked me to go immediately to Bielefeld in Germany to run his household, with the possible promotion eventually to staff sergeant. I was a little shocked but General Tomlinson told me that he would be retiring soon and as the visiting general was a younger man, his equivalent in Germany, and it would serve my career to go.

Julie wasn't that excited about my new job, as she had just started to settle down in the quarters on Shooters Hill, but she was happy for me. Once I had gone through the interview stage and all the paperwork was sorted, she joined me in Germany, and we were given German quarters known as a 'hiring'. Usually they were in a German community, but we were offered a lovely flat just outside the town. Julie loved it, as it was modern, clean and in the countryside.

In Chester I had managed to convince Julie's ex-boyfriend to sell me his V8 Triumph Stag. It was a beauty and I was able to drive it to my new posting in Germany. I had spent a fortune getting it back to its original glory, mostly with my money, but I'd also borrowed quite a lot along the way from various people.

Working with the general was good for me as we got on well and he gave me more and more responsibility. He had a bigger team, and a much bigger house with land attached. There was a chef, a driver, a gardener, cleaners, a handy man and a house corporal. The general entertained more military personnel and also visiting officials than the previous general had, so I was kept busy with a dinner party at least once a week. If it wasn't a dinner, it was a lunch around the tennis courts or on the lawn after a game of croquet. After a few months at the new job my mum contacted me, and I invited her over to stay with us for a week. I hoped it would be better than the time she had stayed with Katie and me.

One evening a few of the lads got together and held a barbecue at the bottom of the flats with friends and family members. There was music and as always a few beers. I was working late, so I told Julie I would join her later and to keep an eye on Mum until I got there.

Before I left my office at the general's house, I called Julie and said I was on my way to the party. She sounded stressed. 'You had better come home now, Paul.' When I arrived, my mother was dancing on top of a table, flirting with the soldiers, who were cheering her on. She was drunk from playing a drinking game earlier with them. I arrived just in time to stop her taking her top off! I went ballistic and took her upstairs. Julie, who had been raised in a smart part of Chester and was well educated, was so embarrassed by the show, while the guys thought it was hilarious. But no one was more embarrassed and ashamed than I was. It reminded me of growing up with her. She was always irresponsible, drinking too much and making a show of herself, making sexual innuendoes and gestures at any opportunity. It took a while for the banter of that event to die down and for my colleagues to refrain from mentioning my mum's antics every time they saw me.

My new job with the general was good but also challenging. I liked him and he liked me. He was a fatherly man whom I admired, but unfortunately I didn't get on with his wife. She was constantly interfering in the arrangements. It would have been fine if her manner had been kind, but most days she upset the staff and the chef. She certainly didn't want to share her home with a strong-minded soldier.

Within six months she had complained to her husband and I was called into his office. 'You are excellent at what you do, Sergeant Cowley. I have no complaints except one; it is very hard for me to defend you to my wife.' I knew he was in a difficult position, so when he asked me where I would like to be posted I replied, 'A fighting regiment, sir.' He agreed, saying that he could never really understand how I got into this type of work in the first place. 'You're a soldier not a butler, Cowley!' he said, and asked me where I would like to go. I replied, 'I don't really care, sir.'

A week later I was packing up our home again and being transferred to the Garrison Sergeants' Mess in Dortmund, another regiment and another married quarters. The Dortmund Garrison contained four different regiments, one of them being 16 Air Defence Regiment, a Rapier (surface to air missile) Unit. I had asked to be attached to a fighting unit but my job was to run the Garrison Sergeants' Mess – not exactly what I'd hoped for but I was happier.

The Garrison Mess served all the regiments, so once again I had a big team to look after. It was, however, really run down and neglected. Raising the standards within a few weeks, people started to notice the difference. My team included privates, lance corporals, and two full bombardiers, one being quite senior. But they were furious with me when I called them all together and explained to them that from now on things would look different in the mess and that included the staff. 'You are a disgrace to the uniform, unfit and overweight.' As the sergeant I had the power to put my team through the army regular fitness tests, compulsory for every soldier in the British Army.

It wasn't long before I had a visit from the senior full bombardier who was in charge of the team. 'Sarge, none of these soldiers have completed a military test for years. That's why they are in this job – to get away from soldiering. They're bar staff.'

'Not any more. They're soldiers first, then bar staff, so get them on parade fully kitted out for a BFT (basis fitness test of three miles) at 6.00 a.m. tomorrow morning, you included.'

The run was complete chaos and I lost 90 per cent of them in the first mile. The road looked like a disaster movie, with bodies lying everywhere. After weekly training they started to improve. However, the job wasn't holding me and I realised I was going nowhere fast. I was now a twenty-seven-year-old sergeant running a Garrison Sergeants' Mess, which was a role usually given to older men who were ready to retire.

Since I had a reputation as a fast runner and keen sportsman, I soon discovered there was a regimental running club. When I found out that the regimental sergeant major (RSM) was in charge of the club I started to hatch my escape plan.

I needed to make friends with the RSM, as he was also the RSM of 16 Air Defence Regiment, which I was interested in joining. After a period of time running with the group, I managed to finish in the top three on a regular basis. However, I was soon advised by a few of the other lads not to ever try and come first, as that was the RSM's position and he wouldn't like it. Apparently, no one had beaten him for years! I always loved a challenge, so one morning, on our run, I was near the front. Coming around the last bend, entering the camp, I flew past the RSM, coming in first.

That afternoon he called me into his office and made me stand to attention as he gave me a severe dressing down for having the cheek to overtake him. No one had ever done that before. 'I can't help it if I'm faster than you, sir', I said.

Looking at me he grinned. 'Sergeant Cowley, what the hell are you doing running the Garrison Sergeants' Mess? How you landed up there I have no idea.' He continued, 'You're a soldier, not a barman, and I think you should become a soldier again.'

6: Face in the mirror

The Falkland Islands landscape, a close relation to the Outer Hebrides where we used to go with the regiment on annual firing camps, may have been familiar to me, but what I hadn't seen before was a military graveyard with new graves. During my first few days on the island I took one of my team to pay a visit. As we looked around at the recently dug graves and makeshift crosses, my young friend said, 'It could have been you or me, Sarge.' It was a sobering thought for two young soldiers, and we walked around without speaking. It reminded me of my tours in Northern Ireland and how I felt walking the streets of Belfast. In places of conflict I have noticed there can be moments of intense noise, but also great stillness and overwhelming sadness.

*

Within two months I was out of the Garrison Sergeants' Mess, having retrained as a Rapier Detachment Commander with 16 Air Defence Regiment, running a detachment of five men. Back in combats, I felt like a soldier again and I loved it.

One day, driving into work, I spotted a magnificent Porsche 911 turbo on the forecourt of a garage. It had been raining slightly and its bronze metallic paintwork glistened in the morning light. It was love at first sight! The next day I went back to speak to the garage owner, and discovered it was a private sale from a local man and the price was within my reach. On the test drive it felt like a wild horse, powerful and strong, and I had to have it.

I sold the Triumph Stag to a guy in the regiment and borrowed some money from a few people. For the first three weeks of owning it, it was in charge of me but I was determined to master it. As a petrolhead I can honestly say it was the best car I have ever had.

One night after drinking quite heavily with Teddy, who was now running the Sergeants' Mess, I offered him a lift home, as he lived near me outside the camp. It was late November, very cold and icy, and it had been snowing. It shouldn't have been a problem for the Porsche because of its huge tyres (225) on the rear that could grip the surface of the road. Unfortunately, on overtaking another car at speed I lost control on a patch of black ice. The car skidded and broadsided into the concrete pillar of a bridge. Fortunately, we were both okay, albeit a little shaken. We left the car in a ditch and walked home. The next morning, I went to assess the damage and was shocked to see that every panel down one side was smashed. That's when I decided to take it to the car park and commit insurance fraud.

Driving to a multi-storey car park in the centre of Dortmund, I parked up and walked away, reporting it stolen to the German police. *Good plan,* I thought. *I'll get it repaired through my insurance once the police have found it and that will be that – all sorted.* About forty minutes later I realised I'd left my wallet and ID card in the glove compartment and it was a chargeable offence not to have your ID on your person at all times. Walking back to the car park, I thought there was no way the police would have been able to find the car in less than an hour. However, as I reached into the glove compartment, I noticed the unmistakable green and white colours of a German police car. I tried to hide near the car park lift, but they saw me and grabbed me by the arm and asked me why I was hanging around a stolen car. As with most of my previous criminal activity I was caught red handed at the scene of the crime. I really should have learnt my lesson by now. I admitted to reporting my vehicle stolen. After being released to the military police I was brought back to the garrison guardroom to the duty officer and the duty sergeant, who knew me.

I was then called in front of the regimental sergeant major (RSM), who was furious with me and threatened to bust me down to gunner and send me to military prison. He was so angry, at one point he even suggested I could be shot! Apart from the crime I'd committed, I think he was disappointed in me because he had had high hopes for me, and I'd let him down badly.

It was a very stressful time for me and for Julie. She wasn't impressed with my behaviour. In the end, I believe the RSM persuaded the commanding officer to deal with the incident, and the German authorities gave me a big fine. There were some more sharp words from the RSM, but I got my car back.

Teddy said he knew a garage in Dortmund where he had a friend who might be able to repair it. Desperate to get my lovely car back in shape I went to see the guy at the garage. After looking at it for some time he told me how much the repairs would cost. It was the same amount I had paid for it. I was depressed and walked away with my head in my hands, while Teddy stayed chatting to his friend. I saw them shake hands and Teddy came over to me and said, 'Don't worry, Paul, we can sort it out.' He had hatched a plan with the garage owner, to fix the car without much cash changing hands, just a lot of contraband. Suffice to say Teddy was as dodgy as I was; neither of us had much of a moral compass.

When I looked in the mirror, I would see my father's face staring back at me. I wondered if I was turning into him. It wasn't just my moustache and the Cowley look. It was deeper than that. Had my upbringing tainted my future? Was I hotwired to be lawless like my father and hot-headed like my mother? Was there no escape? Was it possible that I was a functioning alcoholic like my parents? Studies have shown that having one alcoholic parent can affect a child by causing guilt, anxiety, embarrassment, confusion, anger, depression, trouble forming close relationships and impulsive behaviour. I can confess to having all of the aforementioned.

Looking back, I know that the army gave me a much bigger perspective than a totally selfish existence, as I made friends who relied on me. I was no longer an island. But to my shame, I was unable to really live this out. And on my journey of exploration and growth I was to hurt several more people.

My regiment, 16 Air Defence, was put on call for the Falkland Islands. The operational tour was to be four months and even though Argentina had surrendered, there were still aircraft skirmishes, so I decided to volunteer for the advance party. Julie was not too happy about it as it would mean I would be away from her for six months. But looking for adventure, I was determined to go.

Boarding a Hercules aircraft from RAF Brize Norton, the advance party were soon heading to Dakar in Senegal and then on to Ascension Island, an isolated volcanic island in the equatorial waters of the South Atlantic Ocean. After a few hours in unbearable heat we boarded a bright red Townsend Thoresen ferry called the *Europic Ferry* to take us 6,366 kilometres to the Falklands. We thought it was strange as it was such an obvious target for the Argentinian Air Force: a bright red car ferry with a very large gun mounted on the back. The seas were rough at times and people were throwing up everywhere. A bit like a choppy crossing from Dover to Calais but this went on for ten days and it was exhausting.

Once we had arrived at Port Stanley on the Falkland Islands, my job was to take over an established site from another unit present during the campaign. It was an isolated Rapier missile system on top of a hill, nearly five miles outside Port Stanley. I was responsible for a team of four soldiers, and we slept and lived in a converted shipping container that had been made into makeshift accommodation with a cooker, toilet and beds; not the Ritz, but adequate for the job and it was warm.

*

Visiting that military graveyard was sobering and as soon as I was in the Falklands I wanted to be back home. But it was a pattern for me, always wanting to be somewhere else.

The days dragged by – it was stag on, stag off; duty on, duty off – but when I was off duty there was nowhere to go and nothing to do except eat, sleep and weight train. Most of the time I was stuck on top of a deserted hill with tufts of grass that stuck up in huge mounds making the area where we were stationed difficult to traverse.

Occasionally we got warning of an unknown aircraft in our area and that brought a sense of excitement. My team armed the weapon and waited for approaching enemy fire, but very often we would be stood down again as it was a false alarm and it was back to the boring routine. The only other bit of excitement came from the crew of the Army Air Corps helicopter when they air-dropped our food, supplies and ammunition. They had great fun hovering above our camp, throwing provisions at us – trying to hit us with bags of meat. When they left our site, it was chaos. Jerry cans tipped over, canvases blown away and things strewn everywhere.

In my spare time, of which there was a lot, I'd write 'blueys' to Julie. They were very thin self-sealing A4 pieces of blue paper. As they were free, military personnel wrote thousands of them to loved ones. I missed my wife. I didn't like being on my own and was never really good with all-male company. Unfortunately, I spent all my time with four other men in a confined space. The surrounding area was an unforgiving landscape, covered in a blanket of sheep. The weather was unpredictable, going from winter to summer in one day, and even when the morning chill had lifted it was a desolate place.

In order to stave off boredom the regiment set up a fitness training competition. A gym was established in the main camp at Port Stanley inside a couple of containers. Passing away a few hours each day I ran down the hill for five miles from our hilltop location, did my work-out, and then ran back.

I tried to encourage my team of four to join in, but they were not as enthusiastic as I was when it came to fitness – until I created an in-house gym in our hut on the hill. The gym consisted of a free weights training area. We had a bench press, which was made from a broom handle and two jerry cans filled with petrol. A piece of wood acted as a bench for doing incline sit-ups and a bar was attached to the roof for pull-ups. On the small area of grass outside the container we cleared the stones and created a timed training circuit, consisting of press-ups, sit-ups, squat thrusts, star jumps and short sprints. I was quite proud of the design of my first gym, as it all started with humble beginnings on a faraway island in the South Atlantic.

Each week we gained points as the physical training instructor (PTI) kept the individual scores every time we visited the gym. One of the PTIs told us the event would take around a month to complete. He also said there would be a surprise at the end for the winner, but that they hadn't worked out what it was to be yet. With a prize as bait many of the soldiers embarked on a rigorous set of timed circuits, trying to get as many points as they could for each exercise. Gradually most of my team joined in, as it was a welcome break from the monotony of our container. At the end of the month they announced that the competition would be calculated on who had done the most exercises in the shortest time. That day came and passed, and my team believed the prize had been a scam to get us to work out. Then about a week later a radio message came through to our container: 'Sergeant Cowley?'

'Yes, sir', I replied.

'If you can, get your butt down to the helicopter pad here in Stanley. You and two others have won the inter-regiment fitness competition. You are going home early – that's the prize. You will be travelling back to Blighty with the Royal Navy on a Type 42 destroyer. Oh and did I mention you have around thirty minutes to get down here?'

Since it was a frequent occurrence for the soldiers to play practical jokes on one another, I was convinced that it was yet another prank. 'Have I got time to pack, sir?' I said sarcastically.

'I don't care what you do, Sergeant Cowley, but if you aren't here within twenty-five minutes you will not make the helicopter departure and you will have to stay here for another two months.'

The radio went dead. I turned to a bombardier and said, 'Pack my stuff for me, and get it back to England.' I ran like a bullet, full speed down the hill into Port Stanley dressed in my lightweight trousers, combat boots, heavy wool jumper and combat jacket, with a small rucksack on my back containing a pair of trainers, sports kit, shaving kit and wallet. As I was sprinting down the hillside I was thinking, *If this is a joke, someone is going to pay.*

To my surprise the helicopter was waiting for me on the helipad and within minutes I was flying over the island to the other side, where the three destroyers (Type 42) were waiting to depart for England. As a soldier it was an awesome sight to see three huge destroyers all docked together. One was going home to Portsmouth via the Bahamas, the second one via the Virgin Islands and the third via Bermuda. I was ordered to embark on the one travelling back via Tortola in the Virgin Islands. They had been on a six-month tour and were all heading home with a bit of fun booked in along the way.

The first few days on board were a nightmare for me as I vomited many times due to the rough seas of the South Atlantic. We were strapped into our beds with safety belts at night and I only found my sea legs when we arrived in the calmer seas of the Caribbean. It was then I found out what 'hands to bathe' means. Once in calm and warmer water a net is dropped over the side of the ship, and the sailors jump off into the deep waters below, climbing back up the net and repeating the process. Walking round with my new naval friend to the starboard side of the ship, to my surprise one of the crew was aiming his rifle into the sea, telling me he was on shark patrol. If that didn't put me off going for a dip, then it was the three soldiers with rifles in the small boat circling the swimmers that alarmed me. At the front of the ship, where the bilge pumps pumped out the waste food, I saw several hammerhead sharks enjoying the previous night's dinner. It was then I decided to wait until we docked in port for a swim.

The lads on the ship were very good to me, as I was the only soldier on board and I became like a mascot. They started calling me 'Pongo', a term of endearment used by navy personnel when referring to the army. They gave me their blue uniform, dressing me up as a petty officer (same rank as a sergeant), and totally accepted me as a sailor. After asking permission from the captain, I even got the opportunity to grow a full set – beard and moustache.

During the day I was attached to various crews, so I learnt quite a lot about the workings of a Type 42 destroyer. I was also on painting and cleaning duties most days as the navy paint everything on the ship when they are at sea. That is why the ships always look immaculate when they come into port.

As a soldier I found the confinement of being on a ship for weeks at a time difficult. I have no idea how they can stand it. Give me dry land any day. One way they pass the hours away is in the various messes at night. They certainly have fun! Full of drinking games, arm wrestling and variety nights, which seemed to me an excuse for some of the men to dress up in women's clothing and, when I say dress up, I mean they make a real effort: knickers, suspenders, stockings and make-up. Over-sexualised dancing together went on for hours. All pretty harmless fun but I was certainly surprised.

Arriving on the island of Tortola, the ship was presented with quite a few crates of Pusser's Rum, traditionally given to visiting naval ships. Historically, a sailor's ration of alcohol was beer, with a daily quota of one gallon (or eight pints). This official allowance continued till after the Napoleonic Wars. They must have been semi-drunk all day and certainly alcoholics by the end of their secondments.

From Tortola we travelled on to San Juan in Puerto Rico and spent Christmas Day on the beach drinking, chatting up women and getting a tan. From the Caribbean we sailed home to Portsmouth and on entry to the port all the naval personnel lined the side of the ship. The captain invited me to stand with his crew as we came into port, greeted by hordes of people waving Union Jacks. A military band played stirring music and even though there was no one to meet me, and I had done nothing during the actual conflict, I found the experience exhilarating and was proud to be standing with the navy.

Once I was back home, I took a few days' leave and for a while Julie and I had some fun, but it wasn't long before we were having problems. I started arguments for no reason, just like my mother and father had. I was uninterested in my wife's intensity, even though she was kind. And it seemed that once again army life suited me, but marriage didn't.

On moving back from the Falklands to the UK, 16 Air Defence were now stationed at Kirton Lindsey in Yorkshire. Julie and I settled in to yet another quarters and tried to carry on our relationship, but the conversation always ended up at the same place. Julie wanted children and it was causing a huge rift between us. Clinton had come to visit us a few times and she didn't understand why we couldn't have a child of our own. I had failed as a father once and had no intention of having another go. I was genuinely petrified of the responsibility. I was becoming more and more unsettled, and sensing my marriage was in a crisis I decided to move out of our quarters and into the Sergeants' Mess. I needed to work out what I should do next. Get another divorce? Or try and make this marriage work?

Having taken many courses in my army career, including qualifying as a driving and maintenance instructor (DMI), gaining a Class 3 HGV licence, and also having a track licence (for vehicles with caterpillar tracks), I was able to drive any vehicle in the regiment. As one of the senior DMIs I often helped soldiers get through their heavy goods training on Stalwart, Bedford and Foden trucks.

One morning I collected a truck and, picking up my two trainees, hit the road. As we would be out all day, I remembered I would need some money for lunch and realised I had left my wallet in my other jacket in the Sergeants' Mess. Turning a huge five-ton vehicle around in the street is almost impossible, so it took a while to find a space big enough to do the manoeuvre. Eventually arriving back at camp, I told the lads to stay put while I dashed upstairs to my room.

When I opened my door, I couldn't believe my eyes. Julie was lying on my single bed dressed in her wedding dress with a bottle of tablets in her hand. I panicked, not knowing if she had taken them or not. I went to the sink, got some water and threw it over her. Lifting her into a sitting position, I shouted for help and when the mess sergeant manager saw what had happened he immediately ran to the phone and called an ambulance. Fortunately, she hadn't taken any tablets, but she was in a low emotional state. After one night's observation in hospital she was released.

Taking her back to the quarters, we talked and I told her I was way out of my depth, and she agreed that I should take her to her mum's house in Chester. The RSM of the regiment went ballistic with me and wasn't very understanding, telling me I had one week to sort my life out and then I had to get back to work.

I drove Julie to her mother's house in Chester, but it was an awful journey and I was very scared, as she was constantly trying to get out of the car when it was moving; at times she became quite hysterical. Eventually, after a harrowing journey, I arrived at her mother's home and said, 'You need to take care of her because I can't do it.' Her mother was understandably shocked but took her daughter in.

I then handed back the married quarters and went back to my room in the Sergeants' Mess in Kirton Lindsey. I began drinking far too much. And it was at this point in my life that I was at my lowest ebb. I was emotionally exhausted and completely fed up with being in disastrous relationships. I tried to settle down to regimental life, but I was restless – for what I wasn't sure. I was still only twenty-nine years old, although on some days I felt a lot older.

Once Julie realised the marriage was over she gradually recovered and ended up meeting someone else, whom she married and had children with, which was what she had always wanted.

The only part of my reputation still intact was my fitness ability, so I volunteered to help out in the gym at night to get some of the soldiers fitter. I decided that the best thing I could do was to get away from women, as I seemed to be hurting them constantly. The commanding officer approved of the idea, as he believed I needed time to sort my head out.

I got on quite well with a sergeant who worked out in the gym, and over a few beers in the Sergeants' Mess he told me he was planning on taking a group of soldiers to Cyprus for some adventure training. As I was a qualified joint services mountain expedition leader, I asked if I could go as an instructor and it was agreed that I would spend six to eight weeks teaching rock climbing, map reading, hill walking and survival techniques. I had been told that RAF Troodos was desolate, with nothing but mountains and a few goats. It sounded perfect to me. It was a great opportunity for me to have a break from women and drink.

I needed stability in my life but had no idea how to achieve it or what it looked like. Within a few weeks I was posted to a far outpost of the British Army to run the adventure training summer camp in the Troodos mountains. I thought I would have time to reflect. How wrong was I?

7: Don't let me get caught

At first light, around 5.30 a.m., I woke the two women up. I knew I would be in serious trouble if anyone discovered them in my room. Amanda and Kristina, both twenty-one, had kept me awake telling jokes and giggling but I had to get them out of the camp without being seen. My colleague, who was taking a group of lads for early morning fitness on the parade square, had been briefed, so when I appeared with the women, he instructed the lads to get down and give him thirty press-ups. Facing the opposite direction, they couldn't see us running towards a parked Land Rover. Hiding them both under a blanket, I then drove out of the camp, past security, to a small café on the side of the mountain where an old man served up peppermint tea. We agreed I would come and get them at 7.00 a.m. and take them back to the rock where I would teach them to abseil.

*

It was 1985, I was twenty-nine years old, and the last thing on my mind was falling in love.

I had gone to Cyprus to get away from my second failed marriage and from women in general. Surprisingly, in the middle of nowhere on the side of a mountain, next to a fast-flowing stream, I met Amanda. Having been raised by her Christian mother, she had decided that her faith was irrelevant when she went to study art and dance at Roehampton Institute in London.

With her close friend Kristina, she had travelled to Cyprus on a ferry from Brindisi, on the heel of Italy, via Corfu, landing at Limassol. They hitch-hiked their way to Lemba village, near Paphos, for a month's residency at Cyprus College of Art, established by

Stass Paraskos in 1969. The ramshackle college was embedded in the hills above a banana plantation and visiting students spent time creating sculptures, paintings and drawings in the open air.

Halfway through the month, Amanda and Kristina had taken a coach to the Trooditissa monastery hoping to get accommodation for the night, as it was customary for the monks to open their doors to tourists. But that evening the monastery was full.

Slightly worried about where they would be sleeping, they strolled back down the mountain and spotted a three-ton Bedford truck, one of two vehicles I happened to be responsible for. 'Ah good, the British Army,' said Amanda to Kristina. 'They might be able to help us.'

Unbeknown to me they positioned themselves near where we were climbing, hoping to get our attention.

It was my fellow sergeant who heard them talking.

'Rubbish,' I said, 'there are no women here.' But he insisted, and so in real James Bond style, we abseiled down the cliff and across the stream, making a beeline for the two young women we saw sitting drawing on a rock. I spoke to Kristina, who had short brown hair and was athletic in build, and then Amanda joined in our conversation. She was also physically fit and tanned, with long brown hair and a great sense of humour. Amazingly, she laughed at my jokes. She was also very relaxed about life, a bit of a hippy really, the complete opposite to me.

Having told us their predicament, I offered to take them back to the camp for a barbecue. 'We are both vegetarians', said Kristina.

'I'm sure we can find something for you to eat', I replied.

The soldiers were enthusiastic about two attractive women travelling with them in the back of the Bedford. My feeling at the time, towards both of them, was to be protective. I could see the other soldiers were excited by their presence and one in particular, a lance bombardier called Mark, asked me which one I liked – presumably so that he could have the other one. I told him to leave them alone and that our priority was to look after them. I think at this point in my life I was in shock. I was not interested in forming another relationship that might fail, and just wanted to befriend them, which was odd for me. That night they both asked if they could stay in my room to avoid the advances of some of the soldiers. I agreed and they slept in sleeping bags either side of my bed. It was all quite harmless, except that they kept me awake with their constant storytelling and giggling.

*

Once we were out of the camp, I took them abseiling. Wearing yellow helmets and harnesses, they loved jumping down the steep cliff face, taking turns with the soldiers we were training. Driving them to the local café for lunch I then offered to take them to Limassol, a city on the southern coast of Cyprus from where I was to pick up some supplies from the army base.

Mark and I were both dressed in summer uniform and sat in the front of an open-topped short-based Land Rover, while the girls sat in the back. What I didn't realise was that they were both practical jokers. As we pulled up at a set of traffic lights in the town, everyone stopped and stared at the jeep. People were giving Mark and me very odd looks. Turning round, I saw the girls facing each other with masking tape on their mouths and rope tied around their hands to imitate a kidnapping! At that moment I lost it and barked at them, 'What the hell are you doing?'

I made Mark pull over, and removing the masking tape from their mouths I shouted at them, 'You can't do that! We are in uniform!' They found the whole thing very funny. I was very grumpy as I had had hardly any sleep and it was then that I began to question what I was doing with these two crazy young women.

However, due to a connection with Amanda, I decided to see what would happen. The fact that I was eight years older than her, with a history of failed relationships, did surface in my mind, but we were in Cyprus, the 'island of love', so I decided not to talk about my past in order not to put her off me.

On the second evening, Mark and I had scooters. Amanda travelled with me while Mark took Kristina, and we went into Troodos village. On the way back to the camp, my bike broke down, so Mark went with Kristina to get a Bedford truck. I pushed the scooter to the side of the road, knowing we would have to wait a while for them to come and pick us up. As the sun was setting, I lay down on the dry earth and put my arms behind my head. Amanda joined me. Laying down next to me, she kissed me. I was surprised but happy about it. I was drawn to her warmth and confidence and there seemed to be an unspoken attraction between us. The fact that I was miles from home was liberating and for a while I could remain mysterious. Suddenly, we heard the heavy rumble of the huge truck coming down the mountain. Mark was driving the Bedford and Kristina, sticking out of the cupola on the top of the driver's cab with both arms flailing, was shouting, 'Oooooh, weeeeeee, look at me!'

For five days and nights I sneaked Amanda and Kristina into the camp by hiding them in the back of a Land Rover under a blanket. It was rather stupid because we were staying in a high security area; the camp was a listening post for military intelligence in the Mediterranean. Every time I came through the security gate I prayed, 'Oh God, don't let me get caught!' I was far from being a man of faith but like many people I believed in emergency prayers and I was not in a rational frame of mind.

On the third day, Mark and I met the girls at the usual café at 7.00 a.m. Kristina jumped on the back of the scooter and headed off with Mark, who was still unsuccessfully pursuing her, while Amanda came with me. By 9.00 a.m. the sun was a scorching 38°C. When we got to the coast Amanda shouted, 'Pull over here.' I did as I was told. 'Let's swim!' she said. Dressed in shorts and a t-shirt, we ran like high school sweethearts, hand in hand, into the water. Within fifteen minutes we were back on the bike, albeit dripping wet.

On another trip, this time in the Land Rover, Amanda and I were heading back to the mountains, taking a short cut through some of the old villages. As I was manoeuvring the jeep down narrow streets I turned to speak to Amanda and saw that she was completely topless and giggling to herself. I panicked, especially as I saw a few old ladies staring disapprovingly out of their windows. As I was in an army uniform, I asked her to put her top back on. We laughed so much and once again she took me out of my comfort zone. At that moment I didn't care that this relationship would present me with a whole new set of problems.

The days were filled with mad pranks and playful seduction games. I traded the scooter for a bigger bike, a Kawasaki 900, at a bike shop in Larnaca. When the guy asked me if I had experience on a big bike, I said, 'Of course. Lots of experience.' He then asked for my bike licence and I flashed my HGV driving licence, which he had never seen before. I quickly said, 'It's military. It covers everything.' He nodded and I signed a document. Amanda had never been on the back of a motorbike before, always having thought bikers were reckless, but she was clearly in a reckless state of mind.

As I swerved round a sharp mountain bend, she shouted out, 'What do I do?'

'Lean with me', I said.

'How long have you been riding motorbikes?' she asked.

'Well, I had a scooter as a kid but other than that . . . about an hour.'

Amanda thought that if her mother knew what she was doing, riding a fast bike with no helmet or protective clothing, with a soldier eight years older than her, she would have flown over to Cyprus and boxed her ears.

After five days together, our time came to an end. I took Amanda and Kristina back to the art college, the three of us clinging together on the motorbike around the sharp bends of the Troodos mountains.

The day I arrived back in England I rang Amanda at her mother's home on the outskirts of London and asked if I could see her. I turned up in my Porsche wearing my brown leather jacket. Her mum, Tricia, opened the front door and I could see immediately that she wasn't impressed. Inviting me in, she, along with her new husband Andrew, was soon asking me lots of questions about my background; I assumed she was quizzing me because she didn't feel comfortable knowing her only daughter was now dating a sergeant in the military. It may have had something to do with her supporting CND (Campaign for Nuclear Disarmament) or it could have been my age, moustache or fast car, or just everything about me.

After a few weeks, she told Amanda that she didn't trust me and that I was 'a man of muscle and mystery'! She correctly believed it was unusual for a man my age, and in the army, not to have been married. But I had to keep the lie going, so I just shrugged my shoulders and remained evasive.

I invited Amanda to come with me on an army training week in Tenby, Wales. I was in charge of the fitness each morning and evening but would be free for the rest of the day. Arriving in my car, I went to one of the young officers who had been with me in Cyprus and had met Amanda. 'Sir, I hope it's okay, but Amanda is in the car and if you don't mind, I'd like to pitch a two-man tent away from the rest of the men.' He smiled at me and nodded, 'Sure, Sergeant Cowley.'

At a distance from the twenty or so large green army tents, I pitched my bright yellow civilian tent. Each morning I was up at 6 a.m. taking the lads on a run, returning to shower and then waking Amanda up. We ate with the lads in a disused air hangar on the site and Amanda was extremely adaptable considering she was the only woman. The lads went map reading with the officer, or onto the firing range, while Amanda and I drove into the lovely village of Tenby, to sit by the dock and eat fish and chips, or chat for hours in tearooms. We were physically addicted to each other and able to talk about anything and everything, except faith and religion, and of course the one thing she would have wanted to hear about – my marriages and my child.

On one particular night the rain came down in bucket loads.

Amanda shook me. 'Get up, Paul. We have to go. The water is pouring in.' Gathering our stuff together we made a run for the car, which I then drove into the air hangar. Reclining the seats as best we could we managed to get some sleep. In the morning as I sat up, I grinned. 'Amanda, you had better wake up', I said.

The soldiers, forever practical jokers, had set up the six-foot trestle tables around the car and they laughed victoriously as they saw our embarrassed faces. Amanda was able to see the funny side of it. For the next few nights we moved into another air hangar and I made a bed up in the back of a Land Rover.

Amanda returned to Roehampton to complete her third and final year at college, and we became closer and closer. From the September to the following June I drove from Kirton Lindsey in Yorkshire, a round trip of nearly 400 miles, to stay with her in her rented accommodation. I would leave Roehampton at 4.00 a.m. and drive to get back to camp in time for parade at 7.00 a.m. I decided I would have to get a posting nearer to her.

For Amanda to complete her degree she had to write a 10,000-word dissertation for the art section and produce a ten-minute choreographed piece for the dance section. Deciding to pick one subject for both pieces of work, in order to minimise the reading involved, she chose to study the books and paintings of D. H. Lawrence. She said to me, 'Why don't you read one of Lawrence's books? You might enjoy it, and you will then understand what I'm trying to do.'

What Amanda didn't realise was that I associated reading with school, stumbling over my words while the class giggled at my expense. For me to read a book that wasn't about cars, crime or war was unusual, but I wanted to do it for her because her delight in reading inspired me and I think I wanted a challenge.

I started with *Sons and Lovers* and, even though it was hard going with unfamiliar language, I was determined to finish it. Amanda encouraged me to improve myself, saying that I was smart. I finished it in no time and asked for another. She gave me *Lady Chatterley's Lover*, and then Lawrence's collection of short stories. I devoured them and asked for more. *Women in Love* was followed by *The Rainbow, The Virgin and the Gypsy, Mornings in Mexico* and *The Complete Poems.* After Lawrence, I moved on to Dickens and the Brontës! I was particularly saddened by *Jude the Obscure,* a tragic novel by Thomas Hardy, and when it was finished we spent an evening discussing the characters and the pathos of their situations. I was amazed at the intensity of the writing that years of spy novels had never satisfied. I had an insatiable desire to learn and I was like a sponge, soaking up new words and devouring poetic literature.

At the weekends we went to art exhibitions and sometimes to The Place, in Euston, to see contemporary dance performances. I was so proud of her when I went to the evening showing of her final dance piece and saw her dance in other students' performances. She, in turn, was excited to be able to teach me what was so familiar to her and I even discovered a real love of poetry. As she was a vegetarian I became one too, giving up meat and discovering lentils and tofu and numerous vegetable dishes. It wasn't easy being in the army and insisting the chef cook a veggie meal. When soldiers questioned me, I would say, 'Okay, put your trainers on and we will see who is the fittest.' They soon shut up.

Amanda was always challenging me and no more so than when she suggested I shave off my moustache. I was reluctant because I had had it since I was twenty years old and it was very much part of my identity. It was also a statement in the army, as you couldn't have a beard or long sideburns, so a moustache was something many soldiers had.

One morning I appeared at the door with one half of my moustache shaved off. Just for a moment she didn't notice and then she squealed with delight and told me to get the other half off immediately. She loved my new look and secretly so did I as it felt like a new start. When I looked in the mirror, I no longer saw my father staring back at me. I saw a new man, fresh faced with the possibility of being different.

Meeting Amanda gave me hope when I was in a bad place.

She had a lightness of mood. She was fun and adventurous, and showed an excitement for art, literature, music and dance – things I'd never known much about. In many ways it was the beginning of an awakening for me. In Leo Tolstoy's book *A Confession,* he says, 'Nothing trains a young man, as a connection with a decent woman.'[4]

I have come to realise that it was never the fault of the women I had married when things went wrong. They were both decent women. It was always me. I was a broken man. Amanda managed to steer me upwards because I was willing to be guided. I was in a place where I wanted to open my heart to love and life. But it wasn't going to be straightforward. I was carrying a huge burden of lies and deceit. The more time we spent together the more foreboding it became, but eventually I would be forced, like Leo Tolstoy, to make a confession of my own.

8: Few are chosen

One evening I, along with about fifty soldiers, started packing our Bergens (rucksacks) for the dreaded Fan Dance the next morning. The Fan Dance is the nickname given to a gruelling walk/run across the Welsh mountains. It involves a 24-kilometre load-bearing march. I psyched myself up, having spent an age getting my Bergen to the necessary weight of 45 lbs. If it were found to be underweight, it would mean instant dismissal. By 5.30 a.m. we were inside our sleeping bags trying to keep warm in a three-ton Bedford, listening to the directing staff talking outside about if it was safe to do the exercise. After twenty minutes a member of staff came to the tailgate and said, 'It's not happening today. It's back to camp!' I was relieved but also disappointed because I wanted to get it over and done with. As we left the area we looked out of the back of the truck and saw the snow blasting horizontally! Rumour had it that the SAS had never cancelled the Fan Dance before.

*

My relationship now felt right but I was still unsatisfied at work. I lacked purpose. While Amanda was in her final year at Roehampton, my heart became set on another adventure. I decided to try out for the Special Air Service.

David Stirling established the SAS Regiment in 1941, during World War Two. Along with covert reconnaissance, the SAS deals with counterterrorism, direct action and hostage rescue. Due to my experience in Northern Ireland the prospect of such covert operations interested me. I found out that any soldier who had served three years could apply for the selection process but they had to be recommended by their commanding officer, so I went to see him and he agreed to let me go.

My reporting time was January 1986. It gave me five months to get prepared. I believed I was fit enough but was worried about my map reading skills. Through a contact, I was able to get some accommodation for three weeks at Oakhampton Military Camp in Devon. It was perfect for me, as it was on the edge of the moor, a bleak and desolate area, where my map reading would be tested to the full. When I arrived, there were just a few park rangers who took it in turns to monitor the camp. Once I'd told them why I was there they were keen to help.

Help came in the form of collecting me each morning, blindfolding me and putting me in the back of their Land Rover and driving me to some remote spot on the moor, where they pushed me out, shouting, 'See if you can get back from here.' They found the whole thing hilarious, whereas I was slightly more dubious, having heard stories of people getting lost on the moors and being found dead the next morning. The rangers delighted in telling me ghost stories such as the most popular myth of the 'Hairy Hands'. Over the last eighty years there had been numerous sightings of a gruesome pair of hairy calloused hands that do their utmost to fight you and your vehicle off the road. I have never been interested in ghost stories, but I found the tales unnerving. Dartmoor can be a sinister place, especially when the dreaded mists appear without warning, covering the moor in a blanket of low cloud.

One morning the fog came down and I was completely lost. I had no idea how I would get back to camp. Panic started to set in, and I thought, *Cowley, you could die out here, you idiot! Why didn't you take a radio?* When I heard the sound of running water I was relieved; I knew to follow it, as it was bound to lead somewhere. Eventually I came across some stone ruins and from there was able to find my position on the map. The ruins were called Bleak House, which was apt. It was one of the most remote places I have ever seen.

When I got back to camp, I found out that the rangers were also worried, but not enough to come looking for me. 'After all,' they said, 'if you are trying for the SAS you had better be able to look after yourself!' They had more faith in me than I had in myself, that's for sure.

Thomas Harding, a reporter for the *Telegraph,* stated in his article about the SAS that 'many are called, but few are chosen', a biblical phrase from Matthew 22:14 often quoted during SAS selection, giving 'some solace for the 90 per cent who fail to get through'. In his article, Harding continued: 'The six-month process is regarded as the most arduous in the world: candidates undertake a month of running over the Welsh mountains with 45 lb loads, culminating in the 40-mile endurance march.'[5]

Stirling Lines in Hereford is a pretty daunting experience, partly because the place is steeped in military history, but also because one cannot avoid the myths and legends surrounding the regiment.

Arriving late evening, I gave my name at the guardroom and hoped for the normal welcome you get when you arrive at most army units, but immediately the security guards on the gate were cold and dismissive. Having served in the army for ten years I knew that the psychological testing applied by the SAS had already begun.

I was given an envelope, which contained a briefing document, and then I was pointed in the general direction of my accommodation. The document stated that I was to report to the quadrant at 0600 hours the following morning in lightweight trousers, standard issue combat boots and red vest.

I was in an eight-man room in one of the blocks, and soldiers who had been travelling from various regiments arrived throughout the evening. No one spoke; we just nodded to each other as we took up our bed space. The man nearest to me was a paratrooper.

There was also a Royal Marine and a Royal Engineer. We prepared our kit for the morning in silence, and then went to sleep.

At 5.45 a.m. I stood in the quadrant along with approximately 100 others who were all shapes and sizes. I was very apprehensive, but ready to start. We stood weighing each other up, and then a man looking as if he had just walked off the set of an Arnold Schwarzenegger movie, dressed in lightweight trousers and a vest, shouted through the dim light, 'Good morning, gentlemen. You will start your selection into the Special Forces with a basic fitness test.'

The usual way of conducting a BFT in the army is for it to take place on flat ground. The first 1.5 miles is timed and controlled by the physical training instructor. This is usually a slow run in order to warm up the body and it has to be completed in 11.5 minutes. You then stop and catch your breath for two minutes, a whistle is blown, and the final 1.5 miles is meant to be completed as fast as you can. If you don't get over the finish line in your allotted time, determined by your age, you can try again. If you fail a second time you are put on remedial fitness training until you pass.

I had completed hundreds of BFTs and felt pretty confident that my time was fast, but as we gathered at the start line, we were given a number and a colour (mine was blue 36) and I sensed something wasn't quite right. With Arnie at the front we marched to the top of a hill, where he explained, 'You may have done BFTs before, but I promise you, not like this one.' He went on to say that we would be running at a fast pace downhill for the first part of the test then at a given point we were to turn around and run back as fast as our legs would take us to the start line.

But it's uphill on the way back! I thought to myself.

Then his next sentence caught everyone's attention: 'Forget your timings! The first sixty people over the line will be accepted. The rest will go back to their regiment by midday.' The tension was palpable.

Arnie started sprinting at a ridiculous pace downhill and we all followed. Immediately men started falling back and dropping out. When the majority of the group was at the halfway point the instructor just said, 'Go!' There was no time to stop and catch a breath. The race was on. It was mayhem as everybody took off at speed, uphill, jockeying for position. It was the hardest short run I have ever done.

I crossed the line shouting out, 'Blue 36, sir'; a voice shouted back, 'Twenty-ninth.' I was in! I collapsed in a heap and vomited. Immediately I heard Arnie say, 'Stand up and get a grip of yourself!' He had hardly broken a sweat.

As promised, the forty men who didn't make the first sixty collected a rail warrant and went back to the station and returned to their regiments. Those of us left went back to the accommodation for a shower and breakfast. We then went to the quartermaster stores where we were given equipment, including a Bergen, maps and safety kit for walking on the hills. For the rest of the day, we had lectures on the history of the regiment and were introduced to a few senior ranks, to inspire us for the gruelling weeks ahead.

The next day we went to Pontrilas training area to do an 8-mile timed run and walk, carrying full combat kit and 7.62 mm SLR assault rifle. Knowing the trick of endurance marches is to stay at a steady pace, I was confident I would pass. Eight men failed the test that day and were sent back to their regiments.

*

After the first failed attempt at the Fan Dance, the next morning we went back to the starting areas in two three-tonners. This time the weather was better, and the directing staff (DS) came and shouted, 'We're on! Out you get.' We were divided into two groups and each started from opposite sides of Pen y Fan, an 886-metre-high peak. Although we were put in groups, it was down to the individual's own best efforts to get the quickest time.

My group started at the Storey Arms Outdoor Education Centre. Each man carried a Bergen weighing 45 lbs, a rifle, a further 10 lbs, food and two water bottles, which were essential but still extra weight. We climbed Pen y Fan's west slope (Corn Du) and then we descended on the far side, known as Jacob's Ladder. The rest of the route followed the old Roman road past the Talybont reservoir before going back on itself for the return leg, where the DS took our name and colour before we turned around and repeated the walk back to Storey Arms.

I set off slowly and then jogged at every opportunity, especially coming off the top of the Fan, as it was mostly downhill to the reservoir. The wind bit at my face, the only part of me that wasn't covered, and I completed the return journey in four and a half hours, which was not bad for a winter course. I was pleased with myself, assuming that selection for the SAS was in my grasp.

Little did I know what was in store: the 'Fan' was going to be the least of my problems.

When I eventually got back to my room three more beds were standing on end and I later heard that a few more men from the other blocks had also gone home. It was depressing walking into that room each day just waiting to be next. The hardest part was that no one spoke to me. No one wanted to share any personal information because you always thought you were being tested; it certainly made me paranoid. The experience in the canteen was no better. As I scanned the room everyone was sitting in silence, eating their food, on their own. It was the same at every meal. It was possible to spot the real SAS from the training recruits as they had an air of confidence about them, a sort of 'don't come near me till you're in' type attitude.

In the standard army or 'green army', I was used to lots of banter. By now we would all be sharing stories and having a laugh. The SAS were very different. The psychological pressure of being alienated was the hardest part for me and I experienced it every waking hour.

During the next two weeks we had more weapon training, signals training on radio equipment, milling (boxing, which was later removed from the selection process due to injuries) and swimming tests.

Once the teaching was out of the way, it was on to the hills in pairs. We walked the Brecon Beacons, the Elan Valley (Devil's Bridge) and most of the New Forest, and every day was a test. The threat of failure was hanging over my head and on returning to the accommodation later in the day, there would be another bed stripped and standing on its end. There was no let up and I can honestly say that apart from the psychological stress of walking the streets of Belfast, they were the hardest days I ever experienced in the army.

The fitness testing was at a level not endured by the regular 'green army', but for me I could cope with that side of the testing, as I had trained hard. Most days, when we were out on the road or on track runs, I was near the front. However, the hill work on the Brecon Beacons was soul destroying; long routes over very difficult terrain, always carrying full equipment and a heavy Bergen. I watched as some soldiers took weight out but wasn't surprised when on one route march we were spot-checked, and our rucksacks weighed with a set of portable scales. We lost another three men that day; shipped back home. It was all very unnerving, but again that was the point. I realised that this was all part of the plan to find out who had the mental stamina to see the course through.

Five weeks into the selection course came test week, culminating in a timed 30-mile endurance walk over rough terrain. Test week was as its title suggested: to really test the forty of us who were left. On the fourth day, I was doing a route walk in the Elan Valley. I hadn't seen another human being for around five hours. I was tired, getting dehydrated, and my mind was starting to wander. It wasn't so much this particular route that was making me tired but the five weeks of non-stop fitness, isolation, mental stress and loneliness. Looking at my map I could see I was nearly two miles from my next checkpoint. Having already completed about nine miles in pretty awful weather conditions, I suddenly lost my concentration, tripped and fell, landing face down in icy muddy water. I was unable to get up due to a combination of the heavy

Bergen on my back and sheer exhaustion. I lay there thinking, *What am I doing? What is this all about, Cowley? Do you really think you have the mental ability and stamina to complete this course, and if you do, then what?* It all seemed meaningless.

As I got up, I realised I didn't feel the same. Something in me had snapped. I missed Amanda, her companionship. I hated the isolation and the mind games. I was dissatisfied with work, but the SAS selection process wasn't providing any answers for me.

Arriving at the checkpoint a few minutes late, a zip was pulled down on the small one-man tent and the face of the Directional Staff appeared from a sleeping bag, saying, 'Colour? Number?'

I replied, 'Blue 36, staff.'

He shouted back, 'You're late.'

I just stood there, saying nothing. He said to me, 'Show me where you are on your map.'

With a blade of grass I pointed to my position. 'Here, staff.'

He replied, 'Show me where your next grid reference is.' I did as I was told and then he said, 'Go now or you'll fail. Last chance!' Standing, rooted to the ground, I couldn't move. He shouted a few choice words at me and then he said, 'If you don't move now, you're done, and you can get on the wagon and go home. Now f*** off.' He then softened. 'Last chance, Cowley . . . you are doing okay, son. Come on, push on.'

The words left my mouth before I could think. 'I'm done, staff. I want to get on the wagon.'

He looked at me and said, 'I didn't hear that! Now go! Last chance, Cowley! Come on, lad, you've nearly done this part.'

But I was determined. 'Wagon please, staff,' I said.

He shook his head and went back inside his tent and zipped it up. I climbed on the wagon, got into my maggot (sleeping bag) and fell asleep with two others that were in the wagon with me.

Back at camp, I was told to hand all my kit into the quartermaster stores and then report to the training wing where the training officer would debrief me. They weren't impressed, mainly because I'd passed everything and was doing quite well. I was three-quarters of the way through test week, with most of the hard fitness work behind me. The training officer said I was stupid for wasting their time, money and energy, but then added, 'You should try the summer course, as this winter has been dreadful.' I was told to pack my personal kit and leave the next morning. The officer said a report would be sent to my commanding officer in due course.

Now it was my turn to strip my bed and stand it on its end. When I left that room there was one bed left. I've often wondered if the paratrooper ever made it. I guess I'll never know, because I didn't know his name.

As I walked out through the gates of Stirling Lines and headed for the train station, I thought that at least I had given it my best shot. Knowing I didn't actually fail any part of the selection and wasn't issued with a ticket (three tickets and you are out) helped me deal with the onslaught of abuse that came with returning to my regiment.

Completing selection for the SAS has less to do with fitness and more to do with attitude; how much you can bear the isolation and mind games. If you haven't got rock-solid determination, above all other things, then don't bother.

When I got back to the regiment, the interview with my commanding officer didn't go well. He wasn't impressed with the report from Hereford, as it said I had done well and could have got through to the next phase if I'd put my mind to it. But that was just the problem: I couldn't put my mind to it. I realised that my mind was not as tough as my body and that I needed more in terms of interaction with people. Those who do pass the selection course for the SAS are a certain type. And I have the utmost respect for them. They are unique both in mind and body; a special type of solider, undoubtedly the best fighting force in the world. Thomas Harding, the reporter, concluded his article: 'Light forces that can operate with such gumption behind enemy lines are one of Britain's most valuable military assets. They are also something we should do everything we can to hold on to.'

Apparently, most people who have tried selection find it hard to settle and I was not the exception. Frustrated and disillusioned with myself, I headed for the noticeboard once again, looking for another posting. I was hoping for anything to get me away from where I was. Most days I just wanted to hide, and being questioned about my time at Hereford didn't help; it just made me dissatisfied.

During this time, I was getting closer to Amanda, and seeing her was the best part of my day. She encouraged me not to worry so much – I hadn't failed; I'd just made a life choice, whatever that meant! She was always upbeat and constantly saw the best in me. She suggested that we go and meet my mum and dad. Knowing I could no longer put her off I rang them both and asked them not to discuss my past.

Arriving at my mum's house, the familiar bull's head and crossed swords on the wall, the Spanish trophies decorating every shelf, I was sad to see nothing had changed. Mum was pleased to meet Amanda, asking her lots of questions about how we met and about her being an artist. She brought out a few early photo albums of our trips to Spain. But Mum could tell I was anxious. 'Have you seen your dad?' she asked.

'No,' I replied. 'Not for several years.' I wasn't going to tell her that we were going to visit him after we had left her.

'Please don't leave it as long. Come and see me soon. It's been nearly two years', she said, waving from the door, looking forlorn as we left the house.

'She's not that bad, Paul', Amanda said.

'That's because she is like a hand grenade with the pin pulled out. You never know when she is going to explode', I answered.

Little did I know she had undergone a huge change.

We then went to Dad's sparse flat. He only wanted to talk about himself and his troubles, so I was safe there. He was now in his early sixties, grey and balding but with a thick moustache. While I was at the peak of my physical fitness, he was battling with heart troubles caused by decades of smoking. He liked Amanda, as they talked about drawing. He was keen to show her his sketches and was delighted when she praised him.

I was only just managing my personal life, but it was soon about to implode. Still unsettled in my career, the SAS slogan 'Many are called, but few are chosen' still haunted me.

Little did I know that I would be leaving one selection process for another, equally challenging, but in a different way.

9: What a tangled web we weave

'What is it?' she said.

'Let's go upstairs.'

I made Amanda sit on the bed while I paced the floor.

She assumed I was going to tell her something about my mother. 'What is it, Paul? You're making me nervous.'

'You know I love you, Amanda', I said.

'Yes, of course I do, and I love you too . . . what is it? Tell me.'

'I only didn't tell you because I thought you wouldn't be able to handle the news.'

'What news?' She was getting nervous as she could see I was flustered.

*

In the spring of 1986, I was posted to Bramcote Barracks in Nuneaton, Warwickshire. Having applied for a job as a military skills instructor in the Junior Leaders Regiment, I would only be 100 miles from Amanda in London.

Driving into the camp in my Porche, a soldier stopped me at the gate and saluted me. The car gave the impression I was an officer. 'Don't salute me, soldier. I'm a sergeant!' I said, adding, 'I work for a living!'

Parking the car quickly I headed for the chief clerk's office to present myself and get my room in the Sergeants' Mess. As I walked to the reception area I heard someone shouting, 'Whoever's parked in my parking space, get it the f*** out. And what the f*** is that CND sticker doing in the back window?! Get it moved now or I'll jail them, and when you find them bring the f***** here to me!'

After his tirade, all hell broke loose, and people were running everywhere. I discreetly left the building and went to move my car, spotting the 'RSM' yellow letters painted on the surface of the tarmac. I re-parked and walked in again. Amanda had put the CND sticker in my rear window saying that I could be anti-nuclear and still be in the regular army. I thought she made a valid argument, but I don't think the RSM agreed.

I was soon introduced to my new colleague, Sergeant Grant Ingleton, from the Parachute Regiment, a stocky man with a thick moustache. We became friends immediately.

Grant and I were responsible for training about twenty seventeen-year-old new recruits to become young professional soldiers. Grant suggested we play 'good cop/bad cop', to keep the lads on their toes. One morning we told them to get their dorm ready for a locker inspection. Each young recruit had a bed, a bedside table and a locker holding all their kit. If you were sensible you didn't use the stuff in your locker; you just got double of everything, so that on an inspection day your locker was immaculate, but this was something they would learn with time.

The day of the inspection came, and we decided that I would be bad cop, as they were used to me being the gentle one. The boys all stood to attention by their bunks while I walked up and down. At first, I walked around advising them on their kit and how they could improve. I reminded them that if Sergeant Ingleton saw the state of their lockers he would go mad. I helped them a little, gave them some fatherly advice and said that Sergeant Ingleton would be in within the next twenty minutes. They were worried, as always, about the crazy para.

Grant came in with a menacing look and a pace stick under his left arm. He silently walked around the dorm, took his red beret off and put down his stick. He gathered them all together in the room and as they were nervous he explained, 'Lads, I know I've been tough on you, but it's for your own good. I'm trying to help you be the best soldiers you can be, because when you get to your regiments it will be tough.'

He had their attention and their defences were down. Then he leaned into them and said, 'I'm not sure if you know about Sergeant Cowley? I know you think he cares but he's really damaged goods. He has been through quite a few things in his career and it's unhinged him, so he's a bit mad. So be very careful with him.' He then asked them if I had checked the room and they said I had. Grant said, 'Good, as long as he's happy we should be okay.' They were utterly confused that Grant was being nice to them.

Ten minutes later, I entered the room and they became slightly uneasy. I asked the lads to open the windows down one side of the room, which they did, and then I proceeded to walk up and down in silence. I stopped at the worst-made bed and shouted at one lad to throw his bedding and side table out of the window. He looked shocked, as we were one floor up. I helped him throw out his locker, then the bedding, then more lockers from the room. It was chaos, kit was everywhere – on the floor, out on the grass, under the window. I left the room in silence. Five minutes later Grant came in and said, 'What did you say to him?' They all looked dumbfounded. 'Nothing, sergeant, he just went crazy.' Grant said sympathetically, 'I told you to be careful with him; he's finely tuned.' Grant was nice to them and helped them get their kit back together.

When I look back at this I know it sounds terrible, but I assure you I had the same done to me and it teaches you to take locker inspection seriously. Army life in war zones is not easy and one thing you cannot be is lazy or chaotic. Our job was to take sixteen- and seventeen-year-old boys and shape them into fighting men. We taught them to shave even when they had no growth. We taught them how to keep their feet and their private parts clean. Some of them who came to us were very naive, having had most things done by Mum, while others had had very little parental guidance. Some of the lessons mess with soldiers' heads, but they also instil discipline within a period of just a few weeks, which otherwise would take months to achieve, and the army just doesn't have the time.

Several weeks later I went to Amanda's graduation, which took place at Surrey University. Amanda's mum Tricia and her stepfather Andrew joined us, and after the ceremony we all went back to Froebel College in Roehampton where we had a picnic and some champagne in the beautiful gardens. Talking with Amanda I said, 'I've seen a house for sale in Nuneaton. It's small, just a two-up, two-down. Will you come and see it?'

Amanda was distracted from the day's events. 'Oh, yes, sure', she said.

I was not deterred. 'I was thinking you might come and live with me?' Although we had been together for nearly a year, I sensed she was unsure about making such a commitment. 'Just come and see it', I said.

The house was set up a few steps from the busy Coventry Road, opposite a graveyard. It needed some painting and lacked a proper bathroom. There was a toilet and a shower at the end of a galley kitchen. 'We can make it nice', Amanda said in her usual positive manner, so I purchased the house within a matter of a few weeks.

I liked the local town of Nuneaton and buying my first house felt really grown up. It cost just under £16,000 and the mortgage was £80 per month, which meant it was cheaper than living in the Sergeants' Mess. Since Amanda wanted to earn a living as an artist, and as she was not very materialistic, I was happy to support her financially. After we moved in together, we spent weeks painting the place. We bought pine furniture and Amanda put some of her paintings up. We made a few friends in the town and eventually she went to Leicester Print Workshop and made friends with Angela Harding (now a very established printmaker), who taught her to etch and make monoprints. Amanda was in her element as she produced small etchings, which we framed and sold at local markets. She was intoxicating to be around, always positive towards life and me in particular.

Nuneaton, a small market town, had everything we needed,

and home life was good. Soon Amanda's mum and stepfather moved from their London home to live nearby. I was happy but I was still unsettled. My secret was weighing heavily on my heart. Sometimes I would start to explain and then I would look at her and change the subject. It seemed that my whole time with her had been a lie. I'd completely conned her into loving a man who didn't really exist. There was a struggle within me. My biggest fear was that if she knew my past she would leave me. But now I was deeply in love with her, the weight of the lie was becoming too much for me.

Contrary to me, Amanda was an open book. She had told me that her father, a violinist, had separated from her mother when she was three years old, but that he had always visited her and been involved in her life. She had strong views on parental responsibility. What would she think of me for having dumped my first wife and my three-year-old son because I couldn't really be bothered with them? I knew it was going to blow up in my face at some point, but I was determined to keep my past a secret for as long as I could.

But life has a way of unearthing secrets and that was exactly what happened.

It wasn't long before one of the officers I had travelled to Cyprus with pulled me to one side. 'Sergeant Cowley, I know you are a qualified ski instructor. How would you like to come with me and train the boys for the army Langlauf skiing competition, in Switzerland and Austria?'

'I'm not trained in cross-country skiing, sir', I replied.

'That's okay; you will pick it up.'

Knowing I was the only sergeant he could ask I replied, 'I'm happy to come as long as I can take my own vehicle and you pay for petrol, and I'd also like to take my girlfriend with me.'

'Is she the girl you met when we were in Cyprus?'

'Yes, sir, she is.'

'As long as Amanda can cook I can justify her coming along. And I'm sure we can manage the petrol.'

Amanda jumped at the prospect of three months in Switzerland as a cook. She may have had no idea what she was in for or how things would pan out, but she had a plan to paint landscapes while she was there.

We were due to leave at the end of October 1986. The team was an eclectic group comprised of two officers and two sergeants and twelve lads. The two officers from Sandhurst were like Prince William and Prince Harry, very posh, with impeccable manners and a good sense of humour. The sergeant, meanwhile, had the customary moustache, and then there was me, clean-shaven and eager for adventure.

Since none of the twelve young recruits had ever skied before, the officer got hold of a load of Langlauf skis on rollers, which were used for training on roads and hard surfaces, and every day we went around the camp at Bramcote Barracks for hours at a time in order to train the muscle groups essential for cross-country skiing. Bored of the camp circuits, I decided to take my group of five lads, on roller skis, down into the town of Nuneaton. At first it was fun but as the lads got tired and the traffic increased it became a nightmare. In the end I had to call for the duty transport to come and fetch us from a café in the town. I wanted to avoid a serious accident from happening before the team had even got to the slopes.

Two weeks before we were due to leave in late October, my mum rang the house and told me she was in the process of selling her home in Didsbury and wanted to move nearer to us. I was taken off guard and was nervous about my mum living nearby. I had hardly spent any time with her and when I had it had usually ended in a drama.

In a moment of madness, I thought it might be nice to offer her our house, as we would be away for a few months and she could look for her own property. I put the phone down and relayed the information to Amanda, who, surprised by my kind gesture, said, 'How does that make you feel?'

'I don't know,' I replied. 'Weird, I suppose. I mean it would be great if she was one of those mums that was good to have around, like you read about in books or see in movies, but you don't know what she's like.'

'That's because I have only met her once and hardly spent any time with her before you made an excuse and said we had to leave.'

My rationale for inviting my mother was twofold; first, it would be good to have someone in the house for security reasons and second, she probably wouldn't like Nuneaton and would go back home to Manchester.

A few days before we were to leave, my mum arrived with a couple of suitcases. At the kitchen table she lit a cigarette. 'Not in here, Mum. You can smoke outside if you must.'

'But it's cold out there,' she said. Knowing I wouldn't budge, she put the cigarette out. 'Never mind; it's not good for me anyway.'

I changed the subject. 'What made you sell your house, Mum? It's a bit drastic. You don't even know if you will like it here.'

'Look, son, I thought since you had bought a house here it couldn't be all that bad. At the end of the day, I'm lonely. I don't see much of you and life is too short to waste time. By the time you get back I will be out of your hair.'

Mum was sixty-three years old and looked in good shape except for her nicotine-stained fingers and her dull complexion. Those blue eyes that she had passed down to me were not as bright as they once were, and the dark circles underneath spoke of many sleepless nights. That night, with my mother tucked up in the spare room, I said to Amanda, 'I hope she's going to be okay here on her own. She doesn't know a soul. I don't understand why she's here.'

'She told you, Paul: she wants to be near her son. It's quite clear to me.' She tickled me and I moved sharply away.

'Don't do that!' I was curt. 'It freaks me out, that's all. What is she planning?'

'Well, you had better get used to it. I think she's here to stay.'

Amanda was used to family and wasn't worried about my mum. 'Don't worry, Paul; it'll be sorted by the time we get back.' She paused and lay back down on the pillow. 'I just hope she finds a house of her own.'

Over the next two days the three of us spent time chatting about nothing much – just about the gas fire, the locks, and other practical things. She was a little fed up with us that we were leaving her and going skiing, but I reminded her, 'You knew when I invited you that we were going away.'

Amanda and I loaded up the Porsche with warm clothes and some oils and brushes and a few canvases. When we left for Switzerland, Mum waved at us from the house and, for once in my life, I thought she had behaved well. She seemed a little different, but I couldn't put my finger on it. I thought it was because she was older and had calmed down. But for me it was unsettling, and I didn't really trust her. I wasn't to know then that the change was genuine, and it was for a reason I could never have imagined.

The trip to Switzerland was an adventure; we were in a convoy with two army Land Rovers, both with trailers and loaded with soldiers, rations and ski kit. There was one major disadvantage with my car. It had a problem with its starter motor, which meant Amanda had to push it to get it started. Unless I had parked on an incline, she found it highly annoying and nigh on impossible as the car weighed a ton. Consequently, several of the young lads had to jump out of the Land Rovers to help get the car moving off the forecourt at the many petrol stations throughout our trip. It provided a constant source of amusement for the lads.

Turning into the village of Pontresina, we arrived at the huge rented chalet, our home for the next two months. That night the officer gave permission to order pizzas, as it was too late to shop, and we were all exhausted. The following morning and for the next eight weeks we were out at the crack of dawn. The snowfall that winter had been very poor as temperatures were as low as minus 20 degrees and there was some concern as to whether the ski events would even take place.

Amanda spent her days in a spare room which she had set up as an art studio. She was painting several landscapes of the local area in oil paint. Every day I was training hard with the lads, and when the snow was too thin we took them to the gym or for a run around the lake at St Moritz. After training we arrived back at the chalet to take a warm shower. Sometimes we were in agony, as our Lycra racing suits were no protection against the freezing temperatures and we often sat in tears, holding our private parts until they warmed up! Amanda found all this male activity highly amusing and I would find her giggling somewhere in the kitchen as she prepared a hearty meal for the team.

In the evenings we visited the local village of Pontresina for a drink or a hot chocolate. Amanda and I would often find ourselves counselling the young lads about issues with their parents or girlfriends. Being in contact with so many teenage boys made me think about my son, so I decided to write to Katie. Amanda walked in and asked me what I was doing. 'Just writing to friends', I said.

On 22 December it was Amanda's twenty-third birthday so I bought tickets to hear a classical quartet in the village. One of the lads, Neil, an improbable soldier as he was a surf dude from Devon, wanted to come with us. We arrived at the hall and there must have been about twenty people there. It was a lovely evening, though slightly dull, and because of our long day of skiing I couldn't really blame Neil for falling asleep during the concert. When he started snoring I had to kick him to wake him up. Amanda, however, was impressed that I had found something to do and she thought it was romantic as we left the concert and walked through the village, lit by small lights and Christmas street decorations. I felt so happy that evening, as if nothing could touch us, and I had no idea what was about to happen.

In January we left Pontresina for Fulpmes in Austria for the next round of training. The team was doing well, as we had gained points and good training times, which meant we had a chance of winning something in at least one of the forthcoming competitions. After one such race I showered, then Amanda and I headed into town for a drink. She drew close to me and dropped a bombshell. 'I think I might be pregnant.'

I had a visceral response, which was to nearly throw up over my food. I went into a state of complete shock, fear and panic – I wanted to run, but this time I couldn't. What was I going to tell her now? 'Really? Are you sure?' I was desperately hoping she was mistaken.

'I'm five weeks late', she added.

'That doesn't mean you are pregnant', I insisted.

She could see I was shaken up, so she just sat back and nodded.

The next day, after coming first in a race, the young officer who was with us said we could celebrate with a pizza and a few beers. Arriving back at the chalet late that evening, one of the officers told me that I had to ring Grant at Bramcote Barracks as he had an urgent message for me. Calling immediately, Grant told me that my mother had collapsed in the street and had been taken to the George Eliot Hospital in Nuneaton and that we needed to get back immediately. His wife Maureen then spoke with Amanda, but Amanda was reserved when I asked her what Maureen had said. I went into the lounge and spoke with the officer and some of the boys, who were supping hot chocolate, telling them that Amanda and I would have to leave in the morning on compassionate grounds. Some of the lads were sad, as we had built a rapport with them. 'We will miss your cooking!' one of the boys said to Amanda. 'The officer will make us eat bratwurst every night!'

The news of my mum being ill and the possibility that Amanda was pregnant was the catalyst for me. A perfect storm. I decided that I had to tell her everything, even if it meant losing her. I was in a state of panic. I felt sick. 'I have something to tell you', I said.

*

Taking Amanda upstairs to our small bedroom I sat her on the bed while I paced the room.

'I'm going to tell you everything, all in one go . . . so you must listen to me.'

'All right, I will', she said, looking a little nervous.

'When I was twenty-one I got married. A year later we had a child . . . a son. He's now eight years old. We're divorced . . . but that's not all.'

'Not all?' she said. 'Isn't that enough?'

'I have to finish, Amanda – to tell you everything. I remarried when I was twenty-six and it was over by the time I was twenty-nine.'

'You have been married twice and have a son of eight?' Amanda was visibly shocked.

'Yes, that's right. I know it's a lot to take in but every time I thought of telling you I couldn't bear for it to change our relationship.'

'So why tell me now?'

'Because I was feeling bad about not seeing my son and now my mother is ill she will want to see him, and I can't keep this up any more. I wanted to tell you but was so aware that your father left when you were three and I left my son when he was three. I thought you would never forgive me.'

She started to cry, and then she stood up. 'Well, you may be right, Paul!' Coming at me, she beat my chest with her fists. 'You had no right not to tell me something that big. I would have coped if you had told me from day one.'

'It doesn't work like that, Amanda. We met on a rock in Cyprus, five days went by and I didn't know if I'd ever see you again.'

'Well, in England then?'

'I didn't want to hurt you.'

'Well, you have hurt me.' She pushed me out of the way and ran down the stairs and out into the night. The army Land Rover was parked in the drive, and climbing inside she sat there crying, our conversation playing over and over in her head. What an idiot she'd been. What on earth was she going to tell her mother, her family, her friends?

'God, help me', she said out loud.

I appeared at the window. 'Let me in, Amanda', I said.

'No, go away!' she shouted back.

'Please, Amanda, please . . . let me in.' I stood peering in. It was snowing heavily. Amanda looked at me for a minute, then opened the door. We sat in that vehicle for the next hour in the freezing Austrian winter.

I answered her stream of questions as best I could, but it was getting late. I asked her to come back inside as there was a race the next morning and we were going to have to leave on the long journey home back to the UK straight afterwards.

That night she slept in the single bed and I slept on the floor. We were up at the crack of dawn. Amanda came along to watch the race and, remarkably, we did quite well, coming second. When we were all panting and cooling down from an exhausting cross-country sprint, Amanda came to me, grinning. Whispering in my ear, she said, 'I'm not pregnant.' And to the amazement of twelve sixteen-year-olds I fell down in the snow and hugged her legs. 'Thank God', I said.

Professor Jennifer Argo, who has studied lying in the context of marketing and consumer behaviour, states, 'People appear to be short-term focused when they decide to deceive someone – save my self-image and save my self-worth now, but later on if the deceived individual finds out it can have long-term consequences.'[6]

The consequences of lying to Amanda, for me, were possibly going to be huge. We have both sometimes wondered if what happened next had not happened, whether we would still be together.

10: Not ready to let her go

'I just want to see him, Paul,' Mum said.

I looked at Amanda and she nodded.

Ringing Katie I told her about my mum being ill and asked if she would let me have Clinton for the weekend. She agreed, so I went to meet her at a motorway service station. I hadn't seen him for about a year and a half, since meeting Amanda. He was taller but still familiar with his wide smile and mop of dark hair. He took my hand and we went back to Nuneaton. Amanda was at the front door to greet him. She immediately tried to make him feel at home and that evening she gave him one of her old teddies to cuddle as he slept on the sofa bed in the front room.

The next morning, we went to the hospital and when Mum saw him her face lit up. He was a bit bemused as he couldn't remember her very well. 'Oh, let me look at you . . . you have grown so much . . . I hardly recognise you. How old are you now?'

'I'm eight and a half, Grandma', he said.

'Now I want you to take this money and go with your dad and get yourself a warm coat. They say it will be a freezing February', she said as she handed him forty pounds.

*

It took twenty-two hours to get to the George Eliot Hospital in Nuneaton. The journey was horrible, mostly because the heating system and the heat exchangers were no longer working on the Porsche, and there was ice on the inside of the windscreen. We had to stop the car every hour or so and stomp up and down on the forecourt of petrol stations in order to get our circulation going. Amanda and I then had to push the car to get it started. We wore sheepskin coats, hats and gloves, and talked non-stop as she quizzed me on every aspect of my life, batting to and fro the opportunities of when and how I could have told her.

'How come your mum never said anything?' she asked.

'Because I promised her I would tell you on this trip', I said.

Amanda felt a gamut of emotions: jealousy, anger, betrayal. But she was also a little excited – excited to meet my son sometime soon.

She had one piece of information she was withholding from me and when we arrived at the hospital at 11.00 a.m. on a cold January morning she put her hand on my arm and said, 'Paul, your mum has cancer and Maureen told me it's serious. I'm so sorry.'

I flew out of the car and raced down the corridor; with Amanda running behind me. I found my mum lying in a bed on a busy ward. She was looking frail and yellow compared to the person who had walked through our front door just nine weeks earlier. Within a few minutes of arriving by her bedside, she said, 'About bloody time! Where have you been?' I turned on my heels and stormed out. Amanda explained to her how I had driven non-stop to be there.

Amanda came to me in the corridor. I was pacing up and down. 'Why is she always so ungrateful?' I said.

'Paul, you have to get on with her now because she is seriously ill.'

I nodded, and Amanda took my hand and we returned to her bedside.

I kissed my mum's cheek and she smiled. 'Sorry, son. I'm just scared. I don't know what is wrong with me.'

She had always been a robust woman; but this illness had got hold of her and her vulnerability distressed me. This was not the woman I knew. 'I'll find the doctor', I said, trying to reassure her.

Eventually the doctor arrived and took us to a small room at the end of the ward. 'What's wrong with my mother? Will someone explain it to me?' I said, sharply.

'Your mother has a tumour that is sitting over her heart', said the doctor.

'What's caused it?' I said.

'Well, I believe it is a result of having smoked since she was thirteen years old.'

'Can you cure her, doctor?'

'No, I'm afraid not. The chemo may give her some more time.'

'How long has she got?'

'Maybe six months. I'm so sorry.'

At my mother's bedside Amanda stroked her hand. Mum spoke calmly, 'The first month was fine. I found a house and bought it – a small terraced house about ten minutes' walk from your house – under the arches towards the town, in Duke Street. But then I began to feel cold and unwell, so I went to a doctor, who said if I didn't give up smoking it would kill me. The threat was enough and I stopped that day after having smoked for fifty years', she sighed. 'Two weeks later I collapsed in the street and I've been here ever since. It took a while to track you down. I couldn't bear it on my own without you both.'

For the next week we visited her three times a day, taking food and newspapers and anything she requested. The tumour and the chemotherapy were taking their toll and she was getting weaker by the day. One morning she handed me some keys, as if she was placing a pound coin into a child's hand, wrapping my fingers around them for safekeeping. 'These are for you. I don't think I will get to live in the house . . . I want you to have it, you and Amanda.'

I couldn't believe what I was hearing and said, 'Don't talk rubbish! Of course you will live in the house. Amanda and I will get it ready for when you come out.'

She was uncharacteristically quiet. The ward was very noisy, and she wasn't getting enough sleep. She looked tired and harassed. A man cleaning the floors went past us with a very noisy contraption, like the floor cleaner I had used in Risley when I was seventeen years old. Something inside me changed. I remember thinking, *I am going to lose her; she's going to die.* I was angry, confused and scared. I felt I'd only just got her back in my life and now this. Why? The noise from the floor cleaner was driving me mad, so I took off to the reception. 'Please can my mother be moved into a room? It is too noisy for her on the ward and she is not sleeping.' Unusually there was a room free at the entrance of the ward, and the nurse agreed. Mum was moved that night, and for a day or two she perked up.

Amanda and I went to the terraced property on Duke Street. It was full of taped-up cardboard boxes. A few knick-knacks were above the fireplace and in her bedroom her personal things were on a dressing table. Gathering a hairbrush and some toiletries I put them in her bag to give to her the next day.

Gradually over the next few days she softened. She was even sweet and gentle and very funny at times. We knew she was scared so we tried to reassure her that the doctors were doing all they could to get her well. When she smiled, her eyes twinkled and I thought how pretty she was, despite her yellow jaundiced face. Her eyes were so familiar to me because she used them to speak. When she was harsh she frowned and screwed them up and when she was soft she smiled, and they lit up a room.

Amanda took homemade semolina into the hospital and asked Mum what she would like help with. We were both surprised when she said, 'Can you wash under my arms? I want to smell nice!' Amanda obliged while I sat and read out loud snippets from the paper. It was around this time that she asked to see Clinton. Maybe she knew she didn't have long to live and she wanted to see her grandson.

*

In the hospital Clinton was timid, but I managed to make him laugh when I pointed out he was sitting on his grandma's commode.

It was a strange couple of days with him, but he was a chatty child and I realised, as I looked at him, how little I knew him. He was my son – my flesh and blood – and I'd abandoned him. I felt ashamed of myself. As we got in to the car to take him back to Katie he burst into tears. He must have been so confused. I reassured him that we would get together soon, but I guess he had heard me say that many times before. This time his tears cut deep and I was very upset. Amanda was adamant that we would have him over to the house regularly. She really identified with Clinton's confusion and believed we had to show him that he was welcome with us anytime.

It was 5.00 a.m. on the morning of our tenth day back home when I received a phone call from the sister on the ward, saying that my mum had gone into a coma at 2.00 a.m. I was incensed, shouting down the phone, 'Why didn't you call me sooner?'

She nervously answered, 'We didn't want to wake you so early.'

'How dare you make that decision!' I said and hung up.

Dressing quickly, I then drove like a maniac to the hospital. Amanda and I went straight to her room and saw her curled up in her bed, unconscious. The nurses were fussing around her, so I asked them to leave. I was confused by the love I felt for my mother – confused and desperate to fix things. The heart monitor on the stand next to her bed was bleeping very slowly. Taking her hand, I said, 'Mum!' The monitor sped up but soon began to dip again. 'Mum', I said loudly. The monitor sped up again.

'Can she hear me?' I said to Amanda.

'I think she can. They say that hearing is the last thing to go.'

I barked back, 'Last thing to go? What does that mean?'

Amanda looked at me sympathetically and I knew what she was saying.

We stayed for an hour while the nurses came in and out. This huge thunderous personality, my mum, was reduced to a small frail woman whom I hardly recognised. I turned to Amanda and said, 'I don't know what to do.'

'Paul . . . I think you need to give her permission to go.'

'I'm not ready to let her go', I said.

Amanda shook her head slowly as if to say it wasn't up to me. 'Maybe you can let her know that it's okay to go to sleep.'

'Shall I get on the bed with her?' I asked.

'If you want to, yes', she said, encouragingly. I immediately got on the bed and placed my left arm around her. She looked like a small bird tucked under its wing, her head resting on my chest. She was so still.

It reminded me of when I was small, and my dad was working nights and I would sleep in bed with her. Her familiar smell haunted me; her skin, her perfume, her hand cream. Sometimes people are ready to die; my mum wasn't. She was only sixty-three years old and wanted a new life. A new start with her son.

Amanda took her hand and leaned in close to her ear. 'If you can hear me, Brenda, squeeze my hand.' Feeling a light squeeze, she smiled. 'She heard me, Paul. She heard me.'

And in that moment, I let her go. 'It's okay, Mum, go to sleep if you're tired.' I heard myself saying, 'I'm so sorry, for not being around. I'm sorry for being selfish, I'm sorry for being a bad son to you. I love you, Mum.'

Within seconds my mother had died in my arms.

And that was it, a life gone.

The heart monitor stayed on, omitting a continuous tone, and a single tear rolled down her cheek. Just one. I looked at Amanda, who was crying; we were both bewildered.

Amanda said, 'She will be at peace now.'

But all I could think was, *I don't want her to have peace. I haven't had enough time with her yet.* I felt drained, cheated and angry. All I could say was, 'Why? Why?'

After twenty minutes or so, we spoke with the doctor. He took us into a side room. I was angry. 'You told me six months. You said she had six months; it's been ten days!'

He was apologetic and said that was only an estimate as they never really know for sure. Once I'd calmed down, he told us that the tumour was just too big and that the chemotherapy was possibly too strong for her.

The next few days were a blur as we went from office to office collecting a death certificate, registering the burial and closing bank accounts. It seemed cold and robotic, dealing with my mother's life, but we just got on with it. It was at night, when the emotion had a chance to break through, that I would wake in a sweat, having seen her in a dream, sometimes shouting at me, sometimes smiling. It was all so messed up in my head, the confusion of the last few days and the assimilation of the last thirty-one years of my life. I thought I was going mad.

The funeral parlour phoned, inviting me to view my mother. I felt a need to see her again, her death not having sunk in. Amanda waited for me in the waiting room. An undertaker took me to a small room where the coffin was set on a table, closing the door as he left. Stepping near to the coffin I tentatively looked in but was so startled by what I saw that I took a step back and darted for the door. It wouldn't open, so I pulled and pulled and soon began to panic. The undertaker must have heard the commotion, because he came to slide the door open effortlessly. 'Are you all right, sir?' I bolted for the exit and Amanda followed. I couldn't speak. I heard Amanda calling my name, but it was only when I got to the car that I calmed down.

'What on earth happened in there?' she said.

'She looked nothing like my mother. There was no colour in her face and she looked angry . . . how she used to look when I was a boy . . . I just had to get out of there and when I tried the door it didn't open. I thought I was trapped . . . I had forgotten it was a sliding door and I panicked.' Amanda held me in her arms, and I cried as she tried to reassure me, saying it was most likely the make-up and how they had prepared her. We went to a small country pub and stayed for hours talking about my childhood and the sadness of my mother's death.

The funeral took place at the church opposite our house. Five people attended. Amanda and I, the vicar, Grant, and the officer of the Bramcote Training Centre. The vicar called my mother Barbara, twice, then I corrected him. It was his first funeral and he was nervous. I kept looking back at the church door, waiting for a late arrival. I had called my dad and told him of Mum's death. He had been shocked. He had suffered on many occasions since leaving her, as she had not made it easy for him, especially when she had written to his boss saying all sorts of terrible things about him, trying to get him sacked. When I rang him to tell him she had died he didn't know where to put his anger and sorrow. Having spent over seventeen years with her, he had loved her but there had been no peace between them. Although he had been in a relationship with another woman, Anna, for many years, he thought he should come and support me at the funeral. Having left Manchester in good time on the morning of the funeral he had not anticipated getting so lost.

It was when the coffin was carried out to the burial ground that I saw him pushing open the kissing gate to the graveyard. 'Sorry, son. Sorry I'm so late. Got bloody lost! Sorry, son!' Waving his arms above his head while removing his trilby he ran towards me, puffing as he slowed down. The funeral party stood around the coffin as the gravediggers lowered my mum into the newly dug soil. Dad began to cry so I put my arm across his broad back.

My two military friends turned down the offer of a cup of tea and so did the vicar, who had to go on to take another funeral straight away. Amanda, Dad and I walked across the road to our house. Amanda turned the gas fire on as it was getting bitterly cold. Dad stayed standing near the front door, while I talked about how Mum was happy in the last few days of her life. 'She was softer, easier', I said.

'I'm glad she was different. I loved her one time – you know that, don't you?' he said.

He stayed for a cup of tea but left within half an hour, nervous about the drive back.

That evening Amanda wrapped her arms around me as we stared out of our front bedroom window. It was unsettling looking into the graveyard, knowing that my mum was lying in the cold earth just metres away. It had all happened so quickly – returning from Austria, spending ten days with her, feeding her, washing her, watching her die, and then burying her. It was taking its toll on both of us.

During the next couple of weeks, while I was working at the barracks, Amanda began to sort through Mum's belongings. One afternoon I joined her, putting most of her things in black bin bags to give to charity shops in town. Under the back room window, on a small table, I saw a Good News Bible. I opened the front cover and read a greeting to my mum. At the bottom of the page was a phone number. I recognised the code as Manchester. Without speaking to Amanda, I went to the phone. 'Hello. You don't know me, but I've just found your name in a Bible belonging to my mother, Brenda Cowley. Can you tell me how you know her?' Amanda took the Bible out of my hands to take a look.

The woman said, 'Your mother became a Christian two years ago, and she was a member of my home group. The Bible was a present from the church when she got baptised.'

Baptised? Church? A Christian? My mother? I was genuinely shocked. Being a Christian didn't fit my mother's profile. I told the woman on the other end of the phone that my mother was dead, and I hung up. Amanda interrupted my muddled thoughts. 'That explains why she wanted to come and live near us, you know – to be nearer family?' She smiled and continued, 'Maybe she had an epiphany or something?'

'A what?' I said.

'An epiphany. A revelation.'

'So why didn't she tell me?' I said.

'Maybe she wanted to show you rather than tell you', she replied softly.

The words spoken by the woman on the phone went around

and around in my head. 'Your mother became a Christian . . . your mother became a Christian.'

I thought, *my mother, a Christian? What on earth does that mean?*

11: Let that be a warning to you

Staff Sergeant Eric Martin came into the swimming pool area at 6.00 a.m. on the dot. About twenty of us stood to attention at the side of the pool, in our speedos. Looking directly at us he shouted, 'Cowley, Slater, one pace forward!' My friend Graham Slater (Slats) and I did as we were ordered. He then walked up to us both and said, 'Have you two been drinking?'

'Yes, Staff', we replied.

He didn't look pleased, barking out the order, 'Cowley, Slater, turn to the left. Do forward rolls around the edge of the pool, until you get back to me. Go!'

Slats and I proceeded to do forward rolls around the 25-metre pool watched by the whole class, the staff sergeant insisting that we stay on the raised nobbly bits around the edge. It had to be one of the most painful things I have done. When we finished, he made us stand to attention, shouting, 'Let that be a warning to you all. No one comes on to my parade smelling of alcohol.'

*

After my mother's funeral, I was in a bit of a haze about life, but I was used to blocking things out and moving on. One night in the Sergeants' Mess I was with a few colleagues when someone asked me, 'Have you ever thought of transferring to the Physical Training Corps, Paul?' Although I had seen men in PT outfits throughout my army career and their presence was very strong in Hereford, I had no idea there was an actual corps in the army dedicated solely to fitness. Once I had looked into it, I was hooked. Doing sport all day and getting paid for it sounded like a job I should go for, and I started on yet another plan.

I knew the commanding officer (CO) wouldn't let me go, as I was on a three-year posting to the Junior Leaders and there was no way out of my contract. Discovering that the Master at Arms for the PT Corps was Major Martindale, I made an appointment and turned up at his office in Shrewsbury. I spent two hours with him and we got on really well. He asked me about my army experience, and I told him that I was a good runner, a sniper, skier and climber, and that I was fit and strong, as I worked out in the gym most days. He was particularly interested in my adventure training qualifications, including JSMEL (Joint Services Mountain Expedition Leader). At the end of the meeting he said he couldn't do anything without my commanding officer's permission. I left and returned to my unit a little disappointed.

Two weeks later, I was summoned to see my CO. I thought it was a routine chat to see how the group of young recruits were doing, but as I walked in, his face said it all. He went ballistic with me. Apparently I had done rather better than I thought, as Major Martindale had insisted that I be released immediately to begin my transfer process into the PT Corps. The CO, unable to stop the process, was fuming. After a lecture from him about loyalty I was told to get out and report to the chief clerk's office to start transfer procedures.

My posting orders came through within the week, telling me where to report and what to bring with me. It also instructed me to send through my adventure training certificates, of which I had several, and my PT certificate, of which I had none. A PT certificate was to prove I had completed a basic course in physical training and worked in a gym at some point in my career. Which I hadn't.

I resorted to doing what I had always done at times like this – I bluffed! I walked down to the chief clerk's office and asked one of the team, a young female clerk, to send off all my military certificates along with my non-existent PT certificate to the PT school in Aldershot. She said, 'Fine. Come back tomorrow, sergeant, and I'll confirm we have them all and that they have been posted.'

The next day, I went back expecting to be told that they couldn't find my PT certificate and there was a problem. I asked the clerk if the certificates had been posted and she looked at me and said, 'Of course.' Trying not to look shocked I asked if my PT certificate in particular had also gone, to which she replied, 'I've sent them all, PT certificate included, as that's the main one they wanted.' I walked out of that office confused. How on earth could they have a PT certificate with my name on it?

Within three months from that date, at the age of thirty-two, I was on a one-year selection course for the Army Physical Training Corps at the PT school in Aldershot. There were 118 men who started on that first day, but only eighteen would finish.

The course was physically gruelling, as challenging as the SAS, but in a different way. Split into three sections of four months, the first section, the Advance Course, is where they try to break you with non-stop physical training every day and non-stop sports academic training at night. Then, if you survive that, you're on to the next phase: four months of junior probations. This involves more tests but this time it includes gymnastics. The last phase of the course, senior probation, is mostly education: exams, arranging tournaments and competitions and trying to qualify at an advanced level in most sports. If you are still alive at the end, there is a pass out parade where you are presented with the honoured badge of the red 'crossed swords' and then a posting to any regiment of their choice within the British Army.

It was at the PT school in Aldershot where I was to meet Staff Sergeant Eric Martin; a short explosive man with dark hair, from Cyprus, hated by most, if not all, the students. He had the strange mannerism of staring into space halfway through an order, leaving you waiting for him to finish his sentence. He was a swimming and boxing specialist, among many other things, a very talented man but with the reputation of being a bit of a lunatic.

He became an everyday sight, as he was always instructing us in something, taking great delight in making us struggle to complete various tests. For example, the rope climb, which involved climbing a 30-foot rope with just your arms, keeping your elbows locked into your side and pulling up from the chest with both legs at a 90-degree angle to your body, all the way to the top. It was exhausting. Staff Sergeant Martin made us do the test only to fail us at the end of many attempts, then walked off laughing and saying, 'Again! Tomorrow!'

The course was hard for me because I was older than most of the others and not particularly flexible. We had many early starts and late finishes, which was not a problem, but getting up at 5.30 a.m. for a run and then being expected to do gymnastics at 7.00 a.m. was a bit of a pressure. Many of us became stressed and tired, and injuries started to happen. Men dropped out of the course, as no time was given to recover from sickness or strained muscles. All you could do was hope you didn't get an injury, and if you did you would have to strap the area up and fill up on painkillers. Every day someone left with an injury they couldn't hide.

My fear levels, however, were about to accelerate when, instead of taking part in the mountain climbing phase of the course (due to my JSMEL qualification), I was sent canoeing in Wales. During the canoeing course I almost drowned twice. The first time was when the instructor, another lunatic, decided to take us to the Menai Strait, notorious for strong currents, whirlpools and fishing weirs. Having never canoed before, we were immediately placed in deep water, taught how to capsize and get upright again. But all too quickly the instructor took us out into the middle of the strait and got us to put the nose of our canoes on the edge of the fish weirs. The tidal waters pull huge volumes of water past the coastline with every tide, and the weirs were built to trap fish in small holding areas. They were known as death traps for canoeists and we had to back paddle frantically in order not to get sucked in.

The second time, the instructor took us to Swallow Falls at Capel Curig. This flow of river is over a steep gradient and measured as a grade 5 (risk to life), due to its hazardous rocks and fallen trees. Having only canoed for the past two days I capsized over and over, and was terrified at the speed of the water. I hated that course. Not because of the constant canoeing but because of the instructors who, at times, were irresponsible and dangerous.

About halfway through the PT course, Staff Sergeant Eric Martin walked into my room and asked me and my friend Slats if we wanted to go with him for a drink. When we hesitated, he said, 'Look, I know I am one of your senior instructors, but let's relax. You're both doing well, and I thought that we could have a drink and get to know one another.'

Slats and I were a bit unsure, but we also thought he could help us get through all our tests if he liked us, so why not? That night we went out and had a few drinks and then went on to a nightclub, getting back to the Sergeants' Mess at around 4.00 a.m. At 6.00 a.m. we were due on parade at the military swimming pool at Sandhurst. Slats and I thought that as we were now friends with Eric he was bound to be lenient with us considering the amount of alcohol we had all consumed the night before.

*

I hated Staff Sergeant Eric Martin from the moment he made Slats and me do forward rolls around the swimming pool. He continued to fail me on most of my tests and made me re-do them over and over. When he could see I was at breaking point, he would pass me. This type of treatment in the army is very common, as I mentioned earlier when training young recruits. However, Eric Martin was at a more extreme level of sadistic behaviour and none of us understood his methods. His staring into space and seemingly forgetting what he was doing was increasing, and we all thought there must be something wrong with him.

During the Christmas break of 1987 I went back to my house in Nuneaton and, in one of those bizarre life coincidences, Amanda and I went to a New Year's Eve party at the printmaker Angela

Harding's cottage in Shenton, a tiny village a few miles from our house. There must have been only a handful of people there and when I heard one of the women tell Amanda that she was originally from Cyprus, and her name was Glenys Martin, I had to ask the question, 'You aren't related to Eric Martin in the PT Corps, are you?'

'That's my brother!' she said. 'What's he like to work with?'

'Well, he's a bit of a lunatic, to be honest!' I said, and she didn't seem that surprised.

When I returned to the PT school I went to his office in Fox gymnasium and said, 'Staff, I met your sister at a party on New Year's Eve.' I was expecting a smile or a question about her. I wasn't expecting him to say 'F*** off, Cowley!'

It was at that point I gave up trying to be nice to him as I just couldn't work him out.

A few weeks later he invited Amanda and me for a curry in Elephant and Castle, saying his sister Glenys would be there and that she wanted us all to meet up. That evening was very strange to say the least. I was reluctant to go but Amanda said she thought it was a good opportunity to get to know him. There was definite tension between brother and sister, and when we left that evening Amanda said, 'I never want to spend time with him again. He is sexist, racist, a chain smoker and a bigot,' adding, 'he is one of the most annoying men I have ever met.'

'Welcome to my life', I said.

I wasn't thinking about Eric Martin when I qualified as a PTI. Both Slats and I had got through with sixteen others and we were elated. Tragically, one man died from a broken neck and two men ended up in wheelchairs with broken backs. When I left as a PTI, I was qualified to instruct in boxing, swimming, adventure training, judo, squash, gymnastics, track and field, self-defence, and many more sports. My specialty, however, was as an adventure trainer, otherwise known as a 'woolly hatter' – a term used for the men in the PT Corps who were keen adventure trainers rather than gym-bound instructors.

Now all I needed to know was where my posting was going to be.

One night in the Sergeants' Mess I was on the phone to Amanda when Eric walked past me, stopped and said, 'I hope you can speak Spanish, and I hope you like the heat, Sergeant Cowley.' What on earth did he mean? Where was I going? It had me worried for days and every time I saw him he would just smile and say, 'Ola!'

Eventually I was called into the office and given my posting. I was to go to the 3rd Battalion Royal Green Jackets, who were stationed in Colchester. I was informed that they were heading out to Gibraltar for a three-year tour of duty on the Rock. I was excited about this posting. For one, I loved Spain, as my best childhood memories were made there, and secondly, I thought Amanda could come and live with me and we would have some fun together. However, I wasn't particularly looking forward to going to the Royal Green Jackets in Colchester for four months.

I hit the Green Jackets hard, as I had been warned they were a tough regiment and didn't take to outsiders well, especially from the PT Corps. To start with it was difficult, because they were constantly testing me to see if I was weak – seeing if I would break under pressure – or if they could pull rank on me and pressure me to let them off some of the compulsory physical tests that everyone in the unit (approximately 900 men) had to take. I knew I had one chance at gaining respect and if I didn't succeed I would be totally ineffectual. I made every one of them complete their tests, even failing some of the officers and putting them on remedial PT, which meant they had to train in their own time with me. Apparently, officers hadn't had to do this before I arrived. By the time we went to Gibraltar, four months later, I was respected as a strong PT Corps man who couldn't be bullied by rank.

Although I was happy with my posting to Gibraltar, I was a little worried about my relationship with Amanda. I felt as if I might lose her or that I might sabotage the relationship. Our plan was that I would buy an apartment in Spain and she would come and live with me. Meanwhile, one of the young officers approached me with an idea. He wanted to raise money for charity by cycling the route from Colchester to Gibraltar. After some discussion I was asked to get a group of six men together from the regiment and organise a cycling relay.

The journey started from Colchester to Dover, then across the channel into Calais, then all the way through France, over the mountains of the Pyrenees into the centre of Spain, finally arriving in Gibraltar. It was exhausting but great fun. It took us just over a week to cycle the 1,511 miles and we raised quite a lot of money for a children's charity based in Gibraltar, so the locals loved us when we arrived. It was great for public relations.

Since Amanda and I were not married I was unable to get quarters so had the idea of using the money from my mum's house sale to buy an apartment in Spain – or possibly the 38-foot yacht that had caught my eye in Gibraltar harbour.

Amanda, however, had other ideas. Having been asked to do storyboards for a company making a pop video about a soldier going absent without leave, she suggested they use the real thing. The next thing I knew I was flying home for a weekend's leave and was in Judith Owen's video for 'Tie Me to the Wind'. It was a fun thing to do, dressed in my uniform and running over the Welsh mountains. We still have a copy of it somewhere on VHS. It was a bit of light relief from my day job. Unfortunately, the song wasn't a great success, so my acting career was short-lived.

Having made some connections in TV, Amanda heard that Mentorn Films in Wardour Street was looking for runners. While I was settling into my room in the Sergeants' Mess, Amanda was arriving in the foyer of the film and TV company in Soho, London. Due to her BA in Art, they decided to place her in the art department. I remember the phone call when she excitedly told me she was to start the following Monday. 'I need to earn some money, Paul. I can't expect to live off you.'

'But I thought you were going to come and live with me in Spain', I said. She could tell I was disappointed.

'Well, I still can . . . I could do this for a few months and then come over. I have told my boss that I have a week's holiday booked in four weeks, so I will come and see you then.'

She was trying to reassure me, but I was a realist. I knew myself too well. But what could I do? I was glad she had work and knew I couldn't change her mind. I suddenly felt heavy in my heart. I thought I might lose her, this girl who had made me appreciate life in a different way.

12: God, help me

It was then I heard the shouting, and although I couldn't see them, I could hear them. Scooby's team of five men were stuck on a ledge approximately 400 feet up, shouting for help. They were concerned about Scooby, as they had seen him fall and were all pretty shaken. I shouted up, 'He's okay, just broken his leg. Hold on. I will get you down.'

I was now in a dilemma; it was getting dark and cold, and it had started to rain. It would take hours to go for help and I needed to fix the situation, but I could see that the rock face was almost sheer and way beyond my ability to climb. Without really thinking I pulled Scooby off the rock onto a flat surface, and with the medic straightened out his legs to get the harness off. I picked up the rope that had fallen down with him and, grabbing what I could, started to climb up the cliff face. I was running on sheer adrenalin, feeling way out of my depth.

*

Unfortunately, I had been rather naive to think I could live in Spain and cross the border to work in Gibraltar each day. Buying a flat was not an option, so my home for the next three years became a small room in the Sergeants' Mess high up the Rock in Lathbury Barracks. From the corner of my room, looking out of a narrow window, I could see the Atlas Mountains of North Africa and the port of Algeciras in Spain.

Amanda, meanwhile, was loving her work at Mentorn Films; it was varied and creative and she had no intention of giving it up. I was having a great time in Gibraltar as there was plenty of sun, sea and adventures, especially when Amanda flew out. Taking off in my small red Suzuki jeep, we visited Tarifa, a surfing town along the southern coast. We camped or stayed in hotels, enjoying our time together. In the summer of the first year Amanda had a month off work, and we cycled and slept under canvas. She painted, and we did tai chi and all sorts of other strange and wonderful things.

It was around that time that I was presented with another adventure, and I thought it would keep me out of trouble as I was convinced that my relationship with Amanda was the only one I wanted. I was tired of my roaming lifestyle and, if I could, I wanted to settle down and be with one woman.

Training most lunchtimes in the gymnasium, I had become good friends with Sergeant Ubie, one of the Royal Green Jackets. Known to most of us as 'Scooby' as in Scooby-Doo, he was an interesting character. I was impressed that he was a volunteer basketball player who was able to motivate the soldiers and keep them fit. Although we hadn't known each other very long we had an instant rapport. He liked a drink, one of my favourite pastimes, and he was also respected as a good climber, so we often swapped climbing stories over a few pints.

One night, at one of the many pubs on Main Street, Scooby and I hatched a plan to take a group of men climbing and get the army to pay for it. Scooby, born in Kenya of Asian descent, had a passion to go back and climb Mount Kenya. I suggested I put a proposal together to present to the training major. It would involve taking ten soldiers to climb Mount Kenya and then move on to Mount Kilimanjaro. Since I was the physical training instructor for the regiment and Scooby was well qualified in mountaineering, we were both covered at a professional level and the trip was cleared surprisingly quickly.

Ten soldiers volunteered and soon we started to train them for the trip. I had an idea that as we were in Gibraltar and stationed on the Rock we should abseil down it. I was surprised that most of the team weren't as enthusiastic as I was; in fact, no one wanted to do it as it was thought too dangerous (a 1,398-foot drop). After a few drinks one night in the Sergeants' Mess one of the other sergeants, encouraged by Scooby, dared me to abseil down the Rock for a considerable amount of money. Before I could think, I said, 'Double it and I'll take my mountain bike down with me!'

The bet was on, hands were shaken, and the next day I drew some ropes out of the store, and we drove up to the top of the Rock. I set the abseil up with Scooby's help. Abseiling down with a bike on my back was more difficult than expected, as I had to manoeuvre a knot in the rope halfway down. Fortunately, we had found a cave, so Scooby met me there with the next section of the rope. At that point I did think it was a bit of a stupid dare, but I was committed and finished triumphantly with my winnings presented in the mess that night. I had never asked permission and would have been in a lot of trouble if I'd been caught. After that, there were rumours that some 'idiot' had abseiled down the Rock with a mountain bike on his back.

Training continued, and the final team was selected. Flights were booked, accommodation was cleared, climbing equipment and food supplies were collected and entrance and permission granted by the Kenyan and Tanzania governments to enter the national parks. Scooby was in charge of route planning and logistics, while I was in charge of equipment and morale.

Once in the national park it took us three days to get to the base camp of Mount Kenya. Part of the route involved an area called the vertical bog; it was about three miles of mud that you had to trek through uphill. It was hard going, as we were all carrying a lot of weight and altitude sickness was starting to kick in. After one night at the weather station, at the halfway point, we eventually reached the base camp at 17,000 feet. For a couple of days, we made camp in the wooden hut we had booked in advance and began to train together. It was hard work at that height, as the air was very thin. Even cleaning our teeth was difficult. We needed to acclimatise for a couple of days before attempting to climb the summit at 18,000-plus feet.

After two days we were getting restless and decided to do a little more training. We split into two groups. Scooby wanted to take half the men to do rock climbing techniques, which meant getting them familiar with the rock face and the equipment, while I was happy to take the other group and walk up the mountain to Point Lenana at 16,000-plus feet. This would give us some snow and ice climbing experience and also get us used to the altitude. Each expedition would take around eight hours, so we arranged to be back at base camp for 1600 hours, just before the light failed. Kenya is on the equator and the sun drops really quickly, going from light to pitch black in a matter of minutes.

My team climbed to Point Lenana and at the top we had our photo taken in front of an iron cross which was imbedded in the rock. We sat and looked out onto a sea of cloud and I was in my element. We then traversed back down the mountain heading for base camp. It was a relatively easy walk and climb, but it still felt like an achievement and the young men were excited for our climb the next day. We got back at 1600 hours, expecting Scooby to be back with his lads making a brew and telling stories, but they were nowhere to be seen.

Looking through my binos I hoped to see Scooby's group walking towards the camp. Suddenly, I heard a blood-curdling cry and, following the sound with my binos, saw what I thought to be a person fall off the vertical cliff face. I shouted to the medic and we ran to where I thought I saw the figure fall.

When we got there, I saw it was Scooby who had fallen approximately 800 feet. Having hit a boulder at the bottom of the cliff, his body was arched over the rock and his back was clearly broken. His arms and legs were at distorted angles to his body and there was blood everywhere, as his head and face had also hit the rock. Scooby was no longer recognisable. I checked to see if there was a pulse in his neck and started to push up and down on his chest to resuscitate him. After a while the medic stopped me. He was a young lad and was visibly shocked himself, having turned very pale. He took my arm and said, 'He's dead, boss.'

*

'Sarge, sarge, help us, please. Is Scooby dead?'

Looking up to where the shouts were coming from, I realised the lads who were out of sight were high up on a ledge, stranded, with no way of getting down.

'No, he has just broken his leg. Don't worry!' I shouted back. I was concerned that if they thought he was dead they might panic, and what they needed more than anything was to be reassured and remain calm.

Removing some of Scooby's equipment I made a dash for the rock face. I started to climb and managed to get level with the lads at 400 feet but quickly realised two things. First, a large overhang meant that although I was level with them, I still couldn't see them. I tried throwing a rope to them over and over again, but the overhang was just too large. Second, I didn't have the right equipment to get the men or myself back down. What I needed was pitons, small nail-shaped pieces of metal that you can hammer into cracks in the rock, and carabinas to feed a rope through. Mountain climbing is like climbing a tree; it's easy to get up but difficult to get down and it's also when most accidents happen.

'Just hold on, lads. I will get you down', I shouted back, but after a good twenty minutes I knew I had no idea how I was going to help them.

I stood on that ledge holding on to the rock and I started to shake and cry with fear and frustration. I didn't even think I could get back down myself, let alone help four others. It's the bit in the movies you don't see, where the hero is in a heap, stressed and crying, realising he has failed. As I hid my face in the rock, exhausted, scared, I prayed a desperate prayer: 'God, if you're there, help me. I don't want to die.'

It was then I felt a gentle tap on my right shoulder, and as I turned around, I saw a young man next to me. I won't repeat what I said. But I was shocked. Where did he come from? I can see him now, very lean, long hair and tanned. He just smiled at me. He didn't speak; he pushed me into the rock and secured me on to the ledge and made me safe. He then climbed around me, taking a rope, hammering in pitons as he moved across the overhang, disappearing from sight.

After he had lowered the men to safety, he then came back for me. He put a rope into my harness, pointed down and lowered me to safety. When we were all together on the ground, the four men were horrified when they saw Scooby's body. They had believed me when I said he had broken his leg. We stood for a while in silence, but I could see the men were visibly shaken, so I said we needed to go back to the hut. As we had no way of getting Scooby down from the mountain that night, a park ranger who had arrived on the scene advised us that we should move him first thing in the morning.

Once back at base camp the lads told me what had happened and why they were on the ledge.

Apparently, Scooby was running late, as it had taken them much longer to climb up the mountain than he had anticipated. He was worried that the sun was setting, and they would be walking off the mountain in the dark, so he decided he would do an emergency abseil. With a sheer cliff face of approximately 800 feet and only one rope, he had to do a multi-pitch abseil, which is never recommended as it is dangerous, because after each descent you have to recover the rope. Once the men were safely on a ledge, Scooby recovered the rope and looped it over a rock. Leaning back, the rock split away from the mountain and he fell to his death.

I said to the lads, 'It's a good job the climber guy turned up or we would have all been in big trouble. We must find him and thank him. Did he speak to any of you?'

'No', they said.

We tried to find out who he was, where he'd come from, but he had vanished into thin air.

At daybreak, four of us went back with the ranger and placed Scooby in a body bag and put him on a stretcher. We carried him down to where a helicopter could recover him and his body was taken to Kahawa Barracks in Nairobi.

I radioed HQ at the main camp in Nairobi and asked if they could check the national park's records to see if any other climbing groups were in the park. They told me later that we were the only team on the mountain.

The team was meant to travel from Mount Kenya on to Mount Kilimanjaro, but after Scooby's death none of us wanted to climb or see a mountain again for a long time. It was arranged that we would stay at Kahawa Barracks while the necessary paperwork was carried out by the army.

As an institution, when a soldier dies, the army often goes the extra mile to help a family. Once all the paperwork was completed, Scooby's body was to be repatriated back to the UK by the RAF. Meanwhile, the climbing team was booked on to a flight to the UK for a few days' leave. We left Kenyatta airport on 25 December 1990, and the pilots were suitably dressed as Father Christmas while the cabin crew all wore Christmas hats. After the stress of the previous few days it was a bit of welcome light relief and the glass of champagne we were given sent me off to sleep for the rest of the flight.

Once I arrived in London I headed to Amanda's mum's house in the Midlands. Amanda came to the door and hugged me. I was overwhelmed. I was at last in a safe place and knew I could relax for a few days before my regiment wanted me back for the inquiry into Scooby's death. Tricia and Andrew offered their condolences. I told them that it was as if an angel had come in the form of a climber and saved my life and the lives of the other young soldiers.

On reflection it reminds me of St Augustine who said, 'We cannot pass our guardian angel's bounds, resigned or sullen, he will hear our sighs.' And St Paul who wrote in the book of Hebrews, 'Are not all angels ministering spirits sent to serve those who will inherit salvation?' (Hebrews 1:14).

Staring in the bathroom mirror, my face said it all, and not because it was burnt from two weeks in the African sun but because I had a haunted look. There was a deep ache inside me, and a desperate need for something to change. Scooby's death was a wake-up call. I had seen death on the face of my mother a few years earlier and now I'd seen it on the face of a friend. Scooby was my age, fit and athletic, in the prime of his life, and we had laughed and shared a coffee together on the morning he died. There had to be something more to life and I was determined to find it.

There were two things I wanted, and I intended to get them both.

Part Two

The second half of my life

. . . being confident of this, that he who began a good work in you will carry it on to completion until the day of Christ Jesus.
Philippians 1:6

13: Fear of the Lord

Picking up the bible verse by my bed, I read the words from Matthew 22:13. 'Then the king told the attendants, "Tie him hand and foot, and throw him outside, into the darkness, where there will be weeping and gnashing of teeth."' Suddenly, I was terrified. It hadn't occurred to me that I could be judged by a higher power. The scripture reminded me of violent films I had seen, and nightmares I had had since I was a kid. I felt alone and afraid. All I could think about was being thrown into darkness and there being weeping and gnashing of teeth.

I'm not sure where it came from, but in my mind I saw the picture of an old Ladybird book called *The Lord's Prayer.* On the front were two children kneeling and clasping their hands together in prayer. I got down on my knees and said, 'God, please take away the gnashing of teeth.'

*

Life was short, I told myself, and therefore I should get the two things I really wanted. The first was an Omega diving watch, the one that James Bond sported, and the second was a sheepskin flying jacket. I bought both, and for twenty-four hours I felt vaguely satisfied. But it wasn't to last for long.

I was dreading the inquiry into Scooby's death, which was imminent. Having reached Scooby's body first, I was considered a main witness. The inquiry was to be a series of interviews over a couple of days, carried out by senior officers to assess if Scooby's death was an accident while on active duty, or death by misadventure. If the latter, then his wife could lose all his pension benefits, his army quarters and any allowances she was entitled to. The inquiry lasted three days and all the team were questioned repeatedly about the event, going over it in minute detail. It was exhausting, especially for the young soldiers who had been through quite a traumatic experience. As far as I was concerned he had done nothing wrong; it was simply an accident. Finally, the board of inquiry ruled that it was death while on active service and his family was entitled to his army pension.

I went to my commanding officer and asked permission to drive Scooby's prized yellow Ford Capri and all of his personal belongings from Gibraltar back to the UK to hand over to his wife. The alternative was to box up his belongings and have everything shipped back.

My CO thought it was a good idea and gave me a week off for the trip. I asked Amanda to fly out to Gibraltar and drive back to the UK with me across the centre of Spain. I knew meeting Scooby's wife was going to be difficult and I wanted Amanda there, because at times like this she was stronger than me.

The scenery from Andalucía to the Meseta Central was extraordinarily beautiful; a vast inner plateau in the heart of Spain surrounded by mountains. We had a good time together, but at night I had flashbacks of Scooby's broken body on the rocks. Several times I woke in a sweat as the recurring nightmare of trying to resuscitate him came back to haunt me. I was getting more and more stressed about what I would say when we pulled up at Scooby's front door to meet his wife and children.

When we arrived, his wife greeted us. She had made sure that her children were looked after, as she wanted to speak with us alone. We all sat in her front room with a cup of tea talking about the day Scooby died. Suddenly she said, 'What time did he die, Paul?'

'It was around 4.00 p.m. as the sun was dropping. Why?' I said.

She looked sad, but she smiled. 'When he was leaving for the trip, we said our goodbyes and I had a strange feeling that I might not see him again. And then at 2.00 p.m. on the afternoon he died, which would have been 4.00 p.m. in Africa, I had a sharp pain in my head. I thought then that something had happened to Scooby.'

Amanda and I looked at each other and then back to her. 'You loved him very much', said Amanda.

'Yes,' she said, adding, 'I'd like to see him.'

Scooby's body was by this time at the RAF base Brize Norton in Oxfordshire.

'I don't recommend you see him. It's better that you remember him as he was. Please trust me on this', I said. After my own experience of viewing my mother in the funeral parlour, combined with the knowledge that Scooby had received severe head injuries, I did not believe his wife should see him.

'I trust you', she said.

After Scooby's death, I stayed in Gibraltar for another year and a half.

Clinton came out in the spring of 1991. He flew out on his own, aged twelve. I met him at the airport and took him back to my room in the Sergeants' Mess. Amanda had inspired me to transform my cold, stark room into what was more like a Bedouin tent by putting the mattress on the floor and hanging up a mosquito net. I also painted tropical fish on the wall and put up several photographs and cards. None of this impressed my neighbour, the regimental sergeant major of the battalion, who went red with rage when he looked into my room.

The few days I spent with Clinton were fun but complicated for me, as I had to manage a young boy in an army environment and still do my job. When I look back, I think I treated him more like a young recruit than my son. Maybe because when I looked at him I felt a tremendous guilt as he reminded me of my past – the rows with his mother, and the lack of care I seemed to have for anyone in my life. None of that was his fault, but I was not in a place to understand it all. I therefore resorted to what I knew: fitness and sport. I had him swimming and running, and once I made him cycle up the long steep hill from the main street to the barracks while I ran next to him. But I wasn't able to put in the effort and commitment it takes to form a bond with a child: sadly, he just wasn't a priority in my life. I knew this at the time but it just seemed helpless to change my character.

The three-year posting to Gibraltar was coming to an end; I was relieved because my relationship with Amanda was under strain. She was getting attention from various men in the media world and I was getting interest from women. But I had other things to worry about. I was becoming anxious about my next posting, as I had applied for a position as a 'woolly hatter' in Wales. A phone call came from Manning and Records (the army's human resources) and a friend assured me I would get one of my 'wish-list' postings to the mountain adventure training centres of Wales, Scotland or Canada.

A week later, I received my posting. I was shocked that they wanted to send me to the Guards Depot in Pirbright, Surrey, with promotion to staff sergeant. Even the promotion didn't encourage me. To be gym-bound as a 'tick tock soldier' (slang used for the Guards Regiment) would suffocate me. I knew I couldn't be in the role for two years – not when I was well qualified as an adventure trainer. Something in me just snapped. I was fed up with moving and it was Amanda who persuaded me that I didn't need to rely on the army anymore. She believed I could make it in the civilian world and that I shouldn't be so fearful. Our friends and her family were just as supportive, so I started to think seriously about leaving. It was 1992 and I was thirty-seven years old. It was to be one of the hardest decisions I have had to make. The army had saved my life – rescued me and made me into the man I was. It had also been my home for sixteen and a half years, having fed me, clothed me and housed me. The army had trained me to be ready for anything – except normality.

During the next few months I was back and forth to the chief clerk's office. I resigned one day and the next day I withdrew the request. This happened several times and was annoying for the clerks. In the end I made my decision and started the process. I was discharged in Gibraltar – proud to be the last PTI on the Rock, as the British Army was in the process of handing back its safety to the Gibraltar Army (known as handing over the Queen's keys). I was to serve another three months before the regiment moved back to Dover for its next tour of duty.

Once I was back in Dover one of the hardest aspects of leaving the army was handing in my ID card. It had been with me for the 16 years and 161 days of my career. Handing this in to the chief clerk and going from Sergeant to Mr was a real wake-up call. Packing up my car and saying goodbye to the lads in the mess, I then drove through the main gates of Connaught Barracks for the final time. *What on earth have you done, Cowley? And what's next?* I thought.

The army offered me a resettlement programme, so I decided to take a six-week course in business management in London. I stayed with Amanda, a hairdresser, two specialist decorators and a student in a flat in Great Titchfield Street, a few hundred yards from Oxford Street. Her room was tiny, with a futon mattress on the floor, a suspended hanging rail high above the door for clothes, and two shelves. Being in such a confined space soon began to annoy me.

By the end of the course I was bored, anxious and beginning to feel quite low about my new life. Meanwhile, Amanda enjoyed her work at Mentorn Films, often working late on productions or on her landscape painting, which she was now exhibiting in London galleries.

One day when I was sitting in her office, in walked David Buxton, a printer of entertainment merchandise including T-shirts, pens, cups and jackets. David and I liked each other immediately. He was ten years younger and we had a similar sense of humour. He also seemed to care that I didn't have work and so took me on to work with him in the printing business. After a few months we decided to go into business together, calling our new company Ezee Promotions. For the next twelve months, I learnt a lot about screen-printing, and we were good at making money.

Amanda and I spent our weekends in our home in Nuneaton. Life was looking up on one level, but I struggled with the stress of being self-employed as I always felt the need to get the next job. One Saturday morning, a postcard arrived. It was the catalyst that changed my life.

The card featured a biblical scene. A shepherd on the side of a mountain holding a staff, with his foot on a rock surrounded by sheep. The sun was shining, and a few butterflies hovered over his head. It was a print of a painting from the early 1900s. A circle had been drawn around two of the sheep, with large writing above each one saying 'you' and 'me'. On the back I read, *Paul, I've become a Christian. You need to marry the woman you are living with. Jesus loves you. I am praying for you. Come and see me when I get back to Aldershot. Love Eric.*

My response was to laugh out loud and show Amanda the card. She was not impressed either. *Oh dear,* I thought, *this time he really has lost the plot and how on earth did he get my address? Not only is he a lunatic in uniform, he's now in with the God Squad.* The postmark was from Kathmandu in Nepal. *That's it,* I thought. *He must have joined a cult.* Learning that my mother had become a Christian was one thing, but now this lunatic soldier had succumbed as well. What was going on? It took me quite a few months before I decided to visit him at the PT school barracks in Aldershot, as I was slightly nervous of his erratic behaviour. Nevertheless, I wasn't under his authority anymore, so I decided to go and meet him.

Driving to Aldershot, I parked up and Eric signed me into the Sergeants' Mess for three days. In the mess bar, he told me of the events which had led to his conversion. Apparently, he had been ill for quite a long time. It made sense to me because his behaviour had been so strange at the PT school. It was when his hair fell out in clumps that he began to get seriously worried.

In 1990 he went from Aldershot to Belize in Central America and then to Hong Kong where his health really deteriorated.

A doctor said, 'You are a very ill man. I need to do some tests.'

On his return, she told him that he had been very close to going into a coma with thyroxic shock, as his thyroid was completely diminished.

It seemed an anathema to the doctor that a fit young man could get what was traditionally an older woman's disease, but Eric had his own ideas. He had been stationed in Paderborn in Germany but was on exercise at the East/West German border; as the crow flies he was only 500 miles from the Chernobyl disaster in 1986 in which 100,000 people died. At one point he was bedridden for days with a headache to end all headaches, which he believed was a result of his proximity to the radioactive particles. The biggest long-term health consequence of the disaster was a huge number of thyroid cancers. Eric put in a claim to the army after his twenty-two years of service, but it was rejected on the grounds that it could not be proven.

He was put on thyroxin immediately and stabilised within a few days. Meanwhile, having been given a Christian tract at the airport in Belize he got down on his knees in his barracks room in Sekong on the mainland of Hong Kong. On 14 November 1990, he attended a Billy Graham crusade in a big stadium and gave his life to Jesus.

Eric's story was out of my comfort zone but I was definitely moved by his transformation. His manner was softer, and he had stopped smoking and swearing. He listened to me as I told him about my mother dying in my arms and he reassured me that she was in heaven.

On my last night with Eric he handed me a Christian Bible verse and we said goodnight.

*

Having read the scripture about the gnashing of teeth and having had a restless night I was determined to have it out with Eric the next morning. During breakfast, he asked me how I had slept. I told him, in no uncertain terms, that because of the scripture he had given me I had been terrified.

Without looking up from his breakfast, he said, 'What did you do?'

'I got down on my knees and prayed, "God, please take away the gnashing of teeth"'.

He looked at me and with a big grin on his face said, 'Welcome into the kingdom, Paul.'

I'm sure there are gentler ways to be introduced to God but I needed a sergeant major from the British Forces to speak into my life. For me, kind words about love and peace and forgiveness would have gone over my head. I needed to understand Proverbs 9:10: 'The fear of the LORD is the beginning of wisdom.' I now believe Eric Martin was the man God sent to convict me of my selfishness.

That same morning, Major Jim Noble came into Eric's office and threw a telegram on his desk. It was from the SAS headquarters at Hereford announcing a vacancy for a manager of the SAS squash club in London. Eric and I thought the telegram didn't make any sense – there was no SAS squash club in London. After some research Eric discovered the root of our confusion; rather like Chinese whispers during the First World War, by the time a message travels from person to person, it comes back as something entirely different. 'Send reinforcements; we're going to advance' quickly becomes, 'Send three and four pence; we're going to a dance.'

The job was for the manager of the Bath & Racquets Club (a private gym with two squash courts) in Mayfair, London. As Eric still had four years of service before he was to retire, he handed it to me.

'I may be qualified but I'm not a very good squash player!' I said.

Eric laughed but was encouraging. 'You don't need to play it, mate; you just have to manage the place.'

Neither of us realised at the time that it was Mark Birley's prestigious health club in Brook's Mews, set behind Claridge's.

Mark Birley was a multi-millionaire who owned a string of clubs, including Harry's Bar, Mark's Club and most famously Annabel's, at Berkeley Square in Mayfair. Gavin Rankin, the operations manager, showed me around the club. It was an extraordinary place, with highly polished brass railings, wooden floors and Persian rugs. In the basement there were two squash rooms and I was introduced to Hiddy Jahan, the squash coach (ranked among the top six players in the world from 1970 through to 1986). There was also a small barber's shop, Persian rugs on the floor of the gym and a black marble steam room.

I was offered the job and was delighted to accept. Life was looking up.

But the most astounding thing for me had been seeing the change in Eric. From the man that I had met several years before to the man I now knew, the change was staggering. I had to convince Amanda to meet him again and when she did she agreed he had certainly become a nicer person. He was more caring and he spoke about his faith with such passion that it was attractive.

Amanda and I were now living in West Hampstead in a one-bedroom flat. We spent our weekends with friends, in wine bars and coffee shops, buying clothes and walking on Hampstead Heath. My job at the Bath & Racquets was intense but exciting, as I was training regular members but also people like George Michael, George Hamilton and Tim Jefferies, Ali Al-Fayed, Lord Rothschild, and several film and TV celebrities. There were numerous lords and some of the Saudi royal family. Visitors to Claridge's could also use the club, so I trained Jeb Bush (the brother of George Bush who was the President of the United States at the time), Clint Eastwood, Ralph Lauren and many more. Then there were the MPs, ministers, members of the royal household and dignitaries from around the world – the list was endless. I was thrilled when I got a call saying that Steve Martin was coming in for a visit and could I look after him. I'd seen most, if not all, of his films, so I thought it would be fun to get two of the male trainers to act out the scene in *Three Amigos.* When he arrived, we stood in reception and performed the scene in front of him. He just stopped and looked at us with a completely blank face, then walked past in disgust. It was such a faux pas. We thought it was funny, but he really didn't.

At that time, I was at my physical peak, bench pressing up to 110 kilos. I was happy in my job, making friends with some extraordinary people who took Amanda and me to some wonderful places. One weekend Taqui Aziz (a member of the Aga Khan family) invited us to Monte Carlo to see Shirley Bassey in concert. We lounged on the exclusive beach resort in the day and saw Bassey in the evening. We wanted for nothing. But strangely, there was still something missing in my life, a hole I couldn't fill. I had said a prayer to God and had felt some sense of peace, but I was still restless. At that stage I wouldn't have called myself a Christian. But Eric was on my case. 'We need to find you a church, Paul; somewhere you can learn and grow.'

That night I turned to Amanda and said, 'I want to go to church.'

'Oh, well I think you will be extremely bored! The church is all about the rules you have to follow', she said, which I found annoying because I couldn't imagine my mum or Eric being duped by just a set of rules.

The military is very good at the mental and physical aspects of discipline and training, but where it falls down is in the spiritual discipline of a soldier's growth. I have learnt (late in life, I'm afraid) that we are holistic beings (body, mind and spirit) and all three of those aspects need to be taught and learnt. I had had lots of practice with the first two, but concerning the spiritual area of my life, I had no idea. I grew up in a non-believing home, and to my recollection, the schools I attended never gave me any spiritual input. When I went to prison I never met a chaplain, and after seventeen years in the military I don't recall one conversation with a single padre. So I had no guidance in any spiritual or moral behaviour whatsoever, and I now believe that this left a massive vacuum in my character. I have also learnt that if you have a vacuum in your life, it will be filled with something. Mine was filled with looking after my own interests, regardless of others. I wanted to come out on top – be the best I could be – not get left behind in the race of life. But little did I know that God had another plan for me, and it would be unravelled over the next few years.

14: Come with me

'Listen! My beloved! Look! Here he comes, leaping across the mountains, bounding over the hills. My beloved is like a gazelle or a young stag. Look! There he stands behind our wall, gazing through the windows, peering through the lattice. My beloved spoke and said to me, "Arise, my darling, my beautiful one, come with me. See! The winter is past; the rains are over and gone. Flowers appear on the earth; the season of singing has come, the cooing of doves is heard in our land. The fig-tree forms its early fruit; the blossoming vines spread their fragrance. Arise, come, my darling; my beautiful one, come with me."'

Song of Songs 2:8–13

*

The following Sunday morning I got dressed and went to a church near our flat in West Hampstead. Amanda said she needed to do a shop at Tesco, so we parted and agreed to meet up afterwards. Her lack of interest upset me, but I was determined to find out for myself what this religious stuff was really all about.

The church door was open; the place was dimly lit and smelt musty, and the first hymn was coming to an end. As I walked in, there must have been ten elderly women near the front and an elderly man further back who had an ageing terrier curled up on his lap. I felt as if I had walked through a saloon bar in the Midwest. The faces turned and looked back to see the cowboy, the renegade, who had disturbed the peace. As I perched myself on a pew at the back, the elderly man gave me a smile. I felt out of place. Give me a fifty-pound rucksack and twenty men and I would have no problems taking charge but in this situation I was out of my depth, not knowing what to expect.

When I got home, Amanda made a pot of coffee and refrained from asking me how it had gone. I obviously looked disappointed and she could tell that nothing significant had happened. Eventually I spoke, 'Well, I can see why you said it was boring. How do they afford to run these churches? No wonder they make them into flats!'

'Was it that bad?' she said smugly, serving up some scrambled eggs on toast and pouring another coffee, desperate to add, 'I told you so.'

'Well, there has to be something better. I can't see my mum being involved in a place like that, and Eric was telling me about how exciting it was to be in a Spirit-filled church – whatever that is!'

I called Eric for help and over the next few Sundays, he came and stayed with us on a Saturday night and went with me to various churches; Baptist, Methodist, Catholic, Church of England – it didn't matter to me what denomination they were. What mattered was that I needed to feel something other than boredom.

After a few Sundays I sensed I was on the wrong path. I phoned Amanda's brother James (who had been a Baptist minister for a few years), he advised me to try a Pentecostal church in Notting Hill called Kensington Temple, or Holy Trinity Brompton, an evangelical church in Knightsbridge.

Eric suggested we try the Pentecostal church. When we arrived it was packed, and gospel music was pouring out onto the street. I smiled inside. Here it was then, a full church, lively and vibrant. I weighed up the congregation. They looked happy, business-like and successful. The music was verging on Motown, which I loved, although I resisted swaying and clapping as most were doing. Since we had arrived a few minutes late, Eric and I had been unable to get into the main church so were taken on a small bus to the overspill at Porchester Hall, where the service was relayed on a screen.

The preacher was inspiring and when he invited people to come forward I went to the front with Eric. Inviting the Holy Spirit, he asked us to hold our hands out as if we were waiting for a gift. Suddenly, my hands began to shake up and down. Then my legs went wobbly and I was very unnerved by the experience. Eric reassured me that in the New Testament shaking was perfectly normal, as described at Pentecost when the Holy Spirit fell on people and onlookers thought they must have been drunk.

When I got home in the afternoon I appeared at the door of the front room and gave Amanda a broad smile. I went and hugged her and immediately she looked suspicious and said, 'What on earth's happened to you?'

'Amanda, you have to come next week. It was fantastic! A totally different experience!'

She wanted to be happy for me, but she was annoyed. Her worry was that if I 'got God' it would impinge on our lifestyle. We both had money, a nice flat and we ate out most nights. She didn't want anything to rock the boat.

'Yeah, yeah, sure', she said, pulling away from me and busying herself. She left the room and went and sat on the toilet, her chapel, her confessional. Later she told me that she had cried as she realised she might lose me to God. 'I can compete with a woman', she said. 'A woman, maybe, but not God.'

The following week Amanda came to the church with me and was amazed at how busy it was. People were streaming out from one service and queuing up to get in to the next one. At the end of the service we went forward for prayer and immediately I was taken aside by two men, and several women surrounded Amanda. As Amanda told them that she was living with her boyfriend, they responded with, 'You need to move out of the flat and get married or split up.'

I had the same experience. 'God would want you to make the relationship right', said the two men.

When we got out of the church, I was furious. Amanda was even more furious. What did they mean, *we had to make our relation-*

ship right for God's sake? This was the most 'right' relationship I had ever had. For Amanda it was exactly why she didn't want to be part of a church; it was all about the rules. We left and went to a local pub, both annoyed at what we thought was a judgmental attitude. We sat for hours and discussed the Church, God and faith. It was a rich conversation but at the heart of it was anger. After an hour I turned to Amanda and said, 'Why are we so afraid of getting married? I'm not saying we should, but we've been together for eight years now. What would be so bad about it?'

Amanda looked bewildered. I was meant to be on her side. 'Well, you tell me! You are the one who has been married twice before. We've been over this a million times.'

'I was just asking', I said.

From then on, the relationship became strained. I was convicted that we had to marry and that we should no longer sleep together until then. I didn't really have the words to explain my reasoning. I just knew in my heart that it was what I had to do, even if it meant losing her.

One Saturday morning I walked with her to a coffee shop in West Hampstead. Ordering our coffee, I opened a small package and placed two plain silver rings in front of her.

'What are they for?' she said.

'God has told me we should get married.'

She didn't look impressed. 'Really? Is that right? Well, he didn't tell me.'

What I hadn't anticipated was that Amanda expected a bit more romance than I offered. I was too perfunctory, as if it was a duty rather than a desire. We argued and then she walked out on me, saying she had had enough. That night I went home depressed and sat with a bottle of red wine. Eric had told me that God had a plan for my life. At this point it wasn't looking good.

Amanda went to stay with Kristina and unknown to me was in turmoil. I thought about what she had said to me and rang her the next day and insisted we meet.

We sat for four hours in the Museum of Mankind near Cork

Street in central London unpacking our eight years together. I poured out my heart to her and the hope that I now had to become a better man. At the end of the conversation we had agreed to get married within a few months and Amanda was prepared to come back home with me.

Two weeks after we had been to the Pentecostal church, James suggested we try Holy Trinity Brompton (HTB) in Knightsbridge, led by the Reverend Sandy Millar. In April 1993 Amanda and I walked in on a Sunday morning and found it packed with people singing and raising their hands. At the end of the service, the preacher, the Reverend Tom Gillum, said, 'If anyone would like prayer, please come to the front of the church and one of the team will pray with you.'

Before I could think, I heard myself say, 'I'm going to the front. Will you come with me?' She agreed. Lots of people were there; some were laughing, some were crying, and then I saw a few people fall over. It was then that I decided to leave. Just at that moment the Reverend Gillum stood in front of me and said, 'Would you like me to pray for you?'

'If you like. Go for it', I said.

He asked us to close our eyes and bow our heads, and then politely asked if he could put a hand on my shoulder, to which I agreed. As he prayed, I looked at him, and he appeared genuine. 'Lord, please place this couple in a church where they can grow and know your love. If it's not this church then find them another one. Amen.' He smiled and walked away to pray for someone else. I liked his manner, as I didn't feel he was judging us in any way. There was no pressure and we both appreciated it.

Having left her faith when she went to Roehampton to do her degree, Amanda had looked into Buddhism and other faiths concluding that she was a pantheist (believing that everything is God and no one religion is right). Her return to Christianity was sealed on the following Sunday morning when we went back to HTB. Sandy Millar was speaking and then he invited the Holy Spirit to fall on those people who had a compassion for the broken and lost. Immediately, Amanda felt a weight, a heaviness in her heart, and she started to cry. Eric, who was grinning, said, 'You felt the Holy Spirit, didn't you?'

'Yes, Eric. I did', she replied.

'What was it like?' I asked.

'Like coming home', she said, visibly moved by the experience.

On leaving the church, someone handed me a leaflet for the Alpha course. I looked it over and thought, *Well, I've done so many courses in the army I may as well do a course on God.*

For many years Holy Trinity Brompton was identified as the church set behind the magnificent Catholic Oratory on the Brompton Road. However, with each passing year the Alpha course grew in recognition and the queues that formed outside the church every Wednesday night were unprecedented. The press and media were fascinated that in London, at least, church attendance was on the rise. A few celebrities had been through the course and it was raising eyebrows in the British press.

The Alpha course is an introduction to the Christian faith. It was first created by the Reverend Charles Marnham. The Reverend John Irvine then took over running the course in 1981 and developed the ten-week format which continues to this day. In 1985 the Reverend Nicky Lee took the course on, and in 1990 the Reverend Nicky Gumbel, also then the curate at Holy Trinity, took over running the course at the invitation of Sandy Millar (vicar at that time) and oversaw its revision and expansion.

In 1993 the first Alpha conference for church leaders was held at Holy Trinity Brompton, attended by 1,000 leaders. The course then began to spread all over the UK, in churches of every denomination. Since 1993 more than 29 million people have tried the course in 169 countries. Alpha now runs in every part of the global Church, including the Catholic, Orthodox and all mainstream Protestant denominations.

Amanda and I started on the summer course back in May 1993. Arriving on the Wednesday night, we were shocked to see a packed church. There were about 700 people milling around and lining up for food. The meal was good, and then we sat and listened to the Reverend Nicky Gumbel speaking on 'Who is Jesus?' After the talk we went into a small group led by a lovely man called Geoff Wilmot. The room was tiny and there were about ten of us. I remember being quite argumentative, as I had so many unanswered questions. Geoff was calm and patient and constantly asked others in the group what they thought. He was a good leader: humble and understated. Amanda took to it like a duck to water. I had no idea she knew so much, but of course for her it was all very familiar as she had grown up going to church with her mother and brother.

A few weeks into the course, and at the end of one of the discussions, Geoff said to me, 'Paul, you have so many questions, I can't possibly answer them all. At some point you have to take a leap of faith.' I liked the challenge, and I trusted Geoff. That night I said the prayer of commitment with him: 'Dear Lord Jesus, I'm sorry for the things I have done in my past that have hurt and offended you. Thank you, Jesus, for dying on the cross for me, and please come into my life now, by your Holy Spirit, and help me follow you.'

Christians started to appear everywhere, especially in the media world. Amanda discovered several Christians at Mentorn Films, including Lisa Cole, also a runner (now Lisa Ashton MBE, the founder and CEO of The Winnie Mabaso Foundation). Lisa was a dynamic believer and was thrilled to hear about our journey.

Halfway through the course Amanda and I went on the weekend away at a country house with acres of grounds. The Reverend Nicky Gumbel did the talk on 'Who is the Holy Spirit?' and the shaking at Porchester Hall, several weeks before, made a lot more sense to me. He talked about the gift of speaking in tongues (a spiritual gift, like a foreign language, as described in 1 Corinthians 14) and explained the Scriptures. I was worried that I wouldn't be given any gifts because I had been so bad in my life. I didn't think that God could love someone like me. Surely, he would only want good people who had led clean lives and I certainly wasn't one of them. At the end of Nicky's talk he invited the Holy Spirit and I experienced a powerful presence of God. That evening I went for a long run, trying to process what it all meant. Sitting in the bath afterwards, I felt overwhelmed as I realised that God had chosen to touch me and I started thanking him out loud, which led to me speaking in tongues.

It is hard to describe, hard to put into words, but a peace descended on me and strangely everything felt right. Deep down I knew God loved me unconditionally and I felt genuinely forgiven. The chaos of my life that I'd carried for years started to dissipate and that sense of lacking, that empty feeling, also disappeared. In the session later that evening, I wept during the music, the singing, and during more prayers. My anxiety melted away and my need to be in control diminished. All my life I'd felt as if I was in fight mode – like being in a boxing ring, always wearing gloves – either with other people or myself. At last, for the first time, I could put the boxing gloves down. From that moment on my life began to change radically. If this is what it meant to be a Christian, then I was up for it.

*

On 18 September 1993, due to me having been divorced, we had a civil wedding in the registry office in Nuneaton. The civil ceremony was fun but perfunctory. The church blessing later that day was far more important to us both. Inside a small village church in the Midlands, Amanda held five long-stemmed sunflowers and gypsum in her left hand, while holding firmly on to my arm with her other hand. We walked down the aisle together to the sound of Vivaldi's Concerto in B flat major for violin and cello from a recording in 1977, played by Amanda's father John on the violin and her uncle Peter on the cello. Amanda's friend Kristina, whom I had met in Cyprus, operated the cassette player.

Tricia and Andrew sat in the front row, while Amanda's brother James, family members and close friends were crammed into the pews. I had phoned Clinton to see if he would like come but he had left an answer machine message saying he was busy with friends. His voice message was a little shaky. I sensed something was going on, but I didn't ring back.

Our new friend, Lisa, read from *The Little Prince*, and James read from the Song of Songs, 'Arise, my darling, my beautiful one, come with me'.

After the ceremony the rush of friends and family took my breath away. The bells rang out and we both smiled for hours afterwards. Tricia and Andrew put on a wonderful cream tea at their home and the day ended when Amanda and I went to stay in a lovely Georgian hotel. We were both so happy with our wedding and that night we kept referring to each other as husband and wife as we laughed our way to bed.

The next day, on a cold September morning, a few of our friends who had stayed locally gathered by the river bank. James, Amanda and I stood in a few feet of water and James announced, 'We are gathered together today at the request of Paul and Amanda so that they can publicly confess their faith.' He then read the passage in Matthew 3:16–17: 'As soon as Jesus was baptised, he went up out of the water. At that moment heaven was opened, and he saw the Spirit of God descending like a dove and alighting on him. And a voice from heaven said, "This is my Son, whom I love; with him I am well pleased."'

Being immersed under freezing cold water and rising up with conviction, I felt liberated and refreshed. Amanda grabbed me as she came out of the water and cried into a towel. Some of our friends thought it a weird thing to do but they were strangely moved by it too. But for me, it had taken many years to get to where I was, and I now wanted God to lead me.

The fears that I had had of becoming a Christian were unfounded. It was the most natural thing for me to accept that I needed a saviour. Jesus said that he came for the sinners. I could hold my hands up and say, 'I'm here, that's me, one of the worst!' I just wish it hadn't taken me nearly forty years to get to this point as I felt I had wasted many years walking in the wilderness, causing so much hurt to so many people along the way. I also realised life was short, and there was so much I wanted to do for God. I started running at a fast speed and became hungry for the knowledge of God. I read the Bible and numerous books on the Christian faith.

Through HTB, Amanda and I joined a home group led by Russell and Geraldine Garner. They provided a safe place to explore our faith as a couple. We continued to do the Alpha course and then became group leaders. We were both insatiable for more of God. Our relationship went from strength to strength and it was an amazingly blessed time.

There was, however, someone missing from my life.

But that was about to change when Amanda received a call from my first wife telling her that Clinton, who was nearly seventeen, was out of control and needed my help.

15: Freedom for the captives

'Clinton?' I said.

'Dad?' he replied.

There followed an awkward hug and I suggested we go and get something to eat. As we spent several hours together, Clinton poured out his life. How he had got in with a bad crowd and had missed his GCSEs, eventually being expelled from school that summer. His mum couldn't cope with him and his relationship with his stepfather was also strained. I listened in amazement, shocked by what he had gone through, not having seen him since he was thirteen. Eventually after several hours of talking and tears on both sides I asked him to come back to the flat and stay for a few days. Amanda welcomed him immediately, just as she had done when he was a young boy. She made a bed up for him in our spare room and gave him space and love in equal measures.

*

It was 1995 and life was good, full and prosperous. Amanda and I bought our first flat together in Maida Vale. It had two bedrooms and a small balcony where, once a year, we could sit and watch some of the lorries being prepared for the Notting Hill Carnival. I was enjoying my work at the Bath & Racquets and Amanda had taken over as head of the art department at Mentorn Films. We worked long hours, ate out at restaurants most nights and drove around in a Cherokee Jeep that guzzled petrol at a ridiculous rate.

My son, however, was missing from my life and I sensed I

would have to deal with it soon. Amanda and I invited him to our wedding and to London on several occasions but he had told me that he wanted to spend time with his friends.

Our church home group was a close-knit group of around twenty people who prayed about illness, family problems, work issues and so on, and my relationship with Clinton was often on the agenda.

It was in July when suddenly, out of the blue, my ex-wife Katie rang Amanda at her office. She sounded distressed, saying, 'I'm so glad I've got hold of you as I can't get hold of Paul.'

Amanda replied, 'Is everything all right?'

'Not really; it's about Clinton. I need him to speak to Paul. Can I have his number?'

Katie called me and said she wanted my help. Clinton would call in a few minutes.

Within seconds I received a call from my son. His voice was rich and low. 'Hi Dad. Can we meet?'

'Yes of course we can. When?' I said.

'My train gets in at Kings Cross tonight at eight.'

'Tonight? Okay. Bring some stuff for a few days', I said.

Fortunately for me, we had home group that night, so I rang and left a message for the group leader asking everyone to pray for a good meeting.

On the way to the station I felt quite sick wondering what I would say to my son. I prayed in tongues, but I have no idea to this day what I prayed. I can only say that when I arrived, I felt better and more at peace with the situation and with myself. As the train pulled in, I nervously stood on the platform looking out for the kid I had seen four years previously.

As I was daydreaming, a man appeared in front of me, nearly the same height as me. His hair was almost black, and he was wearing sunglasses.

*

From that night on, Clinton lived with us for the next two and a half years, and it was a powerful time for all three of us. I had to learn how to be a dad: trying to impart a little bit of wisdom, needing a lot of patience and a bit of discipline thrown into the mix.

Looking back, Clinton was a normal teenager with a few insecurities. But in many ways, he was emotionally mature. I wanted to reassure him, over and over, that the breakdown of my marriage to his mum was never his fault. Sometimes I would get upset, saying that I had made such a mess of fathering him, and he would calmly tell me he had forgiven me.

At the Bath & Racquets I was personal trainer to Ali Al-Fayed (who owned Harrods from 1985 to 2010 with his brother Mohamed). He knew some of my story and took an interest in my life. When I told him that Clinton had turned up, he immediately invited us to his Park Lane penthouse flat. Sitting in his private study, overlooking Hyde Park, he offered us tea and cake. After talking to Clinton for a while he offered him a job by way of going to HR under his recommendation.

It was Clinton's first break and he secured a job in the fish department on the ground floor of Harrods. He started to develop a strong work ethic and for the next year he cleaned and gutted fish and learnt how to interact with customers. The downside was that he came home in the evenings smelling of fish, as the men in the department played practical jokes on one another by dropping fish down each other's wellies or placing fish skins in the brim of each other's hats. There was some good camaraderie, and for Clinton it was a place for him to grow up, feel safe and also take on some responsibility.

Every Sunday, Amanda and I went to church while Clinton stayed at the flat. After a few weeks we said we were going away for an Alpha weekend and Amanda asked her brother James to stay and look out for him. On the Sunday morning James asked Clinton to go with him to HTB and Clinton agreed. During the next week Clinton told Amanda and me that he was interested in becoming a Christian. So one evening in our flat, after a short talk from me about the Christian faith, I led my son in a prayer and he gave his life to Christ. It was deeply moving for all three of us. A week or so later he enrolled on the Alpha course, as he wanted to embark on his own journey of faith.

Living with us enabled him to break from the bad crowd he had been involved with at home, and thus he was able to create a new identity and a new life for himself. His mother and step-father were relieved that he had been given a second chance and relations between us all started to improve.

I had now worked for Mark Birley for just over four years and I'd had a wonderful time training some of the rich and famous. It was an extraordinary place but even with all those famous people passing through the door of the club, there was one special guest whom I will never forget meeting. During the day I had a phone call from Mark saying, 'Paul, tell the members that tomorrow the club will be closed as I'm entertaining a guest.'

I replied, 'That may be difficult, sir. They have paid quite a lot of money to be a member and the morning is our most popular time.' I was imagining the angry comments I was bound to receive from members, adding, 'May I ask you who is coming, Mr Birley?'

'It's Princess Diana. I would like her to have the run of the club and also have some privacy.'

'Until what time, sir?'

'All morning! You can open the club up to members again at 1.00 p.m. And if there are any complaints just tell them that it's one of the Royal Family. And there are plenty of other clubs in London if they are not happy!'

The receptionist managed to ring a few key members, but the next morning many of the uninformed turned up as usual and I had to explain to them what was happening. Several people were indignant, so I advised them to speak to Mr Birley directly if they had a problem with it.

Princess Diana arrived with two policemen, two bodyguards, and two ladies in waiting. The policemen went downstairs to check the club. Diana was elegant, and I was certainly a bit in awe of her. She smiled and was polite and gracious. I walked with her to the lounge and Mark Birley greeted her. I left the room and she stayed for an hour and a half. At the end of the visit she thanked me and was quickly escorted away.

It was in my fourth year at the Bath & Racquets when I sensed a bit of tension between me and Mark Birley. Mark had had the luxury of starting the club because he couldn't find a club to his liking. However, the exclusive price tag meant its members demanded standards that were not always in keeping with what he envisaged. I was caught between the two; I realised he was not happy with so much change, even though membership was increasing and the club was now making a profit.

Fortunately for me, one afternoon while I was doing some paperwork in my office I received a phone call from the secretary of a large headhunting firm in the City, saying that Lord Thurso would like to see me to discuss an opportunity that had arisen. Would it be possible to meet me for lunch within the next few days? I agreed.

Lord Thurso had been tasked to redevelop Champneys Health Club in Piccadilly and a health spa in Tring, north London. Under Lord Thurso's eye they wanted it to become one of the most prestigious health clubs in London and my name had been suggested to manage the club. It couldn't have come at a better time as my working relationship with Mark Birley had run its course. They offered me the opportunity to be involved in a multi-million-pound refurbishment, more money and complete control of the club's staffing.

I was offered the role and then met with Mark Birley to discuss the way forward and my replacement. However, he wasn't interested in my opinions and I was given my marching orders. It was a shame, as I was fond of Mark and he had been kind to me during my stay and I had wanted to leave well. It had

Paul with his mum and dad in a pub, Douglas, Isle of Man (1961)

Paul awarded Best Recruit at the Royal Artillery Depot, Woolwich (1976)

Paul in his 'Brick' on Christmas Day in Belfast, Northern Ireland (1976)

Paul teaching Amanda to abseil in Troodos, Cyprus (1985)

Paul in one of the many competitions with the Junior Leaders Royal Artillary Langlauf Team (1986)

Amanda in Fulpmes, Austria (1987

Paul with Clinton (1987)

Paul abseiling off the Rock of Gibraltar with a mountain bike (1990)

Paul in his office in Gibraltar (1990)

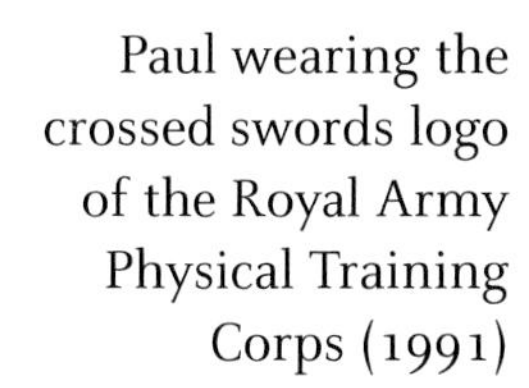

Paul wearing the crossed swords logo of the Royal Army Physical Training Corps (1991)

Expedition team from 3rd Battalion, Royal Green Jackets, at the base of Mount Kenya with leaders Paul (centre) and Scooby (right of Paul) in 1990

Out of the army: Paul and Amanda in 1992

A September wedding with Amanda's mum, Tricia, and her stepfather, Andrew (1993)

James baptising Paul and Amanda the day after their wedding (1993)

Clinton with Paul and Amanda attending an Alpha course at HTB (1995)

One of the first three-day mission trips to HMP Dartmoor (1996)

Paul with Phoebe on the steps of St Paul's Cathedral following his ordination service (2002)

Paul's priesting at St Mary Abbotts, Kensington with Arthur, Amanda and Phoebe (2003)

Finny with his wife Helen

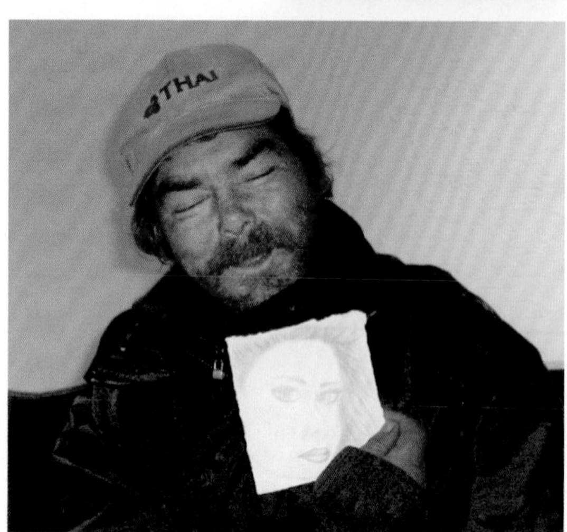

Eddie at Holy Trinity Brompton's Day Shelter (2010)

Phoebe with Eddie at her first photographic exhibition in 2017

Paul with Jack Cowley and Bear Grylls in Tomoka Correctional Institution, Florida (2009)

Paul and Sandy Millar at Emmy's ordination in Uganda (2011)

Paul handing over the knickers to Liness the Chaplain of the women's section of Lusaka Central Prison, Zambia (2012)

Paul with Clinton receiving his MBE at Buckingham Palace (2015)

Paul in robes with Nicky Gumbel (left) and Michael Emmett (middle) at a carol service at HTB Queen's Gate (St Augustine's) in 2017

Paul with Eric Martin and Desmond Tutu in Cape Town, having attended an Alpha Forces Conference (2017)

been a special time for me in so many ways and I had made lots of friends, some of whom I still know to this day.

The entrance to Champneys was at the side of Le Méridien Hotel in Piccadilly. The stairs led down to a grand reception area and a corridor, which opened up to a series of rooms, workout studios and a glamorous, dimly lit Romanesque swimming pool. My first job was to interview and revalue over 70 per cent of the staff. This didn't go down well, and I was soon nicknamed Lord Thurso's hatchet man. But Thurso was a clever man and he wanted a fresh start, so clearing out the old staff with its bias and culture meant the club had a new fresh feel to it. Within a few months, membership was up and refurbishments had started.

My daily routine was to take a stroll around the club and check everyone was where they were supposed to be. I was no longer in gym clothing, just a smart suit every day and a short, neat ponytail. The day was long and demanding, starting at 6.00 a.m. Amanda and I would meet up for supper in Soho and then I would return to the club a couple of hours later and stay to oversee security and lock up at 11.00 p.m.

One morning in 1996, the telephone rang, and my PA looked at me disconcertedly. 'It's that woman from the church again.'

Emmy Wilson had asked my PA if I was available to go with her on a two-day mission trip to HMP Dartmoor. I thought I could just fob her off, but Emmy Wilson was on her own mission and little did I know my part in it.

A tall, attractive woman in her mid-forties, Emmy could easily be spotted at the front of the church in her bold, bright clothes. As a young girl she had longed to be a ballet dancer until she realised she would never make it as a professional. Drawn to nursing, she worked her way up to being the sister of the gastro-enterology department at Chelsea and Westminster Hospital on the Fulham Road, and her patients included many people with HIV/AIDS. In 1985 the same year I met Amanda in Cyprus, Emmy, after fourteen years, gave up nursing when the Reverend John Collins, the vicar of HTB, invited her on staff to start a street ministry in Earl's Court. At the time, HTB had Sunday services and Alpha was in its very early stages, but there was no outreach to the community. On the very same day, John Collins swapped roles with his curate, Sandy Millar, who then became the vicar of the church. An extraordinarily humble act by John Collins. Emmy's first job on the day she started was to organise a welcome tea party for Sandy, the new vicar!

In the same year, Emmy established The Earl's Court Project by forming a partnership with Youth With A Mission, led by Richard Lahey-James. The Earl's Court Project started in the basement of St Jude's, Courtfield Gardens, in the Earl's Court area. It was created to meet the needs of those caught in addiction, including prostitution, drug addiction, alcoholism, HIV and AIDS.

Meanwhile, Sandy had been invited on to the Board of Visitors for HMP Holloway. In 1990 he stopped Emmy outside his house and chatted about his new role and how the prison chaplain had asked Sandy if he could recommend a woman from HTB to help with all the pastoral needs.

Sandy paused and said, 'Actually, I thought of you, Em.'

Emmy's heart sank, and she replied, 'Can I go home to think and pray about it?'

Emmy went home and read in her journal a prophecy which had been given to her two months previously at HTB. John Paul Jackson and Bob Jones (from Kansas City, USA, with a prophetic gift) stated she would be a 'key unto many, unchaining and unshackling those who cannot any longer make themselves free'.

In 1991 she started working with the chaplaincy team in Holloway – at the time, the largest women's prison in the UK. Two years later, the Reverend Bill Birdwood, who was Managing Chaplain of HMP Exeter, in the summer of 1993 went to New Wine (a Christian conference) and attended a seminar on the Alpha course led by Nicky Gumbel. Bill returned to the prison hoping to see God's power at work. He set up a weekly fellowship meeting in the chapel with a group of ten hand-picked, hardened men, and told them about God.

Two of the inmates in the group shared a cell, and they were father and son, Brian and Michael. They were doing a twelve-and-a-half-year prison sentence for importing 4.5 tons of cannabis into the country, packed inside frozen cod in fishing trawlers on the north coast of Devon. They were notorious among the prisoners – respected for their impressive sentence. Brian, despite being 5 foot 5 inches, was not to be messed with; a stocky, strong man with a boxing history. Likewise, his son Michael had inherited his father's good looks and charming ways, although he stood at an impressive 6 foot 3 inches and when he walked into a room, heads turned.

Bill began praying for the group of men in his chapel, but Brian and Michael remained sceptical.

On 14 December 1994 Emmy arrived with a team of six people for a day visit, and Michael and Brian met her in the chapel.

Michael describes the visit. 'Emmy was dressed like Lady Di with sheep on her jumper and red cords and green socks and black brogues. And I was there with my old man, and about twenty-five other prisoners. She then led us in a chorus, "Jesus I love you deep down in my heart". And on the words "deep down" we all had to crouch down and tap the floor with the palm of our hands . . . And then she invited the Holy Spirit, and I won't tell you what I said, but I swore. God touched this sinner, this bad man, and I feel privileged to say this. God bent down and shook my spirit.' Michael also saw how the Spirit of God affected his father, as he ended up on the floor roaring with laughter for ages. It was so out of character and it had a profound effect on them both.

In January in 1995 Bill Birdwood ran the Alpha course and Michael and Brian took part and they received a prophetic word from a local vicar that every prison they went to, the Holy Spirit would break out. Michael and Brian were soon transferred to HMP Swaleside, and the chaplain, a man called Roger Green, visited them in their cell. Brian said, 'We are Christians. Do you run Alpha here?'

Roger replied, 'What's Alpha?'

They advised him to ring Emmy, who once again arrived with a team. Michael and Brian managed to gather together over fifty men in the chapel and when Emmy invited the Holy Spirit, tough men, hardened criminals, ended up weeping and being touched by the Spirit of God. Witnessing this, Roger Green's faith was transformed, and the father and son duo went on to several more prisons and the same thing happened each time.

Knowing nothing of all this backstory, I dismissed Emmy's calls. I told my PA, 'I definitely don't want to go into prison with her. Is she mad?'

I had been trying to stay out of prison since my episode at seventeen. I was terrified at the thought. As far as I could make out, Emmy's role at the church was to hand out tissues at the front when people came up for prayer at the end of the sermon. Little did I know she was dynamite! With such a passion for the prisons she wasn't to be easily thwarted. And the next morning I was shocked to be informed that she was in the reception of the club waiting to meet me. *Couldn't this woman understand the word no?*

Inviting her to have coffee with me in the restaurant, I wrongly assumed that I could humour her and send her on her way. However, in her posh English accent and with her deep-rooted integrity, she told me how she needed someone with a strong testimony to join her and the team of volunteers, and although she hadn't heard my story several people had told her about me. Eventually I agreed to go with her and she immediately rang Bill Birdwood, to get me on the list. As Emmy left the club, I remember thinking, *What just happened? Why have I agreed to go to a prison in the south-west with someone who reminds me of an older version of Princess Diana?*

The plan was to meet the team from HTB at 8.00 a.m. outside

HMP Dartmoor on the Friday morning. They had travelled down the night before and stayed with local people, but I had to stay and lock up the club so I decided to drive through the night. Notwithstanding a good few cups of coffee, I was struggling to stay awake. Apart from my headlights it was pitch black. At 4.00 a.m. I saw the high granite walls of the prison, lit by the security lights. At the time I did not notice the insignia '*Parcere Subjectis*', written on the stone arch that forms the entrance to the outer yard. I just pulled into the car park, reclined my seat and tried to get some sleep. My mind, however, was spiralling with thoughts about going inside. Although I'd told my story in church several times to a receptive audience, I knew a prison audience might not be so welcoming. I thought prisons were full of men who were 'bad', possibly violent, not to mention the paedophiles.

At around 7.30 a.m. a few cars started to appear, and I guessed that they were the morning shift of prison officers. They looked no different from the officers at Risley – I didn't like them then, and I wasn't too keen on the look of these guys now.

Back in the jeep, I dozed on and off until 8.00 a.m. when a loud tap on the window woke me. There was Emmy grinning. 'I'm so excited you got here, Paul. It's going to be an amazing day. Just you wait and see what Jesus is going to do!'

She was far too happy for my liking, especially considering she was full of flu! I greeted her, feeling like a small boy on his first day of school. She then told me that she wanted me to speak first to the regular offenders and then the Vulnerable Prisoner Unit (VPU), which included sex offenders, ex-policemen and politicians. I mumbled something about not wanting to speak to sex offenders and she responded with, 'Paul, everyone needs to know they are loved and can be forgiven by God. If they hear the good news in prison, they may want to say sorry for what they have done and be determined not to re-offend when they come out. Are you going to deny them that because you feel the need to judge them? Leave that to God, Paul. Just tell them your story and let God do the rest.'

That shut me up!

It was a very cold morning and I was anxious to get inside the prison for that reason only, but Emmy made us all gather round to give a quick security briefing. She let us know what we could and couldn't take in and what to do if something went wrong. She then started praying for us and I became rather self-conscious, as prison officers looked at us as if we were mad, standing in a circle with eyes closed and heads bowed, praying out loud. I kept my eyes open, trying to be cool, remaining aloof from this bunch of slightly odd people.

Emmy then enthused about the Reverend Bill Birdwood, who was to meet us at reception, saying how lovely he was and how he was full of God's Spirit. I almost expected him to turn up dressed as Superman with his cape flowing in the wind! I got a surprise when he did turn up.

The Reverend Bill Birdwood may not have looked like Superman, but I realised quickly that he had some super-human qualities. He was a family man, a few years younger than me, but most significantly I witnessed first-hand that he was a man with a passionate faith. Not only did he care for the inmates' salvation like a missionary would, he cared for their welfare like a social worker might. If an inmate's family member died, he would help them get a day pass to the funeral or he would let them use the phone in the chapel office to call a relative. He was a practical man and a gentle man, and sometimes the inmates took advantage of his kind nature. But Bill had the heart of Isaiah 61 'to proclaim freedom for the captives and release from darkness for the prisoners'.

He was aware of being manipulated by the men at times; he also knew that he was well liked by most of the inmates, as they would often rise up in his defence if he was ever bullied by someone new on the wings.

After he unlocked the large iron gate, Bill led us into the chapel. Signalling for us to take our seats in a semi-circle, his assistant John Coppin, a large man with a big grin on his face, then went to make some tea. Emmy sniffed and coughed her way through the meeting, but she was obviously in her element. She led us in prayer and asked God to use us as we spoke, and prayed for the Holy Spirit to touch each inmate with his love.

What happened next was to change the direction of my life for ever!

16: A wretch like me

A man with extreme facial psoriasis walked towards Emmy, asking her for prayer; his face was red raw, and his scalp was flaky like a snowstorm. Emmy, still feeling unwell, took one look at him and beckoned me to come and pray with him. *I never agreed to do that, Lady Di,* I thought. *Me? Pray for a sex offender?* I remember saying under my breath as I stood, 'Please, God, not him. I don't want to pray for him.'

Standing in front of me he muttered, 'I said that prayer. Does that mean I am saved? Has God forgiven me for the things I have done?' I looked at him and saw him more clearly, his eyes full and about to overflow. All my prejudices melted. 'Yes. Yes, it does. If you repent and believe in Jesus. If your prayer is sincere, then yes, you are promised a new life. Now you must walk in faith and learn God's hope for you.'

If I believed that the gospel was true for me then I had to believe it was true for him, otherwise I was spouting rubbish. Lunging forward, he hugged me with an intense body lock, resting his head up against my chest. I was taken aback but found myself putting my arms around him. Emmy looked over, amazed. Within seconds he pulled away and with a radiant face, turned to go and speak to Bill.

*

Bill unlocked the chapel doors at 9.00 a.m. and a few officers escorted the men in. There were about twenty-five inmates, dressed in blue trousers and blue striped shirts, and they were all shapes and sizes; potbellied, shaven heads, muscles ripped with hours of bench pressing displaying a plethora of tattoos, old, young, strikingly good looking and noticeably ugly. Like a group of cowboys from a bar scene in a spaghetti western. Many of them attended chapel each Sunday for the tea and biscuits at the end of the service and to swap stories, share drugs, magazines and other contraband. A few of them had a genuine faith and felt a comfort in the ritual of hymn singing and communion.

Raising his voice above the noise in the chapel, Bill introduced Emmy as the team leader.

Emmy spoke with confidence. 'We are all so pleased to be here with you today and I would love to introduce the rest of the team.'

After the introductions the guitarist from HTB started to play the familiar hymn 'Amazing Grace'. The men joined in, 'Amazing grace, how sweet the sound, that saved a wretch like me', their strong male voices filling the chapel like a group of football supporters on the terraces. The second song was a modern chorus, 'The Name of the Lord is a Strong Tower'. Emmy raised her hands above her head and made the shape of a tower, shouting to the men, 'Join in! Come on, do the actions; it's fun.' She proceeded to do a little jog backwards and forwards as if running into a strong tower for safety, while singing, 'The righteous run into it and they are saved.'

The men raised their hands and followed Emmy's gestures, like children copying a primary school teacher. The officers looked on amazed. They found it hard to get the men to do as they asked. What did this woman have that they didn't?

Bill introduced me and I walked to the front. Looking out to a sea of faces I braced myself. 'Oh God,' I said under my breath, 'help me not judge these men.' Physically, I felt sick. I had to look at my notes for my first line. 'Good morning. My name is Paul Cowley.' I continued, 'Have you ever been in a situation where you felt completely on your own, you asked for help but never got it?'

'Welcome to my life', one of the inmates heckled.

'Well, maybe it's because you're not listening for the answer,'

I batted back. 'As a young boy, my dad was my hero. In his prime he was a big man – nearly six foot three.' Men shuffled on their seats and whispered expletives.

I spoke about my trip to the park when I was eight. How I jumped from the wall and my dad had let me fall on the floor. The men were quiet. 'I remember the argument downstairs. Mum shouting at Dad – Dad saying he wanted to teach me a lesson that I should never trust anyone, because they would always move away from me.'

'That's true!' said a second heckler, a man with 'cut here' tattooed across his neck.

I continued, 'I was born in Manchester. My parents were both alcoholics, and my grandfather was a street fighter in Liverpool – quite a volatile family to grow up in, as my mum and dad often turned on neighbours or each other.'

Glancing at the men in the front row, at the man with a spider web tattoo covering his face and neck, I said, 'I was in the car with my parents when they started to argue and my dad pushed my mum out of the moving car.'

'Hope he did some time for that!' said Cut Here.

'Our parents often do stuff that is wrong.'

'You can say that again', the men chorused.

'So, like many of you guys, I left school with no qualifications – expelled at fifteen. At sixteen I got caught in the middle of my parents arguing over my mother's loss of finances and Dad's womanising. Long story short, my dad hit me and told me to leave. Homeless for a while, I moved into a squat and started to do petty crime, but I wasn't very good at it, so it led to a relationship with the police and I ended up with a short prison sentence in Risley Remand Centre.' Emmy raised her eyebrows – this was news to her.

'I was in Grisly Risley', said Spider Web Man.

'Vowed I'd never go in the nick again . . . how many times have you guys said you won't be back?' More expletives went around the chapel. I knew these men had stories far worse than my own but many of them did not know how to change and were caught in a cycle of re-offending.

I have no idea how long I spoke for but after about five minutes of talking, they stopped interrupting. By the end you could hear a pin drop.

Bill stood and led the men in a prayer they could say in the silence of their hearts. 'Sorry for the things I have done wrong. Thank you, Jesus, for dying on the cross for me and please come into my life by your Holy Spirit.' There was silence. I could see men wiping away tears, shuffling on their feet. Emmy then invited those who had said the prayer to come to the front.

The whole process was repeated in the afternoon session with a group of men from the Vulnerable Prisoner Unit who were not allowed to mix with the main prisoners. Bill mentioned to the team a particular sex offender who had extreme facial psoriasis.

I told my story once more and by this point in the day Emmy was feeling so unwell that she was sitting on the back row. After my talk lots of the men came forward for prayer. Emmy realised she would need to help, so she came to the front.

*

It was then that the man with psoriasis walked up to her and she passed him over to me.

Praying for that man was the key that unlocked my heart. In my life I had sinned badly, but I still judged others. God had to break me down. I understood that no one is too low for God, and that everyone has the chance to be redeemed. I knew, at that moment, that I had arrived at the very place God had intended for me.

That single incident in 1996, in that prison chapel in the middle of a bleak moor, changed my life. I had a profound 'call' from the Spirit of God. I knew there and then that I was going to have to point my life in a different direction. But how I was going to do it was beyond me.

One of the signposts was a trip to Argentina.

Soon after the visit to Dartmoor, I went on my first prison trip abroad. Emmy invited me to go to Olmos prison in La Plata, a city in Argentina, on a three-day mission with a small team of volunteers, including Colin and Stella Armstrong, the Reverend Bill and Clare Birdwood and John Coppin.

Olmos was Argentina's biggest maximum-security prison, home to 3,000 of the most dangerous criminals. In the late 70s and early 80s it had been in the news many times, mostly because of gang murders, rape and security corruption. Due to the violence on one particular wing, the prison officers had refused to enter and the inmates had taken control. Olmos lived with an awful reputation for years and many good men in the chaplaincy had failed to improve things.

All this started to change in 1983 when a young Pentecostal pastor called Juan Zuccarelli felt called by God to go in to Olmos. The authorities said that he could only preach if he was working there so Juan applied to be a prison guard. Remarkably 300 inmates attended his first crusade. Of the 300, 100 gave their lives to Christ. Unfortunately, these men then became targets for other inmates to abuse. So in 1987, as the number of Evangelical Christians grew, Juan proposed to the authorities that they have separate cell blocks. The warden was against the idea, but he let them have a burnt-out cell block because they promised to paint it and restore it. Local churches donated paint and beds and furniture, and gradually the block gained an extraordinary reputation. The first cell block held only twenty-one men, so Juan asked for more. The warden was so impressed by these praying men who were peaceful that he granted Juan his request. Juan and his pastoral team gradually trained up some of the inmates to be pastors on the wings. He broke the prison into areas, or what he called churches or parishes, and there was an amazingly organised team of Spirit-filled men who took services on Sundays, ran Bible classes during the week and allocated mentors to the men to help them on their new journey.

When we eventually got to Olmos we were all exhausted. Most of us had no idea what we were going to see or do. Emmy reassured us, 'God has the plan, so let's not worry.'

Everyone was remarkably welcoming in the prison. At one service I spoke to over 500 men and I will never forget the power of the prayer and singing. But it was when I was sitting in the psychiatric wing, listening to one of the prison pastors preach on God's love to around thirty inmates, that I had a very different physical encounter with the Holy Spirit. I was so touched by the pastor's words of love for the inmates that when we stood for prayer, I fell over. As I opened my eyes I saw the inmates gathered around me praying that God would use me in prison work.

By 2010 there were twenty-four Christian cell blocks in Olmos and 1,600 inmates under a strict regime of prayer and Bible study. Miraculously, a group of inmates became missionaries to other prisons because the government could see the results. Churches were planted within the prisons and now there are over forty Argentinian prisons with church plants originating from Olmos.

I understand that we have to be careful with religion in prison because people can become radicalised and extreme. But where the gospel is preached with an emphasis on repentance and love, it is nothing less than a miracle.

On 6 February 1997 it was Emmy's birthday, so I offered her a day of pampering at Champneys. Without me knowing, she watched me walk around the club in my smart suit and short ponytail and felt God say to her, 'This man is in the wrong job. He should be helping you with the prison work.'

At the end of a staff meeting at HTB she went to Sandy Millar and told him, 'I have been organising trips on my own, speaking and leading the teams. The work is growing, but since the majority of prisoners are male, I feel a man should develop this work.' Emmy was referring to the fact that women make up under 5 per cent of the prison population in England and Wales. Sandy was unsure but encouraged her to write a paper on where she thought the ministry was heading.

I was really starting to enjoy volunteering. Not only was I meeting some amazing chaplains, but I was growing fond of some of the inmates too. In early 1997, Michael and Brian were transferred to HMP Blantyre House and I went with Emmy to meet them. I liked them both very much, with their larger-than-life stories – strong men, very capable, bright and intelligent. I could see that they wanted help with their walk with God and I was delighted to draw alongside them both. They were released later that year and began to attend HTB.

Meanwhile, Amanda, now thirty-four years old, decided she wanted a child. I wasn't totally against the idea but, concerned that I might not be a very good father, I decided to ask for Sandy's counsel. At the end of a church service I followed him down the aisle of the church. Turning to me he said, 'What is the matter, dear boy?'

'Amanda wants a baby, Sandy, and I'm not sure it is right because I left Clinton when he was three.'

Sandy looked genuinely surprised, his blue eyes looking straight at me. 'Paul, nonsense, you are a different man now. You can trust God. Go and have lots of babies!'

And with that advice he turned and walked off.

It was funny really, but it was all I needed to hear. Four months later Amanda fell pregnant and we were both overjoyed.

As time went on my job was no longer inspiring me and the constant complaints from the guests, often about petty things, such as the quality of the towels or smell of the hand cream, started to annoy me, but I was fearful of leaving. Moreover, Amanda was hoping not to work for a while when she had the baby but there was still a mortgage and bills to pay.

I was doing as many prison visits as I could with Emmy while running one of the biggest health clubs in London. All I could do was pray that God would help me and give me my heart's desire. I read in Psalm 37:7, 'Be still before the LORD and wait patiently for him.' So that is what I did – but patience has never been my best asset.

After one year at Champneys I realised the job was too demanding. The financial director resigned and a few days later Lord Thurso called me into his office and said, 'We will replace him, Paul, but it will take a while, so would you mind just holding the fort in that area for a while?' Before I could protest, he was gone.

Working on accounts as well as dealing with a major refurbishment project over a period of eight months, costing well over £1.5 million, was taking its toll on me. I was never at home. I missed my wife and it wasn't the job I had been employed to do.

Two months later, Lord Thurso asked to meet me in the House of Lords for lunch. I knew something was wrong and, in some ways, I didn't mind. I wanted the nightmare to end. Fortunately for me, Lord Thurso could see I was struggling. During coffee he said to me, 'Paul, how are you doing?'

I thought I could do one of two things. I could either lie and say everything was fine, or I could tell the truth. I decided to say it how it was. 'With the greatest respect, Lord Thurso, I'm drowning in paperwork and the job is too much for me. I need you to get me a financial director or I will have to leave.'

'I thought as much, Paul. You have done a great job in getting the club up and running, but I can see the strain it is putting on you. However, I would prefer to have one person do the two roles, in order to cut the budget.'

'Sir,' I replied, 'I think you need a different kind of manager now.'

'Yes, I agree. I want to give you these two envelopes. One contains a very good reference for your next employer, with a personal attachment from me saying what a wonderful job you have done at Champneys, and the other is a cheque for four months' salary.'

And that was it. I worked for a couple more weeks and then left. The cheque made a massive difference and gave me some breathing space, but I was still worried about what I was going to do next.

It wasn't long before a letter arrived from the House of Commons. Lord Thurso had recommended me for an interview to run the health club in parliament. The salary was good and I'm sure the working conditions would have been great, but my heart drifted to HMP Dartmoor and the man I had prayed for. *Wasn't that my destiny? Wasn't that what I should be doing?* So I turned down the interview.

During the next two months I prayed and read the Bible every day, searching the Scriptures for the answer. I just had a sense that something was coming, but that I must wait and get ready.

Emmy invited me into the office to help her reply to letters from inmates. After a few days I said, 'This is boring!'

'Paul, this is really important', she said patiently.

Meanwhile, Emmy, having submitted her paper to Sandy suggesting that I was the person to help drive the ministry forward, was waiting for an answer. Two months later, Sandy and the leadership of the church decided to take me on board. They had never had an ex-offender or a divorcee on staff, and they repeatedly asked Emmy if she thought I was suitable for the job.

Tricia Neill (previously Rupert Murdoch's EA), who was in charge of operations at HTB, invited me to see her. 'There is no money for this work, Paul, so we don't know how long it will last.' After chatting for a while, she eventually offered me a position.

The wage offer was less than half of what I had been on at Champneys, and she went on to inform me that there was also no computer available, no office space, no PA and no extra staff to help me. I remember thinking, *Not the best job offer I've had.* Despite the depressing list of what HTB couldn't provide, my heart leapt, and I felt as if I had won the lottery. And in God's perfect timing the day I started, 1 July 1997, was the last day of Champneys' payout.

I was introduced at my first staff meeting as Pastor for Prisons with the purpose of spreading the Alpha course through the prison system. Asked to say a few words, I got up to speak and felt so excited that I punched the air with joy, shouting, 'This is the most exciting day of my life!' People started to pray out loud and give words of encouragement for the prison work to grow. Emmy hugged me and was just as enthusiastic as I was about the appointment.

God's plan for my life was slowly taking shape.

When I started on staff in 1997 there were around six prisons running the Alpha course. With 158 prisons in the UK, I knew we had to have a strategy. We had to become proactive. I asked Tricia Neill for an office and a small budget. Managing to secure some funding for prison work, Tricia agreed. She also agreed to getting me some administrative help and Thomasin Quibel became my first PA. I started to develop and structure the work, naming it 'Alpha for Prisons'.

Realising that more and more people leaving prison wanted to join an Alpha church, Charlotte Braithwaite transferred from the role of HTB's receptionist to help develop the work of churches wishing to help ex-offenders. Charlotte was very prayerful and gifted in admin and she really helped me expand the remit, as she understood my vision. My love of maps in the army influenced me to put a large UK map above my desk. Every prison in the UK was marked by a green spot, and then a red one as soon as they started Alpha. Emmy and I travelled with volunteers to prisons up and down the country, introducing the Alpha course and speaking on the Holy Spirit.

It was a mad time for me as I was never in the office, always out on the road visiting prisons, and I absolutely loved it. Predictably, as the work started to grow it started to cost money and the budget was diminishing, with no likelihood of it being topped up.

One day, Tricia came to me with a response from the charity Allchurches Trust. Nicky, Sandy and Tricia had given a short presentation saying that this work had massive potential to change thousands of people's lives in prison and that we needed a budget to grow the work. To everyone's amazement we were given £100,000, which was a real boost to the prison department, as I was able to employ more staff.

It was late 1997 when Sandy called me over to the vicarage. Whenever I was summoned by anyone in authority I would start to panic; it was a throwback to my past, always thinking negative thoughts, believing I must be in trouble for something. Sandy was as charming as always, and after the normal polite chat and the offer of tea and biscuits from his wife Annette, he sat me down. 'Paulus [his nickname for me], I've been thinking about your future. I think we need to get you some training.'

I remember saying, 'Why do I need training? I spent nearly seventeen years in the army training.'

He continued, 'I mean biblical training, Paul.' I was shocked. 'Have a think about it. We can keep meeting. You're doing great work with the prisons, but I think there's more.' And that was it. My meeting was over. For the next couple of weeks, I couldn't get his words out of my head.

Amanda and I had been running a home group for a couple of years. Every Tuesday we had about twenty people turn up. It kept us both busy, as we had to organise food, speakers, worship leaders and so on. One evening Meryl, a young fashion designer for French Connection, got our attention. She wanted to play a game. The idea was for each of us to say what we would have liked to be if we were given another chance. Meryl announced she would have been a schoolteacher. The next person in the group said they would have been a fighter pilot – so the game progressed. I started to feel anxious, scared, and I started to sweat. What was going on? Meryl then said, 'So, Paul, what would you have been?'

Before I could stop myself, I said, 'I think I'd like to have been a vicar.' Immediately, I closed my eyes. I couldn't believe I had said it – out loud. I was so embarrassed. I opened one eye, but no one was laughing at me. In fact, most of the group were smiling and Meryl said, 'You know what, Paul, I can see you as a vicar.'

Amanda smiled at me and nodded.

It was the first time I had ever spoken the desires of my heart out loud. Did I want to be a vicar? Could I be a vicar with my past? What sort of training would I need for that job?

Then Sandy's words came back to me: 'I mean biblical training, Paul.' Maybe that's what Sandy was referring to.

I felt sick for days afterwards, not convinced I was vicar material at all. Deep down I was exhilarated, believing that with God's help anything was possible.

I went back to Sandy and discussed the possibilities of training.

It would take a year of going to various interviews before I could get to see the bishop who was able to recommend me for theological training. The main problem didn't seem to be that I had been expelled from school, or that I had spent time in prison, but that I had been divorced. The journey to ordination was not straightforward, but something was driving me on. If I was going to succeed I would have to go to deeper depths of confession, expose myself even more, and throw myself headlong off that wall into the arms of Christ.

17: The secret place

The day before my interview with the Bishop of Kensington, I met up with my close friend Nick Henderson. We had lunch and chatted through what I might say at my interview the next day. At one point during our lunch Nick said, 'You are going to tell them you've been divorced twice, aren't you?'

I looked at him and said, 'Why would I mention it? Everyone thinks I've been divorced once and that's bad enough. Even Sandy and Nicky don't know.'

Nick looked at me and said, 'I think that's a big mistake, Paul.' For the moment I decided to ignore his advice.

*

By December 1997, Clinton was nineteen years old and our relationship with him was really good. As our baby was due in February he decided to follow a job and move north for a while. He felt it was right to give us some space.

Amanda started her contractions at 5.00 p.m. on 3 February 1998. I left work immediately. Tricia and Andrew arrived later that evening.

At 2.00 a.m. the four of us arrived at St Mary's Hospital in Paddington. I phoned Emmy. 'Come now, Emmy. Amanda has gone into labour.'

Amanda had wanted Emmy at the birth as they had become good friends and with Emmy's nursing experience and her dedication to prayer we both knew she would be a support. Dutifully Emmy got a taxi and arrived at 3.00 a.m. But as Amanda was only 3 cm dilated the midwife recommended she take a bath. When her contractions increased she had gas and air in the birthing room and asked for her music to be put on. I can see her now, in between each contraction, with one hand holding on to the gas and air pipe while the other one was raised high above her head, singing her heart out to 'Oh Happy Day'.

It was at around 2.00 p.m. that a team of consultants came into the room and checked all the monitors. One of the gynaecologists said, 'I am not happy with these readings. We need to do some tests.'

Orders were shouted, and Amanda was examined. 'We need to send some bloods from the baby's head to the lab to see if it has enough oxygen.' I watched as the doctor took a tiny amount of blood from the baby's crown. Within about ten minutes the results were given back to the doctor. 'Right,' he said. 'Amanda, we need to get this baby out now as it is stressed. If you can't push it out, we will have to give you a caesarean.'

'I will push it out', Amanda insisted.

Emmy's hand was resting on Amanda's tummy and when she felt the contraction she encouraged Amanda to push. Tricia sat on the chair with her head bowed, deep in prayer, asking God not to let anything awful happen. I held my wife's hand. A second ventouse device was called for as the first one was broken. There was tangible panic in the room. Finally, a small, blue, silent thing was pulled out of my wife and placed on her stomach. There was no sound. Amanda was in a daze. Immediately a nurse took the baby to the side and started working on it. All of a sudden, we heard a cry and the nurse said, 'Your little girl is going to be all right.'

'It's a girl?' I said, amazed.

'It's a girl?' said Tricia, full of tears.

'It's a girl', said Amanda.

Phoebe Jordan was born at 2.20 in the afternoon and weighed 6 lbs 13 oz. We all cried and looked at this funny little thing who was going to have such an impact on both of us.

*

After I met with Nick, I went to the office and started filling in the forms for my interview. I was at the part where it stated, 'Please give any relevant information on previous marriages'. I thought about what Nick had said to me and as my pen hovered over the blank box I sensed someone behind me. Turning around I saw the Reverend Sandy Millar smiling at me. 'Don't let me bother you, Paulus. I'm just checking all the windows are closed and the lights are off. It's the Lord's money we're spending, after all!' After he'd closed one of the windows in my office he said, 'What are you doing here so late?'

I told him that I was filling in the forms. He smiled again and said, 'Is there anything I can help you with? It's a big day tomorrow.' His blue eyes pierced my soul.

I couldn't stand it any longer. I had to tell him. Crying, I said, 'I'm so sorry, Sandy. I'm so sorry for not telling you. You have all been so good to me and I don't deserve your love and trust.'

Sandy put his arms around me and said, 'My dear boy! What on earth is the matter? What's going on?'

I explained to him that I had left out of my testimony that I had been married twice, not once, and I felt like a fraud.

Sandy sat down 'Paulus, you don't have to do all your dirty washing in public. Now how are the forms coming along?'

I told him I was thinking of leaving the second divorce off the form. Without hesitation he said, 'No, Paul, you must tell the truth. It's the Lord that will direct your steps, not man.'

I replied, 'But why would the Church of England take me? I was expelled from school, in prison and divorced twice!'

He looked at me and said, 'I understand all that, but where is your faith, Paul?' He then prayed for the meeting and left me alone.

The next morning, I handed Bishop Michael my forms and a covering letter outlining my past. Sandy had encouraged me to write it out in bullet form, giving a timeline of events, including my two divorces. It seemed like an age before he looked at me and said, 'Okay, Paul, you've certainly led an interesting life. Leave these documents with me.'

I felt disappointed in myself and ashamed of my life. It would appear that I could never escape my past.

Two weeks later I was summoned to see the bishop. As I sat in his office he explained that the two divorces made my application complicated. 'I knew this would happen,' I said. 'I should never have started this journey in the first place. I guess I got it wrong.'

He just stared at me then smiled. 'I said it was complicated, not impossible, Paul. I had to send your forms to the Bishop of London for his consideration and if he is happy he has to send the forms on to the Archbishop of Canterbury. If he's happy, then he and only he can recommend you go forward for ordination training, which starts with a Bishops' Advisory Panel (BAP). If you pass the three-day selection conference, then you can start your ordination process.'

I thought, *What chance do I have of getting through all that?* I felt sick. *The Bishop of London? The Archbishop of Canterbury? Who would be next? The Queen? They would never agree.*

On reporting back to Sandy, his response was, 'Paul, if the Lord is in it, then it will happen. Let's wait and see.'

Getting on with the prison work, I tried to forget the stupid idea of ever becoming a priest.

It was ten days later that Sandy invited me into his study. Placing a shot of Glenmorangie in front of me he said, 'Drink that.'

We clinked glasses and he passed me an envelope, which was addressed to him. 'Read it, Paul', he said. Inside was a small slip of embossed paper with a red wax seal on it. I couldn't believe my eyes. On the piece of paper from Lambeth Palace, signed by the Archbishop of Canterbury the Rt Revd George Carey, it stated that he personally recommended me to go forward for my selection conference. Sandy said, 'Looks like the Lord is in this, Paulus, so I thought we'd celebrate with a wee dram. Well done.'

In 1998 I went on a three-day selection conference to be considered for ordination into the Church of England. It was a daunting process for me, one that I was never sure I would pass. But now I was committed, whatever the outcome.

Arriving for my BAP at a centre in Glastonbury Abbey, I was shown to my room where I unpacked a small bag and placed my books and pens on a desk. At supper I met a few other ordinands, but as soon as I saw Simon Kirby, a man with a friendly face, I put my tray down next to him.

Those three days were a nightmare for me as I was constantly watched and monitored. There were tests throughout and then there were the three dreaded one-hour interviews.

The first interview was with a senior member of the Church of England who needed to determine whether or not I had understood the history of the Church; if I knew the routines of the priestly life: matins at the beginning of the day and compline at the end of the day (two daily prayer rituals). Also, he needed to see if I was familiar with the Bible and the Book of Common Prayer. Fortunately, Sandy had taught me well and by the end of the interview he seemed satisfied.

The second interview was about my pastoral care and discipleship values. The interviewer was very kind, and once I had unpacked some of my life history, especially my military experience – and my two divorces – he thought it would give me a maturity and empathy towards other people's struggles.

The final interview was to be with an educationalist, because they need to know I was up to the standard of education for the two-year diploma course or the three-year degree course. I was particularly nervous of this interview because I didn't think she would be that impressed with my 25 yards swimming certificate.

My army certificates were equally inappropriate, as I'm sure the Church of England doesn't need someone trained as a drill instructor, sniper or tank driver. I had not gained a single 'O' or 'A' level. I certainly didn't have a degree, unlike most of the other candidates whose range of certificates, would have filled the length of a church pew.

Before the final interview began, we were asked to list the books we had read recently. Before the course I had been given a long list of books and I had read several of them in preparation for the selection conference, but at that moment I couldn't recall any. My mind was blank. As I stared at the white piece of A4, I said, 'God, you must give me a book title! Please give me a book title. I read so many of those boring books!' I quickly scribbled down the only title I could remember, but the trouble was it wasn't one from the reading list. I then handed in the paper. When the papers were collected I could see the others had written various titles, including a book I'd enjoyed, called *The Christian Priest Today* by Michael Ramsey. Unfortunately, my ghostly page only contained *All Quiet on the Western Front,* a novel by Erich Maria Remarque, given to me by my good friend Nick.

The interviewer, whom I knew to be a retired teacher, called me into her office. She could see I was nervous, so immediately tried to put me at ease. 'Don't look so worried, Paul,' she said, peering at me over the top of her glasses. 'I have to say, your list of books you read prior to this conference seems to be rather short.'

'I know . . . I am so sorry. My mind went blank. I did read some off the list.'

'It doesn't matter; just tell me about the book you wrote down.' She was kind and I took an instant liking to her.

'Well, it's about two young German soldiers and the friendships that developed in the trenches during the First World War. The book had a big impact on me because, as an ex-soldier, I could relate to the fear and exhilaration they felt through their different experiences. It was about the sacrifice of their young lives, so many young lives, lost for their country. It was all mad and crazy in the trenches, hell on earth, what with the disease, the stench and the starvation. Even though they were the enemy I wanted them to live, but in the end, it was about risk and survival, and the relationships they had formed . . .' I trailed off. Not sure what to say next.

'How can you relate it to your faith?' she asked.

'Well, *faith* is like that. It's sacrificial. Jesus died on the cross for me. He was a young man in the prime of his life. He could have chosen not to do it, but he chose to die because it was his purpose.'

For a moment I became confused and was not sure if I was speaking rubbish but then I had some clarity and continued.

'My faith is about walking alongside people, through the exciting times and the terrors of life. Whatever happens, it's knowing that Jesus went that way too; that he understands us and however bad I have been he can pull me up out of the trenches and give me a hope that I can be a better man, and that makes me want to give others who are stuck in the trenches hope too.'

She looked at me again over her spectacles and smiled. 'I've never heard that book applied to faith in that way before, with such passion.' She paused and said, 'Paul, do you know what I do?'

I replied, 'You're a retired headteacher.'

'I am also a lecturer in English literature, and this is one of the books I lecture on.'

I could not believe it. We continued to talk long past my allocated slot. When I returned to my room I dropped to my knees and let out a groan – a groan that had held in all my inadequacies since leaving school. It had been a burden and I hadn't truly recognised it until that moment. Having cried out for help and asked for the title of a book, God had given me the only book I needed. After that interview and experience I knew God was with me, helping me, guiding me. I started to have more confidence in his plan, and more importantly have more faith. Having watched the birth of my daughter and experienced a deep sense of God's presence in that small college room, Psalm 139 became one of my favourites:

My frame was not hidden from you
when I was made in the secret place,
when I was woven together in the depths of the earth.
Your eyes saw my unformed body;
all the days ordained for me were written in your book
before one of them came to be.
Psalm 139:15–16

I passed my three-day selection and was recommended for ordination training at Oak Hill College in north London.

Sandy insisted that I stay and work at HTB to keep one foot firmly planted in the prison work at the same time as training, so I decided to do the two-year diploma course. I was the first ordinand from HTB to do a non-residential course.

For the next two years I was deeply challenged. Most weeks there were one or two essays to complete. In the first few months on the course I had to read a copious number of books and partake in a day of lectures each week, as well as do a full-time job. I had no idea how to do an essay, but Amanda was able to show me how to construct two sides of an argument, and I gradually started to understand the process of reading and gathering information.

Debates with lecturers and other students sometimes deeply upset me, constantly leaving me feeling outside my comfort zone and challenging my simple faith. I got into conversations only to find I had no answers and would revert back to being defensive in my attitude, which sometimes got me into trouble with staff. Fortunately, my new friend Simon was able to help me navigate through some difficult situations by making me laugh.

Due to my lack of formal education I sometimes wanted to run and hide or stop the whole process altogether. The Reverend

Ann Coleman, one of my tutors, would make me a coffee and sit with me, calming me down by saying I was being too hard on myself. Without Ann's help I really don't think I would have made it through the first year. It was also Ann who encouraged me to go from a two-year diploma course to a three-year degree in theology.

The sense of looming failure that came with this offer was immense.

For some reason my dad had fallen out with me. I honestly don't know what it was about. He was very sensitive. I was able to cut off from him for a while, but then Amanda encouraged me. 'I know he's not an easy man, Paul, but he is the only father you have. He will be gone one day, and you will regret not being in touch.'

'Maybe I won't. Maybe it's just easier to let him go. He never rings me, as a father should.'

'I know, but you have something to say to him.'

'Do I?'

'You have your faith now. You have a hope that things and people can change and be better.'

'Yes, you're right. I will write to him.'

I left it for a few more weeks but somehow he haunted me, so in late December 2000, I put pen to paper.

18: A time to die

'Thanks, son! You know how I like to travel.'

'I know, Dad. Enjoy it; it won't be happening every time.' And with that I left the train and joined Amanda and Phoebe on the platform.

'What made you do that?' said Amanda.

'I have no idea. I wanted to see him happy.'

As the train pulled out of the station, he took his trilby off and reclined his seat in first class. He smiled at me and waved.

That was the last time I ever saw him. He died three weeks later.

*

Dear Dad,

I wanted to write to you because Christmas for me is always a time of pain, confusion and anger, and I can never really work out why. I have everything a man could wish for, but still there are things that are not resolved in my life. A lot of my stuff got sorted out when I met Amanda fifteen years ago. She is an amazing woman, and I thank God for her each day. She has saved me from going mad on many occasions.

Seven years ago, I decided to go on an Alpha course and find out about God. Why? Because I was fed up with who I was, and I had no idea of who God was anyway! As for his Son, Jesus, to me that name was only a swear word. I never did God at school or at home. Not your fault, Dad; that's just the way we were, and I can understand that. I am sure you had enough to deal with just bringing me up.

On the Alpha course I met this man called Jesus and you know what? I liked him. He wasn't what I thought he was. He wasn't weak and feeble; you know the saying 'Jesus meek and mild' (he is sometimes but not always). He was strong and challenging. He made me confront some of the stuff in my life I was doing and saying that wasn't good. Things that I thought I couldn't change because, well, they were me, and a man can never change, can he? That's the way we are made and so you just get on with it. You know what I found out, Dad? It's not true; a man can change, and it's never too late to start, even today, even right now is a good time.

Seven years ago, I was ready to change, and Jesus said, 'Paul, I know you are scared, I know you want to be different, but you will have to trust me if you want me to help you.' So, I did. I took a chance based on what I'd read of him and what other people who knew him had told me and I have never looked back since. It's not always been easy, but you know what, Dad? It's an adventure that waits for all men and women who want to change – even you.

The point of this letter is to say I love you and always have. I want us to be friends. I am your son, and that's got to count for something, hasn't it? But I don't know how we are going to communicate with each other unless we talk. You see, I can't understand why you don't want to see me. Why you don't want to see your grandson Clinton and your granddaughter Phoebe. They are your family, Dad. They love you like I do; you are important to them.

If I have realised one thing in this life it is that people count more than things. Family are people who need to be loved and valued but they are hard work too. I want to love you, Dad; we have a lot of history. I know you have had a lot of pain with family, but a lot of that wasn't my fault. There is also a lot of good to be found in family too, Dad. You just have to look with different eyes.

Anyway, sorry if the letter has upset you. That was never my intention – it's sent in love. A love a son has for his father, and only you and I know how deep that love goes, it is our history. I have your blood running in my veins; there is a part of you with me every day and I don't think there is a day that goes by that I don't think of you.

You don't have to answer this letter if you don't want to, but I pray that you do. I miss you, you are part of my life and your family also miss and love you. We won't go away, Dad. Your son and daughter-in-law, grandson and granddaughter are here to stay (God willing) and we love you and want you to be part of our lives. It can be different if we both try.

Merry Christmas and God bless.

Love from your family

Paul

It was Anna, my dad's partner, who, on a work trip to London, arranged to see me. At a hotel in Hampstead she suggested that I ring my father as he was just being stubborn. I was a bit annoyed because I thought I had said enough in the letter, but she encouraged me to make the call, convincing me he would mellow if I did. She was right. I called him that evening and suggested I meet him with Clinton, as they hadn't seen each other in a very long time.

Clinton and I went to Macclesfield and spent a weekend with him. It was amazing to see how God was reuniting me with my son and my dad. It wasn't the easiest time, three generations of Cowleys together, but it was a start. I didn't mention the letter, but I invited him to stay with us in London and he accepted.

By the end of year three, the stress of working full time as a prison pastor at HTB while developing Alpha for Prisons around the UK, and fitting in a non-residential degree in Theology, was taking its toll, and Amanda and Phoebe took the brunt of it. But I was on my own private mission to do the best I could. People had put their trust in me and I wanted to prove I could do it. I often worked late into the night to meet the essay deadlines. I would then be up in the early hours with Amanda and Phoebe. But we were such a team. Amanda was my rock, bringing me toast and cups of tea when I was up late, and helping me answer complex essay questions.

After what seemed like an age, I finished my Theology degree with a 2:2, which felt like an achievement.

A few weeks later, on 29 June 2002, I entered St Paul's Cathedral and was surprised to see it bursting with people. I didn't invite my dad as Amanda's mum and stepfather came down to stay in the house and I was stressed with the anticipation of the ceremony. I robed with the other ordinands in the crypt of the great church and then went up to the cathedral to greet my guests. Amanda passed Phoebe to me, who was by this time four years old. I greeted Tricia and Andrew and Clinton. 'Hello, everybody,' I said. 'Thank you for coming.'

'I'm proud of you, Dad', said Clinton.

It meant a lot to hear my son say those words to me.

Turning to Amanda, I passed Phoebe back, saying. 'I can't stay long as it is about to start. Come and take your seats.'

Tricia said, 'How many people are being ordained today?'

'Forty men and women altogether. It's one of the largest intakes they have ever had, apparently', I replied, and then I took off, worried I would be late.

I picked up the twenty-page service sheet, printed on heavy-weight cream card. The organ bellowed out, and about 2,000 people stood for the first hymn.

Walking down the aisle with the bishops and forty ordinands was awe-inspiring with the great cathedral towering above me. With the music and the singing, the atmosphere was something of old, its history seeping out from every stone of that ancient building. Like a wave, we settled in two lines opposite the congregation. I smoothed down my white surplice and adjusted my preaching stole. We then proceeded with the two-and-a-half-hour service.

The Bishop of London, Richard Chartres, a tall imposing figure, addressed the flock in a booming voice as if he were reciting *Hamlet* or *King Lear* at the Globe, and yet his soliloquy was about the duties and honour of working for Christ. Each ordinand then approached the bishop and knelt at his feet. Placing both hands upon their heads, he prayed quietly over them.

When it was my turn I knelt, and as he laid his hands on my head, he said, 'Come, Holy Spirit, on your servant Paul, and help him do the work of a priest.' The importance of the ceremony and the responsibility of serving Christ was felt in the weight of the bishop's warm hands on my head.

The service drew to an end, and the voices filled Sir Christopher Wren's dome with a beautiful final hymn: 'Here I am, Lord'. The congregation stood, and the Bishop of London proceeded to walk down the aisle, smiling broadly while singing, followed by many more bishops and the recently ordained priests. I had the biggest grin on my face as I walked past my family, feeling as if I had truly been given the biggest gift ever. Walking out of the doors at the back of the cathedral we were met by a huge crowd of tourists and guests who had left before us to capture the moment on their cameras.

I was, at last, the Reverend Paul Cowley.

Back at the house, the sun streamed through the patio doors into the kitchen, where there was a large gathering of friends. Walking down the stairs to the basement kitchen, I was greeted with cheers from all my closest friends. I was now dressed in a smart dark suit with a black cotton shirt splashed with the white of a dog collar at the neck. At the bottom of the steps I was greeted with the gift of a granddaughter clock. 'Is that for me?' I said.

The plaque stated, 'For my son-in-law Paul, on his ordination day, 29th June 2002. With love from Tricia.' I later found out that the clock had been given to Tricia's father and mother, Leigh and Gertrude Waller, when Leigh became the minister of the Burrowbridge Baptist Chapel, in Somerset. The clock is in our kitchen chiming the hours of the day. It is a reminder of the years I have wasted and the years I have left. Psalm 90:12 comes to mind: 'Teach us to number our days, that we may gain a heart of wisdom.'

One year later, I was priested at St Mary Abbots in High Street Kensington. I invited my dad and Anna, and it was a good experience for me as my dad was on good form and after the service we all had a tea and celebration at a hotel near Gloucester Road. Soon afterwards I was commissioned, by Richard Chartres, to be an Alpha missioner. It was a brand-new post and it recognised the work I was doing with Alpha for Prisons internationally.

Meanwhile, my dad, now seventy-six years old, was in poor health. Having had his first heart attack at sixty-three he had struggled on and off with his heart. On one particular visit, Anna tapped on our bedroom door in the early hours of the morning.

'I'm sorry to disturb you both but Arthur is not doing too well.'

We both got up immediately and went upstairs to the guest room.

'Dad,' I said, 'what's the matter?'

He was obviously distressed and was struggling to breathe.

Amanda called an ambulance and two paramedics struggled with getting a 6-foot, 15-stone man down three flights of stairs, but eventually my father was in the ambulance. Amanda and I followed in the car while Anna stayed with Phoebe.

The doctors kept him in for tests and decided he needed a pacemaker.

On the day of his operation I went in to see him. I had been taking a service at church and was wearing my dog collar. Standing over my dad while he was lying in bed, we chatted about everything except the imminent operation. I could see my father was nervous and uncomfortable but, as always, I didn't know what to say to him. Two nurses entered the room and said that they would take my father to the operating theatre and I could walk with them if I wanted to. Just before they opened the doors to the theatre one of the nurses said, 'Aren't you going to pray for your dad?'

At this point, I had prayed for hundreds of people but never my own father.

My father said nothing but closed his eyes. It took all the courage I could muster to pray for him, even though I was dressed for the part. Placing a hand upon his chest I fumbled through a short prayer. I think after that he was less nervous about the operation, but only because I'm sure he would rather be operated on than have his blabbering son pray for him.

Having a pacemaker helped regulate my father's heartbeat but it made him feel anxious. Unsure of how it worked, he felt it was a foreign object inside him. He joked about being on VHF and having a bad reception. Anna was very supportive and I believe she kept him going for years longer than he would have lived had he been on his own. She made sure he was fed and clothed well. She helped him with his flat and issues with the council.

*

It was in 2004, on a trip down to London, that I took Dad and Anna to the Guards Depot near Buckingham Palace. Since I was friendly with the head padre, he showed us around. Dad was delighted with the trip and enjoyed showing Phoebe, who was now six years old, all the war memorabilia.

As he and Anna boarded the train at Euston, I had a sudden desire to do something nice for them both. I ran to the guard and asked to upgrade them.

'Let's move you down to the first-class carriage', I said.

His face was beaming. 'Now this is what you call travelling in style', he said, as he took his seat. I gave him a hug and said goodbye.

It was three weeks later that the phone rang, and Anna spoke to Amanda.

'There is no easy way to say this, Amanda, but Arthur died from a heart attack at 2 o'clock today.'

'Oh, Anna, I'm so sorry. Let me get Paul.'

Anna went on to tell me that he had been enjoying the day and had wanted to mend the fence in the garden. 'He had a daffodil in his trilby and had been telling jokes. When he didn't appear for his tea I went to look for him, but the car boot was up, and I couldn't see him. I found him on the floor in the garage. I tried CPR and then I dashed to call the ambulance. I went back to see him lying there. He was still, and I said, "This time, Arthur. I have to tell Paul." They were very good, Paul; they tried to save him . . . but it was too late.'

Thanking Anna, I put the phone down. I was numb. I didn't know how to feel. This huge character, my father, my dad, was gone. A chapter in my life closed shut.

The Reverend Ric Thorpe (now a bishop and a dear friend of ours), offered to take the service. I said thanks but that I would do it myself. Ric insisted, saying I might not realise how emotional a family funeral can be and therefore he would take the service and I should do the eulogy. I was so grateful to him on the day.

On the morning of the funeral, we headed off on the long drive up the M1. The sky was unforgiving. Clouds hung low over the road and the rain hit the tarmac as soon as the wheels graced the motorway. Phoebe sat in the back protesting, but soon the journey was over, and we arrived at the hilltop crematorium outside Manchester. At the end of the service, we all went outside, and the heavens opened again. The earth was thick and cloggy. It reminded me of my mother's funeral, although there were more people there, including my father's brother and sister and their children, whom I hadn't seen since I was very young. Several of our friends came from London and I was grateful for their support. After the service, Amanda said, 'Well done, Paul. The eulogy was moving.'

'I didn't see enough of him!' I said. I had wanted to cry, but I couldn't.

Sometimes in life God can throw you a coincidence so big that no one can persuade you it isn't a miracle.

In June 2004, just three months after my dad had died, I met with Ali Hanna at an Alpha conference in Washington DC. He was a softly spoken Irishman, retired from McKinsey & Co as a senior partner, and he had set up an office to run Alpha North America. He introduced me to a tall man with a rugged face, a bit like John Wayne. He was dressed in a short-sleeved white shirt, blue jeans with a steer's head buckled belt, and black crocodile skin cowboy boots. When he opened his mouth and said, 'Howdy, friend', I thought I was in an episode of *Bonanza*.

But it was what he said next that really got my attention. 'I'm Jack Cowley! Pleased to meet ya.'

I almost fell over. Jack Cowley?

At the time, Jack was freelancing but had been working for Prison Fellowship (PFUSA), the highly respected organisation, established in 1979 by President Nixon's right-hand man Charles Colson, who had spent time in prison due to his involvement in the Watergate scandal.

Jack and I immediately bonded. For me it was like meeting an older brother. We even looked a bit alike. We chatted for a couple of hours and Jack told me about his experience of being a prison warden for thirty years and his work with Prison Fellowship.

I told Ali, 'This guy is extraordinary.' He agreed and decided to put me in front of the Alpha North America board, who were meeting in the hotel. I made my pitch. At this point in my ministry I was travelling almost 170 days a year. I told them that I couldn't keep coming over the pond to do this work, and that we needed someone in the USA. 'The perfect person is downstairs', I said.

I dashed downstairs and said to Jack, 'I truly believe we have a God moment here. There are too many coincidences for it not to be. We should be working together. Come and work for Alpha.'

Jack was given five minutes to pitch to the board. They loved him, and he was hired instantly. That was the official start of Alpha Prisons USA.

Jack Cowley has been working for Alpha for the past fifteen years and has been a huge asset, as he has managed to get the course into 557 prisons, running 1,571 courses, impacting 33,000 inmates.

One of our trips together in 2009 included a visit to Tomoka Correctional Institution in Daytona Beach. Jack asked me if I could get Bear Grylls to speak. Bear was becoming well known and he happened to attend HTB, so I knew him a little. He and his wife Shara were on holiday in Florida so I asked Bear if he would like to do a prison visit. It was Bear and Shara's first trip into a prison and Bear was quite nervous when he stood and spoke to around 200 inmates. He told them how his experiences in the wild may have been similar to what the inmates were going through in prison. For him it was the fear of the unknown. Being away from family and having to depend on his faith in the Lord to get him through tough situations. He talked about how Alpha helped him in building a relationship with the Lord and that during those times of uncertainty he was confident that God would guide him in making the right decisions. He added that it was through the Alpha course that his life had changed, as he began to understand how God was relevant in his life.

You could have heard a pin drop as the prisoners were obviously moved by his story. Moreover, the chaplain said it was the best 'non-sermon' he had ever heard and that many of the men were drawn closer to Christ.

Apart from prisoners, there was another body of men I felt compelled to reach with the love of Christ; and that was soldiers. Having been one myself for many years, I had a heart for them to discover the hope I now had.

19: I vow to thee, my country

To my amazement, the army chaplain started to walk forward for prayer. He was an argumentative and determined character who had stood at the back of the room, wearing his conservative theological college tie. All morning he had been quite negative about Alpha, saying it was just a new-fangled attempt to change the gospel and the only reason he was there was because he had been forced to attend by his superior officer. I watched in amazement as Nicky Gumbel prayed for him . . . and then *wham,* he was knocked to the floor by the Spirit of God. The other forty chaplains looked on amazed and the atmosphere of cynicism started to shift as more men came forward for prayer. The chaplain who fell down in the Spirit that day was soon running Alpha at Catterick Garrison in North Yorkshire. Suffice to say, he was full of joy after his encounter and went on to do amazing work with the soldiers.

*

'I Vow to Thee, My Country' is a poem by Sir Cecil Spring Rice that was set to music by Holst and published as a hymn around 1925. It is sombre in tone and was written in honour of the huge loss of life during the Great War, 'The love that asks no question, the love that stands the test / That lays upon the altar the dearest and the best.'

Military personnel are intrinsically meshed into our British history. Civilians care deeply for their welfare, as seen clearly in the profile of Help for Heroes as well as many other initiatives, including the Invictus Games for wounded and sick veterans, founded by Prince Harry.

On operational tours professional soldiers will face life and death situations and as Christians it is important to honour these men and women by telling them what we know and believe. Romans 10:14 seems particularly poignant: 'How, then, can they call on the one they have not believed in? And how can they believe in the one of whom they have not heard? And how can they hear without someone preaching to them?'

With nearly seventeen years in the military I hope you will appreciate my passion for service personnel. I understand first-hand the pressures they face and have also been struck by the statistics. The British Forces are made up of mainly young men: 92.5 per cent of personnel are male, with an average age of thirty to thirty-three. This is the same age group as the majority of men in our prisons in the UK. It is this group that is missing from our churches, and yet, strikingly, 75.5 per cent of regular forces in the UK profess to be Christian, though often they may not actually understand or believe the gospel.

At HTB in 2003 we were having the usual Tuesday morning staff meeting where staff members give feedback on churches around the world that are running the Alpha course. Several of the places mentioned were very familiar to me as they were military bases I had been associated with through courses, military exercises and postings: Bielefeld, Osnabrück, Paderborn, Dortmund, Sennelager.

Suddenly I had a lightbulb moment! What about Alpha for the forces? I wanted to get a planned initiative on how to get the Alpha course into all the military establishments in the UK – the army, the navy and the Royal Air Force – and then into the forces around the world.

In that staff meeting, Alpha for Forces was born, and it became official when I asked Jerry Field, a remarkable young man who was volunteering in the prisons office, if he would help me to get it going.

A few weeks later we invited all Christian military that were connected to HTB to a consultation day to see how many of them were interested in running the course within their regiments. Rhett Parkinson, who later became Membership Director of the Armed Forces Christian Union (AFCU), was a key person in helping to bring the day together. Sergeant Major Mark Davis 'Canada' (SAS soldier for seventeen years) turned up, as well as Major Grant Ashton, who was a senior army chaplain. The day went well, and it seemed that the chaplains were generally very interested.

It was about a year after this event that Jerry left his job in the City and came on staff full time as the doors for Alpha for Forces started to open. Although Jerry had not served in the forces, he was a polite and gentle character, who was adept at securing meetings with people of all ranks and it didn't take long before we had two big breakthroughs.

The first one came when Jerry and I went to meet the chaplain general for the army, Major General John Blackburn. John agreed to give us funding towards the first Alpha for Forces promo video and also an endorsement from the British Army, thus encouraging more chaplains to use the course. The second breakthrough was meeting Major Grant Ashton, who was promoted to Lt Colonel and was given the role of a training officer running Amport House, the British Armed Forces Chaplaincy Centre (AFCC). This enabled us to give a presentation to all the chaplains on the Continuous Ministerial Education programme, which included the training for all chaplains entering the British Army. Alpha gained credibility as an official course in the military.

*

I will never forget the first official training session, as I had asked all the big guns to be a part of the event. Sandy Millar came to speak as he was a friend of the Adjutant General Sir Alastair Irwin Hastings, and he had encouraged him to open the conference. Later that day, Nicky Gumbel gave the talk on the Holy Spirit and at the end he said, 'If anyone would like prayer please come forward.'

To my shame I thought, *No, Nicky, not now; it's too soon! These men are chaplains and they are far too stuffy to want prayer.*

When the rather cynical army chaplain came to the front and proceeded to fall over, I think we were all amazed.

Two important military endorsements for Alpha followed. The first was from Major General Tim Cross, who had served as Director General, Defence Supply Chain, until 2002, when he became involved in planning the invasion of Iraq. He was the most senior British officer involved in the planning and in the Coalition Provisional Authority, receiving the CBE for his humanitarian work in establishing the refugee camps in Bosnia. The second endorsement came from General Sir Richard Dannatt (now General Lord Dannatt), who became the Commander of the Allied Rapid Reaction Corps (ARRC) in 2003 and led the ARRC headquarters in planning for deployments to Iraq and Afghanistan. These two high ranking officers have continued to support the work of Alpha for Forces across the UK.

One of the high moments for both Jerry and me was at an Alpha launch for the Royal Engineers in Chatham. The chaplain put on a beer and curry evening for about a hundred squaddies, and Mark Davis gave a talk about his time in the SAS and his Christian faith. Mark is not large in stature, but he is an undeniable force, a gentle man with a strong faith who has a powerful story of transformation.

A perk gained from being involved with the forces work was when Major Mark Goodwin Hudson invited me to become the sessional padre at the Household Cavalry barracks at Hyde Park. As the padre I was instantly given officer status, and because of my age most of them assumed I was a major. One morning, on a riding session around Hyde Park, a troop of around sixty soldiers on horseback dressed in their stunning uniforms were coming back to the barracks after the changing of the guard at Buckingham Palace. As they passed me on my horse wearing my clerical collar, the sergeant at the front gave the order 'eyes right' and the whole troop saluted me! I returned the salute and rode off chuckling to myself!

During my time with the regiment I led two carol services in the stable block and gave my testimony to the soldiers sitting on hay bales. The regimental sergeant major stood up at the start and shouted, 'Right, lads! The padre is here, so sit up and shut up and sing up . . . Padre, over to you.' Telling your testimony makes you vulnerable but it's also the strongest way to convict others. Generally, people are not interested in being Bible-bashed. But they are interested in hearing stories of change. As it states in 1 Peter 3:15, 'Always be prepared to give an answer to everyone who asks you to give the reason for the hope that you have. But do this with gentleness and respect.'

At the end, when we were drinking glühwein, the RSM said, 'Bloody hell, Padre, you have been around the block a bit!'

I find it strange when people say that Alpha doesn't work in their church, because I have seen or heard it work in the most unlikely places – from under trees in Africa, to Saddam Hussein's former palace where soldiers were baptised in his swimming pool, to Gambia where over 500 soldiers attended Alpha in a predominantly Muslim country. Six soldiers on that course in Gambia have gone on to become the first chaplains in the Gambian Army and remarkably the chaplain to Gambian servicemen was ratified by the Vice President.

In 2006 Jerry Field went for ordination while still working at HTB. He is now the vicar of St John's Hampton Wick. Without Jerry's passion and hard work, I believe this ministry wouldn't have got off the ground and I am eternally grateful to him for laying down such good foundations.

Charlie Lacey was Jerry's successor. When I walked into the room to interview him for the role, he was dressed immaculately, and he was literally standing to attention. I thought, *You're hired!* Charlie was an ex-Royal Marines Commando who served operationally in Afghanistan in 2001/2 and Iraq in 2003 with forty Commando Regiment and in Northern Ireland (South Armagh and East Tyrone) in 2004. He had a spell in the Military Corrective Training Centre (MCTC) and left the forces as a confessed drinker, fighter and womaniser, but eventually turned his life around when he met with God on his travels. He joined Alpha for Forces in March 2007.

The military is a very strong institution and a close-knit family, so getting church volunteers on to the camps can be difficult. Having the new Alpha film series has been a real benefit because it means the chaplain doesn't need civilian speakers.

General Sir Richard Dannatt at the Cavalry and Guards Club was so earnest in his desire to see the gospel proclaimed throughout the armed forces that he organised a dinner. We were given the opportunity to speak about Alpha to the three senior chaplains from the army, the navy and the air force. He emphasised that he would like to see the course running throughout the military, which was an impressive endorsement.

One of the most dangerous trips Charlie and I went on was when we went to Yenagoa in Bayelsa State, Nigeria, at the request of Precious Omuku, a former Shell executive (and now a bishop). Nicky Gumbel had been invited by one of the directors of the state; unable to go himself, he offered me up! When I researched it, I realised it was a fairly volatile area, as the government advised against travel due to kidnappings. Charlie and I handpicked the team – including Mark Davis (ex-SAS) and Billy Gilvear (ex-British Army officer, now Baptist minister). An unlikely team member was Josh Smith, a verger at HTB, whom I said no to at first until he told me he was a qualified trauma medic. I decided he might be useful if one of us got shot!

Yenagoa is known as a kidnap area, as militia are continuing to kidnap oil workers to use as bargaining tools against the big oil companies. Therefore, upon our arrival at Lagos we were given a close protection team, which meant an armed vehicle in front and behind. As we were being driven along dry dirt roads Mark Davis suggested that if we were ambushed he and I should take the guns from our armed guards, as they were decidedly sleepy. Fortunately for us nothing of the sort happened and the trip went incredibly well. We managed to speak to 150 pastors in a church hall.

Charlie and I were also invited to go to Sierra Leone and Liberia. As both countries are extremely poor we decided to raise some funds for the two Alpha offices. While Charlie did the hard bit by entering the Marathon des Sables (251 km ultramarathon), I raised money through my contacts. Charlie completed the race and Joseph Francis Williams (National Director, Sierra Leone) and John Aaron Wright (Forces Director, Liberia) were both happy recipients of a 4x4 vehicle.

There were so many trips, just too many to mention, but the work grew around the world. After four years of working hard on Alpha for Forces, I encouraged Charlie to go for ordination. I knew he would be a kind and inspiring vicar, just like Jerry, his predecessor.

Twenty-five countries were running Alpha in their military but I now needed a replacement for Charlie. Amanda said to me, 'What about Eric?'

Eric Martin? The crazy staff sergeant who had given me that scripture about the gnashing of teeth? *Yes, he would be perfect,* I thought.

Having left the army after twenty-two years of service in 2003, Eric was living in Cyprus with his wife Angela and his two children. Having owned and managed two successful diving schools in Larnaca he had sold them both and started a company called Discount Ten, importing British goods for his four supermarkets serving the expat community. But he quickly realised this line of business was tedious, so he sold his share and was looking for something else to do.

He readily agreed to the job but wanted to run Alpha for Forces from Cyprus while being able to visit chaplains around the world.

In February 2011 we went on our first mission together to train chaplains to engage with Alpha in Cape Town, South Africa.

The team included Billy Gilvear and Andy Shilling. We trained a total of 100 military chaplains and lay leaders by running an Alpha conference on a military base. With live worship, excellent food and refreshments, the four of us presented polished talks filled with war stories and anecdotes, and finally finished off handing each delegate a set of Alpha resources to carry the work forward. Six months later they had not run one single course and when we researched the reason for their apathy we discovered that having presented such a good show, the delegates' response was, 'We can't even get close to running Alpha if that's what is required.' That was a lesson well learned!

After that conference Eric changed the structure of training to make running Alpha as easy as possible. He produced software on credit card sized USB cards with a camouflage design. The excellent Alpha film series, along with the USB and the camouflage designed pamphlets, really opened doors for us. Alpha for Forces training went to Canada, the USA, New Zealand, Australia, Africa and South Africa as we were invited to different countries. The biggest of these was a conference in South Africa where I was the keynote speaker; I was able to speak to representatives from almost every country in Europe, while Eric was able to equip them with Alpha resources.

During this period of activity, we also applied for a grant from Lloyds of London and were given £100,000 to promote the Marriage Course devised by Nicky and Sila Lee. In the British military, marriage breakdown is prolific. The result was a huge interest among the chaplains and welfare services and as a result we had reports of rescued marriages and improved relationships.

Currently, after ten years in the post, Eric has advanced the newly revitalised and aptly named Alpha Forces. It is now operating in sixty countries around the world, including the Palestinian Police Force. Our most recent mission to Kenya resulted in seventy-two chaplains and lay leaders trained and charged with a new-found zeal to evangelise their troops.

On a trip with Eric to Hohne Garrison, I mentioned the

Portakabin I had lived in as my first married quarters to the chaplain, Pat Springfield, and he said, 'Paul, come with me. I want to show you something.' At the back of his chapel there was a Portakabin he was using for storage, one of the original emergency quarters. All the memories of my time with Katie flooded back and I became tearful. Eric hugged me. The experience prompted me to write an email to Katie and apologise for my behaviour and what I had put her through. She was gracious enough to write back and say, 'Thank you, but I knew what I was getting into when I married a soldier.' I am aware that not all soldiers behave as I did but I was grateful for her understanding.

Alpha Forces has run in every theatre of war including Iraq and Afghanistan operational tours. Alpha is now running in the Falkland Islands, Okinawa with US Marines, West Indies on British guard ships and South Sudan with the UN mission. In the navy it takes place on destroyers and submarines.

Eric has been extraordinary and has carried the baton of this ministry into being the biggest Christian ministry to the British Forces around the world. He has also developed partnerships with every other organisation working in this field.

Tragically, in 2018 there were 8,500 former members of the armed forces in UK prisons. According to the Ministry of Justice, veterans represent approximately 10 per cent of the prison population. Frances Crook, Chief Executive of the Howard League, said that several factors contribute to the number of veterans entering the prison system, including alcohol abuse and post-traumatic stress disorder.

Any Christian military or ex-military who are reading this, I urge you to speak to your chaplains and get behind Alpha in your present or past regiments. We need to encourage and help our tri-service chaplains. They do an amazing work as they speak to men and women who are sometimes placed in the most extreme situations imaginable and who, on our behalf, suffer serious injuries and often return from war with trauma issues. When you think that there are 147,000 regular forces in Britain, including the reserves and the Ministry of Defence personnel, there is a huge ministry out there, and if you include direct relatives affected by soldiers killed or wounded on various military operations, then you can probably triple that number at least.

The gospel transformed my life and the lives of Lance Corporal Charlie Lacey, Sergeant Major Eric Martin, Sergeant Major Mark Davis, Major General Tim Cross and General Lord Richard Dannatt, and it has the potential to transform all those in the armed forces, despite gender, disability or rank.

20: Go and make disciples of all nations

When you enter Lusaka Central Prison through the small door, like the 'eye of the needle', the stench hits you immediately. It is a harsh smell: a mixture of men's sweat and excrement, and boiled whitebait cooked in pots around the yard. Your hands will work overtime as you flick the flies from your eyes and mouth, and the heat will rise up through your shoes and slow-cook your ankles. It is a dry heat, a desert heat with no breeze, and on the day we went into the men's prison it must have been hitting 44 degrees. It's important not to show any fear on your face as over a thousand pairs of eyes peer at you with a mixture of inquisitiveness, aggression, sorrow and hope. I was conscious that having a lockdown in Lusaka Central Prison would not be my idea of fun, especially as I had my wife and fourteen-year-old daughter with me.

*

Before I was ordained, and since, it has been a real joy to travel thousands of miles and visit prisons all over the world. Matthew 28:19, 'Therefore go and make disciples of all nations, baptising them in the name of the Father and of the Son and of the Holy Spirit', really comes to life when you can get on board a jet plane and cover thousands of miles in a matter of hours. I have had wonderful experiences with Michael, the ex-offender from Exeter, in Korea, Canada, Singapore and Africa, both of us speaking about the transformative power of the Holy Spirit in our lives. Once, we sat with Emmy in a shed with a tin roof, in Zambia. Emmy prayed with a woman who was dying of AIDS. She had nothing.

Michael left that shed deeply moved. He wanted to give her some money, but I took hold of his hand and said, 'Prayer is better for her now, Michael. She doesn't have long left.'

The missionary in me came alive when I went to Africa. The sun lit up the sky like a blood-red orange across the plains of the Sahara, and I knew I had found a mission field far from London. I started going twice a year and two trips in particular were poignant for different reasons.

In the May of 1994, Amanda and I were sitting every Wednesday night in a comfortable church attending our fourth Alpha course, quite oblivious to what was happening only a few thousand miles away. One of the worst international atrocities ever to take place was well under way. It became known as the Rwandan genocide, the mass slaughter of the Tutsi tribe in Rwanda carried out by members of the Hutu tribe, who were the majority tribe and the core political elite. An estimated 500,000 to 1,000,000 Rwandans were killed during the 100-day period from 7 April to mid-July, constituting as much as 70 per cent of the Tutsi population. The genocide and widespread slaughter of Rwandans ended with the military victory of the Tutsi-backed and heavily armed Rwandan Patriotic Front, led by Paul Kagame, who became President.

In July 2009 I went to Rwanda and met with Paul Kagame, a devout Catholic and a man of prayer. I was able to thank him for allowing the Alpha course to run in his prisons. It was a slightly surreal situation, sitting in his office with some of his senior staff with our heads bowed praying to the Almighty to guide our paths. I remember thinking that this man, a powerful military man, had toppled his government and now I was praying with him. After the prayer session we had tea and biscuits, followed by a short discussion about his vision to make Rwanda the best country in Africa.

On entering Kigali Central Prison, the first thing I noticed was the overcrowding. Built to hold around 500, it was nearing 4,000 and the smell was intense due to the heat and the number of men and women present. Pastor Deo Gashagaza mentioned that ten people died every day and as many were taken to hospital with pneumonia, dysentery or typhoid. He also informed us that most of the prisoners were Hutus charged with some involvement in the genocide. My lasting memory of that prison is not the stench or the overcrowding but my time in the main chapel, where I was asked to share a gospel message.

The chapel was rammed with a thousand inmates. Three hundred of them were women, their eager faces looking at me. The men and women had two things in common: shaven heads and shining faces. The women all sat together, following my every word, their Bibles open on their laps. Most of them were taking notes. Many of them had murdered their neighbours and relatives.

In Rwanda, when you preach that God forgives all our sins and offers forgiveness through his Son Jesus, it is hard not to think of the bloodshed and the victims of mass murder. In Africa I saw with my own eyes that there is no depth of depravity and no amount of evil that God cannot reach into and pull us out of, if we are prepared to forgive and trust that he will help us.

*

In September 2012 I was able to take Amanda and Phoebe on a trip with me. My desire was that this experience would impact our daughter in a way that nothing else could. All the lectures about people in the world being worse off, or starving children in Africa, never really resonated with her. Having spent most of her life in West Kensington, she liked nothing more than to meet her friends on the King's Road, eat at Nando's and shop in Westfield shopping centre. I'm glad it was a far cry from my upbringing, but still! I thought it was a great opportunity to whisk her away to a continent which was less than predictable and certainly without the privileges she was used to. Amanda had some concerns about taking our daughter into the prison but she trusted my judgment.

Paul Swala, the Alpha team leader in Zambia, met our team of fifteen outside Lusaka prison's gates. The team included Tricia Neill and some supporters of Alpha from Malaysia who had a heart for prison work.

The moment I met Paul Swala, my African namesake, I admired him. A stocky man with skin as black as coal, and brown eyes that told a story of both great suffering and great joy. He had one of those God stories that made my eyes widen when I first heard it. His faith was giant.

Paul was involved in the coup against the Zambian president in 1997. He was arrested for treason and along with sixty-two soldiers and three officers was expecting a death sentence. Sent to Lusaka Central Prison, for two years he had very little hope, as he lived with the daily fear of his trial. One day he visited the small and humble prison library and picked out a thin red pamphlet entitled *Who is Jesus?* by Nicky Gumbel.

Paul committed his life to Christ and prayed that Jesus would give him the chance to get out of prison. 'And I promise you, Jesus, if you do that, then I'll continue serving you. I'll even come back and serve you in this prison.'

The day of Paul's trial came around and when Paul stood in front of the judge, the judge said, 'Accused number 6, Paul Swala. The law has found you innocent. Go home.' Three times the judge had to repeat it as Paul was stunned. 'Go home', he insisted. Fifty-eight of Paul's friends were given the death sentence, commuted to life imprisonment.

Paul left the prison that day and joined the Alpha team in Zambia. He has been going back into prison preaching the gospel for the past nineteen years.

Lusaka Central Prison, built in 1923 for 200 men, held 1,145 on the day we visited. The sleeping conditions had stirred up the human rights campaigners as men were being packed into cells at 5.00 p.m., sitting in between each other's legs in a circle formation, and not released until the following morning. For two years Paul was living inside Lusaka prison, often waking up to the smell of death pressed up against his back as men died in the night from epidemics of tuberculosis and cholera. He told Amanda, 'Having a dead man lying up against you all night is enough to drive you mad.' More than half of the prisoners were still awaiting trial and sometimes they died before they could hear their innocence declared. Sometimes they were in prison for just having an expired visa, while others were very dangerous men.

I was conscious that taking a fourteen-year-old girl into one of the most deprived prisons in the world might seem foolish to some – my wife in particular. At the gate I had second thoughts when Amanda said, 'Is it safe, Paul?'

'You are both safe with me', I answered, as if I wore a cloak and had the word 'Superman' slapped across a blue Lycra top. Amanda didn't look convinced as we stood in the area between the exit door and the interior door of the prison. Armed guards sitting with fully loaded rifles on top of the warning towers were some consolation, but I knew Amanda well, and her instincts of being a mother hen over our little chick were showing on her face.

But it was singing that welcomed the team that day. It was incongruous to say the least, but very reassuring. Groups of men were singing about salvation and Jesus. They lived in the pit of hell and yet they sang of the joys of heaven. Many of them were on fire with faith and my talk was almost redundant. Although there are always those who have not heard the message, there are always those who are desperate for salvation.

Escorted to the centre of a large courtyard, we sat under the only bit of shade, a rickety structure with corrugated iron sheets for a roof. The inmates sat under the blaze of the midday sun. If the men were going to revolt, they had reason to do it then. 'I feel really uncomfortable being the privileged white woman', said Amanda. My wife being a very non-confrontational person was out of her comfort zone.

'Don't worry,' I said. 'Just smile and stop looking so scared.'

'This is a bit mad, Paul. I don't think Phoebe should be here', she added.

It was simply too late to make a fuss.

Now I could see nervousness on my daughter's face too as she looked around the courtyard and saw over a thousand black male faces staring back at her. She stayed close to Amanda and I was suddenly struck with the thought that I may have got it wrong. It was one thing going into these prisons around the world as a single man, but another thing to involve my wife and child.

The team took their seats and Paul Swala, familiar to the inmates, took the lead at the lectern. He introduced the guests and we received cheers and clapping.

I then stood, and my blue cotton shirt was no protection from the sun's intensity as sweat began creating rivulets down my back.

'Hello, everyone', I bellowed down the microphone. Paul was at my side repeating my every word in his language. As usual, I gave a testimony and, when I had finished, I asked people who wanted to give their lives to Christ to stand. Literally hundreds of men stood, so I asked those men who were already Christians to pray for the men next to them. Out of nearly 1,200 men I would say there must have been 70 per cent standing and praying.

On leaving the men's section we were then shown the women's section; it was a dirt courtyard with simple brick buildings which held around 120 women and their babies. Phoebe was noticeably moved by one young girl of the same age who was in prison for killing her baby after being ostracised by her village.

Amanda asked the chaplain, Liness, what the women did for underwear and sanitary products. When Liness said they only had the underwear they came in with, Amanda decided that that needed to change. 'I have at least ten pairs of pants and they have one or two? For goodness sake! And no sanitary towels? We have to do something.' I could tell she meant business, but didn't realise what that would mean for me.

Later that week, accompanied by David Thomson, Chair of Alpha Zambia, and Father Frank Hakoola, Alpha Zambia Director,

I had a meeting with the Vice President of Zambia, Dr Guy Scott, to discuss the deteriorating conditions within the prison. When I asked him what his prison policy was, he said with a straight face, 'We don't have one of those.' He called up his team for Social Justice and we sat around the table as he fired questions at them which they couldn't answer. The Vice President, rang his Minister of Justice and insisted that she go into prison with me on my next visit.

Once we were back in London, Amanda made an announcement for women in the congregation at HTB Queens Gate (St Augustine's) to bring in packs of knickers. For the next few months, bags of new pants were deposited in a basket in the church. The brief (pardon the pun) was for plain, size 12 and above, black or white pants. What we received was a motley collection from thongs size 8 to huge pink polyester pantaloons, to sexy lingerie. Amanda and Phoebe spent quite a few hours laughing at the proceeds; my daughter held them up saying, 'I don't think the women in Lusaka prison need these, Dad!'

A few months after the visit with my family I went back. We shipped out boxes of sanitary towels and knickers ahead of time, but knickers were still being donated, which meant I had to take a suitcase crammed with approximately 200 pairs of women's pants as part of my luggage. I have done some crazy things in my time but going through Lusaka airport laden with a suitcase full of women's underwear must have been one of the silliest. Imagine if I had been stopped!

We had also been given numerous donations and were able to buy mattresses locally for some of the cells, and an oven was delivered for the women's side. However, as a result of the Minister of Justice coming into the prison with the team that day, and being appalled by what she saw, she was keen to work in partnership with Alpha to improve conditions. Although she was a lawyer and had represented prisoners she had never been inside and seen their conditions. She was determined to do something, and within eight months, having sorted out many of the visa violations, ninety-eight women with children and eight very old women had been released.

The phrase 'Do not be afraid' is frequently found in the Bible. One of my favourites is from Psalm 27:1: 'The LORD is my light and my salvation – whom shall I fear? The LORD is the stronghold of my life – of whom shall I be afraid?'

The point of this story is to show you how my wife felt the fear but acted anyway. She was motivated by the appalling conditions and realised she had so much more than the women in Lusaka prison. And what impact did the trip have on Phoebe? It certainly woke her up, as I had hoped it would. She now has a real interest in prisons around the world and has more recently been into several UK prisons. It was like jumping into the Devil's Pool on the edge of the Victoria Falls (we did that too!); it seems a stupid thing to do but overcoming one's fears can be thrilling, because often the fear is unfounded and the pay-off for taking a risk is what adds to the rich experience of life.

With regard to encountering ex-offenders, I can understand why people are fearful, but there are solutions and I was determined to find one.

21: Caring for ex-offenders

From the age of three to sixteen, Jason's mother had physically abused him. By the time he was sixteen he decided he could no longer put up with it and, he explained, 'When she threatened to stab me and throw me over the balcony, I knocked her out.'

Very shortly after that, Jason got his first sentence at a magistrates' court in Yorkshire for assaulting a man who threatened him with a brick. Placing his hand on a Bible, he told me, 'I thought I had better behave myself. Just tell the truth on the Bible. It felt disrespectful not to. My dad always tried to instil good morals into me. I know I was a thieving git, but I had a moral code. I never broke into churches or mugged old ladies.'

A captain in the army sent a letter to the judge suggesting that Jason go straight to basic training with the Marines and thus avoid prison, as he had passed the entrance exam. Unfortunately, the judge decided otherwise and gave him a six-month sentence at HMP Everthorpe. It was the beginning of his repeat offending. Between the ages of sixteen and twenty-seven, Jason never spent more than six weeks out of prison.

*

By 2004 I had been working for HTB for seven years and had been ordained for two. Having visited most of the prisons in the UK and spoken to thousands of men and women up and down the country, I had started to feel a burden for those coming out of prison.

In Matthew 25:35–36 Jesus says something that doesn't appear often in Scripture: 'For I was hungry and you gave me something to eat, I was thirsty and you gave me something to drink, I was a stranger and you invited me in, I needed clothes and you clothed me, I was ill and you looked after me, I was in prison and you came to visit me.' Jesus personalises a ministry to the poor, so much so that if we ignore them, we are ignoring him. 'Truly I tell you, whatever you did for one of the least of these brothers and sisters of mine, you did for me' (v. 40).

As I was helping on an Alpha course in a prison on the south coast, one of the inmates in the chapel said to me, 'I've become a Christian now and I'm out in a couple of weeks. What shall I do?' I told him to grab the Alpha newspaper (no longer in print) as on the back was a list of all the churches running Alpha in the UK. Shortly after that conversation, I received a letter from him saying he was back in prison. Although he had done what I had suggested, when he got to the church he received a very cold welcome, as they were nervous of him. Not feeling as welcome as he did in the prison chapel he reoffended just to get back inside.

It became increasingly frustrating that offenders were coming to faith in prison, being supported by chaplains and church volunteers, only for them to leave prison with very little support on the outside.

Apparently people inside prison make around 200 decisions a day, while people outside prison have to make around 2,000. Once outside, offenders often become overwhelmed as they deal with problems such as housing, unemployment, addiction and divorce, and especially rejection. Churches were often rejecting ex-offenders when they arrived at their services, mainly due to fear and preconceived ideas about them.

Funding for Alpha for Prisons continued to pour in as the congregation at HTB heard testimonies from ex-offenders. Meanwhile, more and more ex-offenders started arriving at HTB, looking for community, help and advice. When a parishioner notified the police that her car had been stolen from the church car park, I was in disbelief that it was one of our own ex-offenders. But it turned out to be true and I realised that we needed to protect the congregation as much as we needed to care for the men trying to change. Subsequently, it was my statement that helped get him arrested. However, because he was repentant, I visited him inside prison and upon his release was there to meet him at the gate. We had to wise up and learn to understand former inmates' needs and shortcomings first-hand.

*

I first met Jason in March 1997 in HMP Brixton when he was twenty-seven years old. He was emaciated, with short cropped hair. Although we were both from the north of England he saw me as an authority figure and took an instant dislike to me. Six months earlier, Emmy and Georgie Wates had prayed for him after an Alpha appetiser. He felt a big weight in his head travel through his whole body and he ended up jumping around and speaking in tongues. At the time, he was at HMP Leyhill – a category D open prison. Having been on the run for a few days he had decided to turn up at HTB for one of the services. Emmy and Jamie Haith persuaded him to go with them to the police station and hand himself in.

Emmy had insisted that I met up with him because she thought he needed a strong man in his life. When I arrived at HMP Brixton I let him know that Emmy and Georgie were unable to visit him and immediately he swore at me. He said that everyone always left him and they were the same. Not willing to put up with the swearing, I got up to walk out and he said, 'You're just like them. You'll leave me as well.' So I went back and sat down and from that moment on he softened. I agreed to meet him upon his release.

When he was officially released, I met him at the prison gate in my Cherokee Jeep, which as an ex-serial car thief he loved, and we went for breakfast. At church, his skills came in very handy when a member of the congregation locked herself out of her car; he opened it within seconds.

For many years Jason was employed as chauffeur to a wealthy individual who decided to take a risk on him. Jason now lives in Devon and has never been back to prison. We chat every so often and I am hugely proud of him. It doesn't mean Jason hasn't had his struggles, he certainly has, but nevertheless he has done well.

Reading William Booth's *In Darkest England and a Way Out* I was inspired by Booth's Prison Gate Brigade. Booth was the founder of the Salvation Army in 1865. His wife Catherine became known as the Mother of the Poor, as she organised soup kitchens for the needy around London. Booth stated that you can't talk about the love of God if a person's belly is empty, and you can't tell them that God loves them when they are almost naked, freezing, with no roof above their head. First, you have to feed them, clothe them, and through your actions they will then start to listen to you about the love of God. Back in the 1860s he created the Gate Brigade. A team of men arrived at a prison gate in a horse-drawn carriage. They invited prisoners leaving that day back to a safe refuge to have some food and to be washed and clothed. Booth coined a catchphrase known as the three Ss: soup, soap and salvation.

The strength of the Church is twofold. First, all Christians, irrespective of denomination, share the 'Corporal Acts of Mercy' inspired by Matthew 25, which includes 'I was in prison and you came to me'. And second, they have a network of volunteers that surpasses that of any other institution. Having spent over sixteen years of my life in the military I know what a command is and this one is issued by our Commanding Officer! My aim was to form an army again, an army that was passionate about aftercare. The Church is called to confront poverty and injustice and in doing so we *rescue* those in crisis situations, *restore* those caught in addiction, debt, homelessness and crime, and *integrate* those individuals back into our society as Contributing Members. Nims Obunge MBE, Chief Executive of the Peace Alliance, put it succinctly when he said, 'It is the duty of the church to be the epicentre of this work for the marginalised in our society.' With personal experiences with the likes of Michael, Jason and many others, I felt compelled to start a charity.

The significance of the carving on the facade stone of HMP Dartmoor, *Parcere Subjectis*, now made sense to me; that we should 'be kind to prisoners' and help them upon release. After founding Caring for Ex-Offenders (CFEO) I was able to put a team together and soon established a network of over 700 churches that were interested in being trained to help with aftercare.

In 2004 Caring for Ex-Offenders was launched at the Cavalry and Guards Club, Mayfair, hosted by Paul Boateng (Minister of State with responsibility for prisons and probation in England and Wales) and endorsed by Simon Rufus Isaacs, 4th Marquess of Reading, Jonathan Aitken and Michael Hastings, Baron Hastings of Scarisbrick.

There was also an eclectic group of about fifteen ex-offenders who had all come to faith through the renamed Alpha Prisons, and who were all being looked after by the CFEO team based at HTB.

The three main principles of CFEO are:

- Holistic Ministry: we, the Church, come alongside ex-offenders to support and encourage them in all aspects of their lives and faith.
- Local Church Teams: CFEO is expressed within the local church as part of the body of the Church, rather than it being separate from the Church.
- Long Term Community: from a formalised entry into the Church, the goal is for an ex-offender to be integrated into the Church just like any other congregation member would be.

On our CFEO mentoring training, we use the acronym BRIDGE to teach mentoring skills and the mentoring process, because we feel that mentoring serves to help ex-offenders build a bridge between prison and their new lives. The stages on the journey are summarised as follows:

- **Build Rapport:** to put in the building blocks needed to create a positive, trusting and safe mentoring relationship and developing friendship. Ideally this stage should begin while the individual is still in prison.
- **Invest:** to invest in the relationship so you can move towards identifying and achieving goals.
- **Direction:** Direction and its partner, Goals, function as two halves of the same stage. The aim of Direction is to begin to identify the direction your mentee wants to go – it's about mapping out the future they want for themselves and working out what's really important to them.
- **Goals:** to identify your mentee's specific goals and plan how to reach them.
- **Empower:** focus on how independent your mentee has become and empower them to continue their journey. Support your mentee in engaging with the church and local community on their own, introduce them to a home group, and stop referring to them as a 'mentee'.

We started gathering statistics for CFEO in 2006. From that year, the charity has supported at least eighty-two ex-offenders at HTB. During this time we have had a re-offending rate of less than 15 per cent at twelve months after release. This is considerably lower than the national average for all offences: 46 per cent, or 69 per cent for those serving less than a year.

For many years CFEO's office was based in one of the most beautiful churches in London, St Augustine's Queen's Gate in South Kensington. How this came about was certainly not by the conventional route, but it all stemmed from Nicky Gumbel asking me to do a job that was out of my comfort zone.

Having been asked by the Bishop of Kensington to take on St Augustine's, Nicky asked me if I was interested in leading the service. I was intrigued. The church designed by William Butterfield was beautiful, but attendance was very low and it was likely to be closed down and sold off as a spa. In a prime position in South Kensington, any developer would have loved to get their hands on it.

One Sunday I went on my own to the service. I sat at the back and just watched, having had no experience of a High Anglo-Catholic service with all the robes, incense and formality. I went to Nicky and said, 'Do you know what goes on down there? I can't take that sort of service.'

He replied, 'Of course you can do it, Paul. You just need to learn it.'

The second Sunday I went there, my heart melted on hearing the music sung by a small professional choir. The kindness of the faithful few who were left moved me to tears. So, I went to Nicky and said I would give it a go.

I robed and began to lead the service. For several months I had to have Alastair, a server, take me through each step of the service, his forefinger guiding me through every line of liturgy. I often made mistakes, and he would whisper in my ear, 'You've forgotten the creed, Paul. Say it now.' Over the next few months, the church began to grow in numbers and I was given David Walker, a wonderful curate, to help me. We moved our less formal 9.00 a.m. service from St Paul's Onslow Square to St Augustine's and retained the 11.00 a.m. High Anglo-Catholic service.

Changing the church into a functional space for outreach work wasn't going to be easy. As a Grade II listed building there was not a lot you could do to make it fit for purpose. However, the archdeacon was on our side, and when I said I needed to remove the pews in order that the homeless could sleep on the floor during the winter months he said he would support me, as we would be in for a fight. I told the archdeacon and the journalist Ruth Gledhill when she interviewed me: 'All this history is fascinating but what is it doing as a church? It needs to be reaching out to more people within the community.'

The ministries I was responsible for were growing and we

needed more space to work, so eventually we converted the space in the basement into offices and I formed the William Wilberforce Trust (WWT), inspired by another great Christian social reformer. It became the umbrella charity for the all social action projects which HTB was now embracing, including anti-trafficking, dealing with depression course, a recovery from addiction course, Crosslight Advice (debt counselling), a day shelter and night shelter (at HTB Queen's Gate), Alpha Prisons, Alpha Forces and Caring for Ex-Offenders.

Although I was instrumental in founding these ministries, the day-to-day operation has been carried out by an incredible group of people and it has been a privilege to work with them. At HTB we have a small team dedicated to the work of CFEO in London, but unbeknown to me it was also going to go to many countries around the world.

In February 2015, on a freezing cold day, Amanda, Clinton and Phoebe went with me to Buckingham Palace where I was to be awarded an MBE by the Queen for my work with ex-offenders. I had always longed to meet Her Majesty, so was slightly disappointed to be presented with the award by HRH Prince Charles, but he was very friendly and we had a chat about prisons. It was a momentous day for me – something I could never have imagined in all my wildest dreams when I was walking around the exercise yard of 'Grisly' Risley. It is funny how life turns out.

In 2013 I was in Canada speaking in prisons in the Toronto area under the auspicious leadership of Sue Bennett, who was developing the Alpha office there. Just as I was leaving a women's prison, my phone rang and Nicky said, 'Where are you, Paul?' I replied, 'I'm in Canada.' He then said, 'Oh brilliant, you're not far away. Can you get on a plane and come to Sydney?' I laughed. 'Why on earth do you want me there?' Nicky was at the Hillsong annual conference, which had around 20,000 people in attendance. He added, 'You need to get here ASAP. We have an extraordinary opportunity to grow the work you are doing.'

I booked a flight immediately.

Nicky asked me to share my testimony as part of his talk. The next day I gave a seminar on social action with about 2,000 people attending. Unbeknown to me, the Head of Alpha Australia, Melinda Dwight (a powerhouse of a woman), and her youth worker Jono Green were in that seminar. They came to me and said, 'We need to do this work here. Will you be on our board?' That very day Melinda began the process of establishing a variation on WWT called the William Wilberforce Foundation, and it is still going strong today. It is having a tremendous impact on the prison system and it is also starting to help with aftercare through CFEO. Every year I am invited out to do a whistle-stop tour of speaking events. I am thrilled to be involved with developing Australia's aftercare for prisoners as it has a long history of working with prisoners, and ex-offenders. Interestingly, most of Sydney's waterfront warehouses were built by deported prisoners from the UK.

There are thousands of ex-offender stories around the world about men and women being transformed by God. Eddie's story is just one.

'As a child I started sniffing glue and gas and drinking far too much. In 1984 I came to London and got introduced to amphetamine, acid and cannabis. I started taking Ecstasy to get high and Valium and temazepam to come down, then went on to heroin and crack cocaine, and I became a chronic alcoholic.'

The first time I met Eddie was at the day shelter when he was causing a disturbance. He swore at me and took a swing at me but missed, and spun around falling on his backside. Picking him up, I escorted him out of the church, and he walked off.

Eddie's condition soon deteriorated. 'I went into hospital in

October 2010 with severe hypothermia and DVT in both my legs. I had cirrhosis of the liver, bleeding varicose veins from my heart to my stomach, hepatitis C, a messed-up head and a broken heart.'

Eddie returned to the day shelter and the team at HTB secured him some counselling. He told me, 'I felt loved, accepted, for the first time in years.' He ended up doing the Alpha course and was put in Michael's group. At this point Eddie was still bearded and unkempt and very smelly. Turning up to one of the Alpha evenings drunk, he got a plate of chicken supreme, went to his group, but lost his balance. Falling back against his chair, he spilled his food everywhere.

Eddie was barred from church that night and was not allowed back until he was sober. In Eddie's words it was 'a wake-up call. You see I had never seen my addiction before, not really. I lived in a bubble.'

When Eddie turned up to church again to do Alpha he was welcomed back in Michael's group. It was on the Saturday afternoon of an Alpha weekend away that the leader invited people to seek some prayer. I turned and looked at Eddie and I walked away. I thought, *Not him, I don't want to pray for him.* As I walked out of the room, I felt God say to me, 'Turn around, Paul, and go and pray for him.' Eddie told me it was his last chance to get better and that he needed God to help him. He then fell into my arms sobbing. I led him in the prayer giving his life to Christ and then I left.

It was several months later after a service at St Augustine's that Eddie came to me. 'Eddie? Is that you?' I said, hardly recognising him. His transformation was remarkable. He even smelt amazing. Having completed six theology courses at St Mellitus College and his levels 1 and 2 in health and social care, he was a walking miracle. He told me, 'Jesus took the afflictions and broken pieces and healed and restored and renewed my mind, body and spirit. But I am work in progress. It is a daily reprieve.' Eddie is now the manager of the night shelter for the Glassdoor homeless charity based in Chelsea.

It is the most natural thing to pass on good news to people and soon I came to realise, after some research, that there was no prison conference in the UK – no forum which brought all the elements of prison work together. In November 2006 I was given permission by Nicky to hold the first Prison Ministry Conference (PMC) in the UK at HTB, and 145 people attended.

As the years passed the event grew in popularity, and by the sixth conference on 7 November 2016, almost 700 men and women came. Those attending included prison chaplains (Christians, Sikhs and Muslims), governors, officers, politicians, probation services, police and the general public; all sharing a common interest in breaking the cycle of crime. I had the privilege of interviewing Eddie at the 2014 conference. I showed a photo of him before his transformation and then I called him up on stage. There were gasps from the audience and a well-deserved standing ovation for Eddie.[7]

22: Can the cycle of crime be broken? Part 1

In 1987, Jack Cowley was the warden of the Joseph Harp Correctional Center, a high security prison in Oklahoma. He told me the story of John, who had mental health issues.

John was in his cell and threatening to kill his cell mate by thrusting a sharpened pencil into his ear and through to his brain. The guards were dressed in riot gear to storm his cell. Jack was in his office when a call came through informing him of the situation. He told them to stand down until he got there. John was vicious. He was still shouting that he would murder his cell mate. Everyone was in a heightened state of anxiety. But Jack had known him for years, so on opening the cell door he was able to reassure him: 'John, it's Jack. I'm coming in.'

Immediately John threw his cell mate aside and rushed at Jack, flinging his arms round his neck and kissing his cheek over and over again. The situation was diffused, and the cell mate was removed. John was appropriately sectioned for his behaviour and Jack continued to help him.

*

Breaking the cycle of crime is a huge subject and there have been many excellent books which tackle it in more detail, but I have come up with three suggestions informed by my years of working with inmates and officers, chaplains, governors and government prison ministers. Prior to these suggestions I will touch briefly on six points that are helpful in order to set the scene. They are: the formative years; the political situation; the physical state of our prisons; more training for all prison staff; mental health issues; and spiritual input.

Would it surprise you to know that there are nearly 93,000 people in our UK prisons[8] and only 3 per cent will never be released due to the horrendous nature of their crimes? Therefore, we are dealing with 97 per cent who will be released at some point. Let us remember that the Ministry of Justice stated in July 2016's 'Proven Reoffending Statistics' that 'adults who served custodial sentences of less than 12 months had a proven reoffending rate of 64.9%'. This means that within one year, approximately 65 per cent of those released will be back in prison. That is a pretty shocking statistic. So how do we break the cycle of crime in a person's life?

Released prisoners typically re-enter society less equipped for life than when they entered prison, as demonstrated by the high rates of recidivism. And it is shocking that the risk of death is more than three times as high, and the risk of death by overdose almost thirteen times as high, for a released prisoner than it is for the average citizen. Moreover, women account for 20 per cent of self-injury behind bars, and are twice as likely to report mental health issues as male prisoners. We are failing in our duty as a society to help those in prison to change and better themselves physically, mentally and spiritually. Winston Churchill's words to the House of Commons in 1910 sum up my thoughts so much more eloquently:

> The mood and temper of the public in regard to the treatment of crime and criminals is one of the most unfailing tests of the civilisation of any country. A calm and dispassionate recognition of the rights of the accused against the state and even of convicted criminals against the state, a constant heart-searching by all charged with the duty of punishment, a desire and eagerness to rehabilitate in the world of industry of all those who have paid their dues in the hard coinage of punishment, tireless efforts towards the discovery of curative and regenerating processes and

an unfaltering faith that there is a treasure, if only you can find it, in the heart of every person – these are the symbols which in the treatment of crime and criminals mark and measure the stored up strength of a nation, and are the sign and proof of the living virtue in it.[9]

The formative years

There are many advisors within the care system better able than I to comment on issues including those in fostering, adoption and education, who are able to redirect a young person away from crime. We cannot ignore what happens in the formative years, before a person commits crime. There are no excuses for crime, but there are many reasons for it; criminal behaviour can be established early within a child's mindset, birthed in low self-esteem, trauma or copied behaviour.

At the time of writing this book the largest group of prisoners in the UK are white males, making up 74.3 per cent of the prison population. Statistically they come from broken homes, are poorly educated and have drug or alcohol dependency, and a high percentage are dealing with some level of mental illness.

I believe focussing on the family and schooling is paramount in preventing crime. Positive environments within schools and homes need supporting and encouraging with more financial commitment from the government. If the statement released by the *Bromley Briefings* (Autumn 2015) is true, that 'three-quarters (76%) of children in custody said they had an absent father and a third had an absent mother', and '39% had been on the child protection register or had experienced neglect or abuse',[10] then we as a community have to take the information and translate that into radical care earlier on.

According to the Centre for Social Justice the direct cost of family breakdown is estimated at £24 billion per year. The criminal justice system needs to engage better with schools and the wider community in preventing people from ending up in prison.

The police also need to work alongside schools, as they may be the first to discover abuse in the home. They can then take immediate action to protect the children before it is too late. And because the very poorest pupils, those on free school meals, are four times more likely to be permanently excluded from school, there needs to be more transparency between the public services, not less. To me, it's like having a broken fence at the top of a cliff and having medics at the bottom catching people as they fall off. Surely, it would be better to fix the fence at the top of the cliff. We need to become more proactive and less reactive in our approach to the problem.

Working with young offenders is crucial, as they can be prevented from climbing up the criminal ladder into adult prisons. The Reverend Matt Boyes, Managing Chaplain at HM Prison Feltham, the largest young offender institution (YOI) in Europe, said, 'Young offenders in particular use strong relational terms such as "fam", "blud", and "bro" when referring to each other. This desire for connection and significance is key for prison workers who are able to build trust, as their positive interactions can be the key that unlocks the potential for rehabilitation.'

Benjamin Lindsey, a world-renowned judge of the juvenile court in Denver, in 1909 wrote, 'All the courts or probation schemes on earth can never effectively correct the faults of the child as long as there remain the faults of those who deal with children in the home, schools, in neighbourhoods, in the community itself.'[11] Today we have so many more opportunities to work with experts in the field of fostering, adoption and educators.

The political situation

Since 1997 I have met with over ten Ministers of State for Prisons shortly after their appointment, advising them on reoffending issues. Productive conversations have taken place, only for them to be moved, in a matter of months, to another role within the government. Each minister comes up with interesting ideas which are often changed by the next minister. Fortunately, Michael Gove's

(Secretary of State for Justice 2015-16) idea for a Teach-First-style scheme, in which graduates work in prisons to help educate offenders, now has an equivalent in 'Unlocked Graduates' which has been running for the past three years with over 200 highly motivated graduates working as frontline officers in fourteen prisons.

When Rory Stewart took over from Liz Truss, he developed the '10 Prison Project' which highlighted ten prisons to serve as models of excellence for the rest of the prison estate and this has proven to be a success. Stewart wanted to concentrate on improving security and the living conditions within the ten worst prisons. He also believed in piloting a prison run on military principles in order to teach self-discipline and self-respect but resigned before he could explore the idea. During his time in office Stewart did manage to change all the windows in HMP Wormwood Scrubs, thus resulting in less litter and drugs being passed through broken windows and therefore a cleaner courtyard due to fewer rats and pigeons. This was simple but effective. Michael Segalov, in his article for the *Guardian* on 3 May 2019, stated that Peter Dawson, Director of the Prison Reform Trust, told him, 'There will be a good deal of regret at the loss of Rory Stewart from the prison's brief . . . if only because he had stayed in it long enough to begin to understand the complexities of repairing the damage done by previous administrations.'[12]

Governments are reluctant to spend huge amounts of money on prisons as they would appear to be a lower priority. But the changes needed by the prison system demand long-term solutions and therefore have to become part of cross-party policies, otherwise we will keep going over the same ground.

The physical state of our prisons

Many of our prisons are in a diabolical state. Most need to be renovated or rebuilt and many need repositioning. In the UK there are ninety Victorian prisons and they are simply not fit for purpose, with an increasingly ageing and disabled population. Peter Dawson, Director of the Prison Reform Trust, stated, 'We should not tolerate a situation in a civilised society where . . . prisoners are forced to share cells designed for one, eating their meals next to an unscreened toilet; where violence and self-harm have risen exponentially; and where a fifth of prisoners spend less than two hours a day out of their cell.'[13] Moreover, the *Bromley Briefings* 2018 stated, 'This level of overcrowding has remained broadly unchanged for the last fifteen years.'[14] But what we don't need is huge American-style megaprisons. In the past three decades, the US prison population has increased nearly five-fold, whereas the UK prison population is relatively small at nearly 93,000 compared to the 2.2 million inmates in the US.

*

Jack Cowley, before he came to work for Alpha Prisons (USA), was the warden of an American correctional facility and he knew first-hand that inmates like John needed meaningful interaction with others, otherwise their mental health could seriously deteriorate. Since we are often dealing with people who have come from emotionally impoverished backgrounds what we do not need to do is isolate them further. Integration and knowing an inmate well can produce fertile ground for change to take place.

Large prisons are impersonal and usually built too far away from public transport, which is not conducive to families on low incomes being able to visit. One governor said to me, 'The problem with megaprisons is that they are trying to act small and it doesn't work.' In William Booth's *In Darkest England and The Way Out* he stated, 'The process of centralisation, gone on apace of late years, however desirable it may be in the interests of administration, tells with disastrous effects on the poor wretches who are its victims.'[15]

Interestingly, although Booth wrote his statement in 1890, more recently in the May 2017 *Prison Service Journal,* Yvonne Jewkes, a research professor in criminology at the University of Brighton, writes,

> The current Government seems committed to building warehouse-style "mega-prisons", despite a multitude of academic evidence and Inspectorate reports showing that small prisons are more operationally effective and are better than larger facilities at housing prisoners in safe and secure conditions, providing them with meaningful work, education and training, encouraging purposeful activity, and fostering healthy relationships between prisoners and prison staff.[16]

Unless someone is dangerous to the community it is essential that the community, with all its resources of care, including doctors, mental health specialists and drug centres, be utilised to help offenders directly rather than paying to set up those organisations within prison.

More training for all prison staff

With an increase in staff sickness levels and lack of adequately trained staff, the prison system is under huge strain. Each year HM Chief Inspector of Prisons for England and Wales writes an annual report, which is essential reading for anyone interested in a comprehensive understanding of the state of our prisons. Referring to category B and C prisons (which account for the numerical bulk of prisoners) he states, 'Staff shortages had been so acute that risks to both prisoners and staff were often severe, and levels of all types of violence had soared.'[17]

Prison Officers' Entry Level Training (POELT) takes ten weeks from application to working on the wings. Having spoken to various prison officers recently, I was told that they are highly stressed because they don't know how to cope with the inmates' level of mental illness, especially the violent prisoners and self-harmers. John McCrae, Custodial Manager at HM Prison Onley, said,

> The staffing shortages created by the austerity measures and flawed recruitment process, used over recent years, has caused significant issues within prisons. The unions will state safety of staff is at risk. This is true; however, the most fundamental part of our role is also at risk, the rehabilitation of those in our care. Staff do not receive enough time to be the positive roles models we aspire to be.

John has hope that the new apprenticeship training may bring positive results, but this is not yet compulsory.

Having spent two days visiting Norway's maximum security Halden Prison, I saw with my own eyes a radically different institution from the ones I am used to. Hoidal, the prison governor, said, 'I want the inmates to be calm and peaceful, not angry and violent.' During my time there I saw officers interacting with inmates, eating together, playing sports together; they talked to them and motivated them. Hoidal calls it 'dynamic security', reminding me, 'We don't have life sentences here, so we are releasing your neighbour.' A sobering thought. However, in Halden Prison it costs £98,000 per person per year to house a prisoner, compared to between £40,000 and £50,000 in the UK. It takes two years to train their officers but they do have one of the lowest reoffending rates in the world. Laura Paddison in her article 'How Norway is teaching America to make its prisons more humane' stated, 'Norway also seeks to keep inmates connected to the outside, importing services like health and education from the community. The aim is to connect prisoners with services they will use when they're released and link the community with the prisons – demystifying and destigmatising them.'[18]

On 14 September 2018 a news headline by Harry Cockburn for the *Independent* stated, 'Prison strike: Government seeks court injunction to stop officers walking out over "unprecedented" wave of violence'. And a staff union leader stated, 'I'm fed up of hearing of my members receiving smashed eye sockets, broken arms, broken legs . . . enough is enough'.

Why do we think in the UK that ten weeks' training is acceptable? We can't possibly be valuing our prison staff enough.

Mental health issues

Jack Cowley told me that everyone was shocked by John's response when he attacked his cell mate, but then he reminded me that inmates have complex needs. They have to be known, and connection takes time, resources and money. Jack had spent time getting to know John and he knew that all he needed was to be listened to. Jack raises two important issues. First, inmates with serious mental health issues should not be in our standard prisons because they not only impact the prison staff, they also impact other inmates. Second, prison staff are not trained to deal with them; they need to be in specialist care. The criminally insane need to be in secure mental institutions like Broadmoor, a high-security psychiatric hospital run by the NHS. But we only have three in the UK: Broadmoor, Ashworth Hospital near Liverpool and Rampton Secure Hospital in Nottingham, and these are at capacity.

As a volunteer chaplain at HMP Wormwood Scrubs, I visit men on the healthcare wing who are often locked in their cells for twenty-four hours a day. They are known to throw faeces and urine at the guards when they open the small sliding window in the cell door. Often an officer has said to me, 'I wouldn't visit him today, Father. He is throwing things.' Now I know what they mean. How on earth are these men going to get better? This type of rehabilitation takes time and money, and far better facilities are needed. Suicide watch (an officer sitting outside a prisoner's cell door, checking an inmate's behaviour every fifteen minutes) is costly and time consuming, and needs to be dealt with by people far more experienced. It is unfair to put the weight of severe mental health issues on often young, inexperienced officers who are not trained. It makes an officer feel inadequate and stressed when their job should be keeping order and facilitating men and women to get to their daily work and rehabilitation courses. For the inmates' safety, a senior officer informed me, 'There should also be no transfers or release from prison on a Friday, as men and women have no hope of getting help from essential service providers and end up wandering the streets.' I would also add that the same goes for releasing men and women who have no family or friends to go to over the Christmas and New Year periods.

Spiritual input

Interestingly, crime was recorded at its lowest in the UK between 1880 and 1920, and it is not a coincidence that this was also when the largest number of children under fifteen years old attended Sunday school. Sunday school helped children to read and write and taught them a moral code based on the Ten Commandments.

The multi-faith chaplaincy teams in our prisons have a unique role and they should not be dismissed because people are concerned about radicalisation. Radicalisation is not about repentance, forgiveness or spiritual growth; it is about control, domination and suppression. I have it on good authority, from some excellent prison chaplains who are imams, that we now have big problems in London and other major city prisons during Friday prayers. Muslims are threatening inmates who won't convert to Islam or won't attend prayers. This behaviour is born out of an increasing gang culture, which is rife in our prisons, rather than the result of faith.

An increasing number of prisons are cancelling activities (work, education, visits) because they need to redirect their prison officers' resources to manage these incidents. One article in the *Evening Standard* reported that there was a rise in violence at HMP Wormwood Scrubs during Friday prayers, whereby some Muslim prisoners had arranged a fight to take place at the Eid celebrations.[19] This behaviour is not accepted by imams, who see it as disrespectful to God.

Through my relationship with Peter Welby, a consultant on religion and global affairs specialising in the Arab world, I have now attended two conferences of Shaykh Abdullah bin Bayyah's Forum for Promoting Peace in Muslim Societies – one in Abu Dhabi and one in Mauritania. Meeting so many Muslim leaders has given me hope; many come together from around the world, focused on defeating extremism and building more peaceful relationships both within Islam and with other faiths.

In the light of the recent terrorist attacks in the UK, where innocent members of the public have been murdered, it is crucial that we have a better understanding of how to deal with such terrorists in our prisons and upon release. Equally, we wouldn't want Christian fundamentalism in the prisons; it is unappealing and against Christ's teaching. This issue needs governance around it, but it should not thwart the good work of chaplaincy. The alternative is to have no spiritual presence in a prison and this would be counterproductive, resulting in more depression and lack of self-worth.

In *More God, Less Crime*, renowned criminologist Byron R. Johnson states: 'Religion is a powerful antidote to crime . . . faith-motivated individuals, faith-based organisations, and the transforming power of faith itself are proven keys in reducing crime and improving the effectiveness of our criminal justice system.'[20] He also provides a review of over 270 published studies on the impact of religion on crime, and concludes that faith also helps reduce drug use, teen violence, gang activity, recidivism, domestic violence and other forms of pathology.

Pastoral care is very important. During the induction process it is carried out by the chaplaincy team who ask how an inmate feels and what their concerns are. This can make a big difference at the point when they have lost their freedom. A chaplain can bring a sense of *shalom* (peace) even just for that short period of time. I often think back to my time in Risley. If someone in authority had said, 'Come and sit down, son; have a cup of tea. Things will get better', it would have meant the world to me.

So why aren't there more partnerships between prisons and faith-based groups? Why aren't all the churches involved in this work? Especially in aftercare. The easy bit is speaking about hope in the prison, the hard part is engaging the churches to help ex-offenders upon release. If you are a member of a church near a prison, think seriously about getting involved. Your priest or pastor may be too busy to organise training days and visits, so take it upon yourself to find out what needs doing.

Harbour Church Portsmouth are doing a fantastic job in this area, as the Reverend Alex Wood facilitated a wonderful woman, Lauren Meredith (who raised her own salary), to work for them. With a BSc in criminology, she is in the process of completing her master's, and her ministry is to build connections with prisoners, chaplains and local statutory organisations, with the aim of integrating prison leavers into the local church. She has been achieving this by working closely with CFEO and Alpha Prisons, who delivered all the training for her volunteers.

There are some extraordinary stories of transformation, not least that of Shane Taylor, who was one of the top six most violent criminals in Britain and had a profound experience of God on an Alpha course in prison. He now spends his days ministering to those less fortunate than he is. When a repeat offender like Shane changes for the better, the impact upon society is unquantifiable. If we are to find the 'treasure' in every person then faith-based courses in prison, such as those sponsored by Alpha Prisons and Prison Fellowship, must be encouraged and resourced as they present compelling and comprehensive evidence that religious practice and programmes help with reconciliation, reduce recidivism and promote social engagement.

23: Can the cycle of crime be broken? Part 2

I first met Finny in HMP Dartmoor in 1996. He was a striking young man with a shaven head and tattoos. I discovered that by the age of nineteen he had been given eleven years to serve in prison. Finny told me he had been looking for 'the truth' for years. He was inquisitive and intelligent, but his life was a crazy roller-coaster of drugs, arson and madness. Through it all he asked himself what life was all about and why he was here. Looking into ouija boards and occult practices, he found them unsatisfactory and one day he said to God, 'Reveal your truth to me. I know you are out there. I need to know your truth.' That very same day Finny was in court and felt compelled to tell the truth about the crimes he had committed. Although he was given a six-year prison sentence he knew God was doing something profound in his life.

*

With the previous six factors in mind I believe there is a three-part strategy to help break the cycle of crime: repentance, rehabilitation and mentoring.

Repentance

I put 'repentance' first because, in my opinion, it is the most important. However, repentance often comes about due to an inmate having attended a course for rehabilitation, so they often go hand in hand. St Augustine said, 'The confession of evil works is the first beginning of good works.' Repentance is crucial for change. Its definition is to have 'sincere regret or remorse'. The Greek word for repentance is *metanoia*, which means 'change of mind'. For an offender to recognise their part in a crime and having a heart to repent and change will result in them taking responsibility and acknowledging the consequences. In America the word for prison is often penitentiary, from the medieval Latin *paenitentiarius*, meaning 'repentance'.

But how does a person change? It is a question pondered by parents, pastors, physicians, politicians, educators and therapists. From twelve-step programmes, public awareness campaigns, management techniques, virtually every occupational sector offers ways of encouraging and equipping people to identify, address and eliminate their addictions and diseases. There are few concerns as pressing or as important as the reformation of character, and few tasks as difficult. And nowhere is the issue of character reformation more urgent, or the stakes higher, than in the realm of crime and punishment.

Often when I visit men and women in prison, they tell me they are innocent, and they believe it, even when there is overwhelming evidence to the contrary. Admittedly, there are occasional miscarriages of justice, but generally it takes a while for them really to embrace their part in a crime: what they did and whom they hurt. But when that revelation comes it can be a real release and also devastating at the same time, because suddenly the burden for their crime rests on them. Once you get a conscience and start to have empathy for your victims, change can truly start to happen. The act of 'repentance' can be without God, but in my case and with many others it was only when God was embraced that I truly repented.

*

Finny, in his confession in court, is a great example of what St Paul says in 2 Corinthians 7:10–11: 'Godly sorrow brings repentance that leads to salvation and leaves no regret, but worldly sorrow brings death. See what this godly sorrow has produced in you: what earnestness, what eagerness to clear yourselves, what indignation, what alarm, what longing, what readiness to see justice done.'

I was definitely guilty when I was given my sentence at Risley. I was a thief. I had no conscience until I was much older and I realised that people worked hard for their 'stuff' and actually I had no right to take it from them just because I could. In the British Army I learnt that respecting authority is essential, and I believe because of that training and imposed self-discipline I started to become a better person. However, I still needed something bigger in my life to truly change me deep within. Something that would compel me to become truly repentant. God enabled me to see my sin and make that change. I am so grateful to God for making me turn that truck around and return to the Sergeant's Mess all those years ago. When Julie, my second wife, contacted me through social media many years after we had divorced, I told her I was happy for her that she had become a mother and she was pleased I had stayed with Amanda. She considered doing an Alpha course and I told her how to find out about it. Saying sorry, or repenting, is a hugely powerful act. It should be encouraged and facilitated as much as possible, and if you find yourself in prison it's a good place to start.

Rehabilitation

Prison is never a neutral experience. Prisons will either school an inmate in new forms of criminal behaviour, or hopefully set them on a road to change. Rehabilitation is the key to unlocking the prisons but also to making society safer. I know it can seem that too much emphasis is given to the criminal and not enough to the victim. Criminals need to be punished and victims of a crime need proper care and support, and to have a sense that justice is being properly carried out. However, we have to remember that most offenders will be released one day and therefore the question we have to ask ourselves is: do we want them to be rehabilitated and transformed as human beings contributing to society, or do we just want them to stay on the treadmill of reoffending? Christian Jarrett wrote an article for the BBC on 1 May 2018 titled 'How Prison Changes People'. He stated, 'As the long-term prisoner becomes "adapted" – in the true sense of the term – to the imperatives of a sustained period of confinement, he or she becomes more emotionally detached, more self-isolating, more socially withdrawn and perhaps less well suited to life after release.'[21]

Courses that involve anger management, drug awareness and withdrawal, victim awareness programmes and spiritual courses, create an environment for confession, repentance and the restoration of self-worth as opposed to boredom, drugs and gang culture, which do a lot of harm in prison. Nicola Marfleet, a prison governor, states that her number one commissioning intention is '. . . to ensure a rehabilitative culture that motivates offenders to make positive changes in their lives'.

In prison, Christian courses like Sycamore Tree, run by Prison Fellowship (a victim awareness programme which teaches the principles of restorative justice), have had a huge impact on offenders as they learn to become more in touch with how their actions impact their victims. The Alpha course is obviously about God but other courses including Alcoholics Anonymous, Cocaine Anonymous and Narcotics Anonymous all recognise a 'higher power'. These programmes must not be cut due to budget restrictions or staff shortages as they all address an inmate's conscience, making them aware of their addiction and their responsibility towards family and community.

Work is also an essential part of rehabilitation. Skills in woodwork, making clothes or electrical engineering are encouraged, but are often interrupted with lock-downs and staff shortages. Getting inmates to their education or work courses is paramount in deterring them from boredom and anxiety, which can lead them to drug-taking.

I asked a previous governor of HMP Wandsworth about the state of his prison and he said that drugs and alcohol were the main problem. When I first met Finny at HMP Dartmoor, twenty-plus years ago, he said the same thing. 'It was in the secure unit that I learnt about chemicals, namely amphetamine, known on the streets as speed. And I developed a taste for it. So mixing cannabis with the alcohol, then with the speed is a very dangerous cocktail. And that's when my violence kicked in.'

Jonathan Aitken was very struck by the drug use in prisons: 'I saw time and time again a young person come into prison who really didn't have a drug problem, but who got one . . . In English prisons, drugs flow through them like a river, and a pretty well unstoppable river as far as the authorities are concerned.'

Nothing much has changed in twenty years except the drugs have become even worse. New chemical substances like spice are causing severe mental health problems and behavioural issues which prison officers are facing on a daily basis. One of the problems with spice and other chemical substances is that once they have been detected, the drug dealers change the chemical compound, which is then untraceable. As soon as the sniffer dogs learn to detect one version, a new one will take its place. It is hard for the prison authorities to continually outwit criminal minds. We need to think differently. The only way to stop men and women taking and dealing drugs in prison is to offer something better. John McCrae, a managing officer, stated, 'Not enough is done to combat drugs in prisons, again down to a lack of resources and partnership working between all of the agencies. The drug misuse has increased due to boredom and a lack of regime.'[22]

Temptation is everywhere. Therefore, if prison can become a powerhouse for rehabilitation instead of just a place for punishment, we could create a very different environment. In Proverbs 13:12 it states, 'Hope deferred makes the heart sick, but a longing fulfilled is a tree of life.'

I am aware that there are many people who are hugely

passionate about this subject and who are in a position to make changes. In March 2018 a good friend of mine and also a great prison advocate, Lord David Ramsbotham, introduced the Rt Hon David Gauke MP, Secretary of State for Justice, at the Prison Reform Trust evening. In his speech, Gauke said,

> There is an important need to ensure that prisoners who make moves in the right direction are properly rewarded. To put it into a two-word phrase: incentives work. I think we need to do more to look to sharpen some of those incentives, and to make sure that we have got a prison system that meets all of its objectives. One is about protecting society, and two is that there is a need for punishment. But three is about rehabilitation. A balanced approach requires us to deal with all of those things.

It's as if we need a paradigm shift in our outlook on prisons. Instead of seeing them as punishment centres, we should start to see them as rehabilitation centres. Swedish prisons are closing down due to their success at rehabilitating prisoners. On 10 November 2016 BBC news reported, 'Dutch prison crisis – a shortage of prisoners – in the past few years 19 prisons have closed down.'[23] Van der Spoel, the deputy governor of Norgerhaven, a high-security prison in the north-east of the Netherlands, said,

> In the Dutch prison service we look after the individual. If somebody has a drug problem we treat their addiction, if they are aggressive we provide anger management, if they have money problems we give them debt counselling. So we try to remove whatever it was that caused the crime. The inmate . . . must be willing to change but our method has been very effective . . . persistent offenders are eventually given two-year sentences and tailor-made rehabilitation programmes. Fewer than 10% then return to prison after their release.[24]

When will the government be radical in the way it deals with crime? When will it be prepared to spend millions of pounds to address these long-term issues and change our antiquated prison system into thriving rehabilitative centres?

Mentoring

As you have read, my own rehabilitation took many years and came about through the army and through meeting with God, but it also came about by having an extraordinary number of wise men and women advising me over the past twenty-five years of my life. If a person does not have these friends and elders in the community then they have to be provided, and this is what we call mentoring. The mentor is the glue that holds the ex-offender together.

Even inside the prison there is more potential to utilise mentoring between older prison staff and younger recruits. John McCrae from HM Prison Onley stated, 'The wrong people are training staff. In the Second World War, the USA took their ace fighter pilots away from the front line where they were dying, to teach at the flying schools in order to train the next generation of pilots . . . why does HMPPS not follow this approach? Those of us with the years of experience are not being used to train the new staff.' Moreover, the 2020 BBC TV series 'The Choir: Aylesbury Prison', hosted by Gareth Malone, was a testament to how prison staff, with Gareth as a mentor, were able to transform the lives of inmates, showing how rehabilitation is truly possible.

In 2018 I was asked to join the board of Crossroads Prison Ministries, based in Grand Rapids, Michigan, USA. Their mission statement is to connect prisoners with mentors in Christ-centered relationships so that lives, prisons and churches are restored through the Gospel. Sometimes unlikely friendships are formed, and the lives of both prisoners and mentors are changed as they exchange letters, study God's Word and apply biblical truths to their lives. Even after working for twenty-three years in the prison system around the world I never really understood the power of a letter. Letter writing is a lost art. In a world of email, text messaging and social media, many of us are missing out on the joy and intimacy that can be found in the exchange of letters. I remember what it felt like when I was on operational tours in the army to hear my name called at mail call and receive a letter. It was the best feeling. This is a valuable form of mentoring.

As I've mentioned, the average person has to make 2,000 decisions in a day, yet an inmate will make 200. You can give a person a house or a flat to live in but if they are not ready, they will sabotage it. You can give someone employment but if they are not ready, they will leave. A person can find a partner, get their kids out of care; but if they are not ready, they will self-destruct. If they have a mentor, however, someone to talk to when they can't pay the bills, or when they are struggling with their partner or their job, a potential nightmare situation can be averted over a coffee. Coming out of prison is often a huge adjustment for an offender to make and having someone walk with them through it can be greatly comforting and empowering.

This work can be facilitated by faith groups and charities, not for recruitment purposes or for money, but for the genuine welfare of an offender and ex-offender's practical and spiritual needs. At HTB we run training courses for mature Christians to become mentors in a voluntary capacity through the charity Caring for Ex-Offenders. The training presents the definition of a mentor as 'A person or friend who guides a less-experienced person by building trust and modelling positive behaviours. An effective mentor understands that his or her role is to be dependable, engaged, authentic and tuned into the needs of the mentee.'

Eddie was mentored by Michael and me, and subsequently he has helped run the Recovery Course (for addiction) at HTB. He is a truly gifted man in giving practical advice, and his understanding of the Bible is second to none. Finny, meanwhile, has gone on to run a successful landscape gardening business. He is married to Helen, the daughter of a police officer, and they now have three boys. Finny said that all his worries about his aftercare 'were quietened with the love that the church gave through their care. It's a very powerful thing.'

These three points are not new. They are almost as old as civilisation itself and have been put into practice, to varying degrees, by governments and organisations over the past decades. But unless we are far more rigorous about making our prisons centres of rehabilitation we could be on a trajectory to disaster. What with mental health issues, overcrowding, staff shortages, lack of finance, violence and shifting government policies, things look very dim. The crucial thing is that we have to think differently about the men and women in our prison system as they need more, not less, investment. Believing that we are all made in the image of God, and that each of us is given a divine spark at birth, a spark sometimes hidden so deep that it's almost extinguished, should propel us to look for that spark in the prisoner. But we on the outside may have to look with different eyes. In the words of John's Gospel, 'The light shines in the darkness, and the darkness has not overcome it' (John 1:5).

Identifying and encouraging what works in reforming lives and character is an urgent matter for the public good. This is my passion not just because I'm a Christian, a priest or a social reformer, but because I'm a husband and father, and I want our streets safer for my own family and for yours.

Epilogue

Writing the story of my life has been like cutting down an old oak tree and seeing the concentric growth rings. Each ring marks one cycle of seasons, or one year, and it can even tell us what the weather was like in that year.

As you will see from reading the first part of my life, it was packed with some seriously bad weather. I always had the belief that once I was out of prison my life would get better. If I had a job it would be good. If I were married it would be great. If I had a child everything would be okay. If only I was divorced it would be easier. My journey was to always look for the next fix, the next job, the next woman. It was as if I was in a state of perpetual homesickness.

In all honesty I can say to you that unless Jesus had come into my life and turned me around in 1993, part two of my life would have been very different. I don't think I would have married Amanda, been reconciled with my son, or had a daughter. I certainly would not have gone in to prison or become a priest. I believe I would have pushed through with my army career and pursued a life of promotion and material gain.

In St Paul's Cathedral there is a famous painting by Holman Hunt called *The Light of the World.* Jesus stands at a door that is covered with briars and thistles. He is holding a lamp and is knocking on the door. I think he must have been knocking on my door for years and years, but I never heard him. Reflecting upon my past I can appreciate how a divine hand has directed me. A hand that I tried to avoid in my youth but one which nevertheless steered me home to him.

Now I am so grateful for all that I have, and it is summed up in a few verses from Psalm 18 in *The Message,* a contemporary version of the Bible:

God made my life complete
when I placed all the pieces before him.
When I got my act together,
he gave me a fresh start.
Now I'm alert to God's ways;
I don't take God for granted.
Every day I review the ways he works;
I try not to miss a trick.
I feel put back together,
and I'm watching my step.
God rewrote the text of my life
when I opened the book of my heart to his eyes.
Psalm 18:20–24, MSG

Now I have a family I love and who love me back. My marriage to Amanda is extraordinary, as we are a great team and she is a continual support to me. I love her creativity, energy and optimism. My son, a successful businessman and full of wisdom, is one of my best advisors and he is very much involved in our lives. My daughter, who is creative and bright, is on her own journey and it is a joy to watch it unfold.

When I think of my children and my relationship with both of them, I see that it is nothing like the one I had with my own father, which was often difficult and strained. But we trust 'that in all things God works for the good of those who love him' (Romans 8:28). Now my father has become part of my story, which I have the privilege of sharing on the Alpha film series, the guidance talk. I talk about my father and our last moments together, three weeks before he died. That story has been watched by millions around the world and I'm often stopped by people who tell me how their story is similar to mine and how it has helped them to forgive. The irony is that we have now become a double act for the gospel, especially in prisons. I can't wait to see his face when we meet again.

I also have the wider family of the church. They have loved me, despite my flaws. They have nurtured me and believed in me. When I have struggled with work or faith, they have drawn alongside me and lifted me up. The Christian walk is not about walking in perfection. Nelson Mandela sums it up when he said, 'Do not judge me by my successes, judge me by how many times I fell down and got back up again.'[25]

In my own life I have experienced many battles. I have had to recognise my part in them and also my desire to climb into new behaviour, seeking counsel, advice and prayer from people I trust. Working in the areas of prison and homelessness and within the institution of the Church of England has never been easy for me. On the contrary I have often wondered what on earth I am doing. Having seen the film *The Darkest Hour* recently, about Churchill and his first days as Prime Minister in 1940, I hugely identified with his conversation with the king when he said, 'My emotions are unbridled. A wildness in the blood I share with my father. And my mother also. We lack the gift of temperance.' This has been both a strength and a weakness for me, as often I feel misunderstood. My northern bluntness and my personality have been a tool for orchestrating change but at times are perceived as overbearing. It is only by casting my burdens on to Jesus Christ and having the support and love of an extraordinary set of people in my life, including a wonderful trauma therapist, Jan, that I now have awareness and insight into my past and a few tools to manage my low moments.

On 4 June 2018 I was licensed as Minister in Charge of St Francis, a small church built in 1938 for the people on the Dalgarno Peabody Estate – not far from HMP Wormwood Scrubs and the Grenfell Tower. The church is linked to HTB's parish and is growing into an exciting and vibrant Christian community.

At the same time that I became Minister in Charge of St Francis, I also became a part-time chaplain at HMP Wormwood Scrubs and HMP YOI Feltham. I mentioned earlier that Nims Obunge believed it was the duty of the church to be at the epicentre of work with the marginalised, and I have had the privilege of seeing this firsthand. On a recent visit to the Scrubs, I had the opportunity to encourage men to attend the Alpha course, run by Gavin Cutler. On the first course there were fifty men and on the second, forty, of which nine were baptised. These were the first baptisms to take place in the chapel for sixteen years. Four men, upon their release, were met at the gate by Luke Smith (CFEO) and brought to a service at St Francis. Three are now regular members of the church; and as I see them united with their families and praising God, it inspires me to continue to minister to the prisoners.

If you are going through bad times, please seek support and counsel from those willing and able to help. And pray. Get down on your knees and cry out to God who will hear your prayer and call you to live a fuller life with Him by your side.

It is my belief that we are all unremarkable people whose lives can be made remarkable by God.

Notes

1 Newberg, M. D. and Walderman, M. R., *Words Can Change Your Brain* (London: Penguin Random House, 2013).

2 Northumbria Community, *Celtic Daily Prayer: Book Two: Farther Up and Farther In* (London: HarperCollins, 2015).

3 Salter, S., 'Why Do We Lie?', *Psychology Today* (22 September 2013), http://bit.ly/2C7D7UJ.

4 Tolstoy, L., *A Confession* (London: Merchant Books, 2009).

5 Harding, T., 'SAS: The chosen few who are a force like no other', *Daily Telegraph* (25 April 2011), http://bit.ly/2PBn9KJ.

6 Argo, J., 'Why We Lie', *Live Science* (15 May 2006), https://www.livescience.com/772-lie.html.

7 See https://youtu.be/PtvtbCSDeFk.

8 Sturge, G., Commons Briefing papers SN04334 'UK Prison Population Statistics' (House of Commons Library, 23 July 2019), https://researchbriefings.parliament.uk/ResearchBriefing/Summary/SN04334.

9 Churchill, W., Speech in the House of Commons, Hansard (20 July 1910) vol. 19, cc1354, https://api.parliament.uk/historic-hansard/commons/1910/jul/20/class-iii.

10 Prison Reform Trust, *Bromley Briefings Prison Factfile*, Autumn 2015, page 6, http://www.thebromleytrust.org.uk/files/bromleybriefingsautumn2015.pdf, citing figures from Jacobson, J., et al., *Punishing Disadvantage: a profile of children in custody* (London: Prison Reform Trust, 2010).

11 Greenwood, P. W., *Changing Lives: Delinquency Prevention as Crime-Control Policy* (Chicago: University of Chicago Press, 2006), page 21.

12 Segalov, M., 'Rory Stewart's promotion to DfID is bad news for Britain's prisons', *The Guardian* (3 May 2019), http://bit.ly/2JKoIix.

13 Bulman, M., 'Prison conditions "most disturbing ever seen" with staff now accustomed to jails not fit for 21st century, watchdog says', *Independent* (11 July 2018), https://www.independent.co.uk/news/uk/home-news/uk-prison-report-conditions-inspectorate-disturbing-jails-21st-century-a8442111.html.

14 Prison Reform Trust, *Bromley Briefings Prison Factfile*, Autumn 2018, page 16, http://www.prisonreformtrust.org.uk/Portals/0/Documents/Bromley%20Briefings/Autumn%202018%20Factfile.pdf
15 Booth, W., *In Darkest England and The Way Out* (London: The Salvation Army, 1984).
16 Jewkes, Y., 'Prison planning and design: learning from the past and looking to the future', *Prison Service Journal*, vol. 231 (3 May 2017), pages 15–21, https://www.crimeandjustice.org.uk/publications/psj/prison-service-journal-231.
17 HM Chief Inspector of Prisons, *Annual Report: 2018 to 2019* (9 July 2019), page 8, https://www.gov.uk/government/publications/hm-chief-inspector-of-prisons-annual-report-2018-to-2019.
18 Paddison, L., 'How Norway is teaching America to make its prisons more humane', *Huffington Post* (22 August 2019), http://bit.ly/2r1GQ3W.
19 Bentham, M., 'Rise in "Friday prayers" attacks at Wormwood Scrubs prison', *Evening Standard* (7 January 2020), https://www.standard.co.uk/news/crime/rise-in-friday-prayers-attacks-at-wormwood-scrubs-prison-a4328256.html
20 Johnson, B. R., *More God, Less Crime* (West Conshohocken, PA: Templeton Press, 2011).
21 Jarrett, C., 'How Prison Changes People', BBC Future (1 May 2018), https://www.bbc.com/future/article/20180430-the-unexpected-ways-prison-time-changes-people.
22 Personal email to the author.
23 Ash, L., 'The Dutch prison crisis: A shortage of prisoners', BBC News (website) (10 November 2016), https://www.bbc.co.uk/news/magazine-37904263.
24 Ibid.
25 See 'Nelson Mandela, in his Words', *Wall Street Journal*, Excerpt from an interview for the documentary 'Mandela', 1994, https://wsj.com/articles/nelson-mandela-in-his-words-138628093.